STUDIES IN CULTURE AND COMMUNICATION

General Editor: John Fiske

UNDERSTANDING NEWS

STUDIES IN CULTURE AND COMMUNICATION
General Editor: John Fiske

Introduction to Communication Studies *John Fiske*
Understanding News *John Hartley*
Case Studies and Projects in Communication *Neil McKeown*
An Introduction to Language and Society *Martin Montgomery*
Understanding Radio *Andrew Crisell*
Popular Culture: The Metropolitan Experience *Iain Chambers*
On Video *Roy Armes*
Film as Social Practice *Graeme Turner*
Television Drama: Agency, Audience and Myth *John Tulloch*
Understanding Television *Edited by Andrew Goodwin and Garry Whannel*
A Primer for Daily Life *Susan Willis*
Communications and the 'Third World' *Geoffrey Reeves*
Advertising as Communication *Gillian Dyer*
The Ideological Octopus: An Exploration of Television and its Audience *Justin Lewis*
Textual Poachers: Television Fans and Participatory Culture *Henry Jenkins*
Key Concepts in Communication and Cultural Studies *Martin Montgomery, Tim O'Sullivan, John Hartley, Danny Saunders and John Fiske*

UNDERSTANDING NEWS

John Hartley

ROUTLEDGE

LONDON AND NEW YORK

First published in 1982 by
Methuen & Co. Ltd
Reprinted twice
Reprinted 1987

Reprinted 1988, 1990, 1994, 1995
by Routledge
11 New Fetter Lane, London EC4P 4EE
29 West 35th Street, New York, NY 10001

Printed in England by Clays Ltd, St Ives plc

British Library Cataloguing in Publication Data
Hartley, John
Understanding news. –
(Studies in culture and communication)
1. Mass media–Social aspects
I. Title
302.2'3 HM258

Library of Congress Cataloguing in Publication Data
Hartley, John.
Understanding news.
(Studies in culture and communication)
Bibliography: p.
Includes index.
1. Journalism. I. Title. II. Series
PN4731.H34 1982 302.2'3 81-22314
AACR2

ISBN 0–415–03933–9

To DAFYDD ELIS-THOMAS, MP
in solidarity and in answer to a question:

If the relationship between intellectuals and people/nation, between the leaders and the led, the rulers and the ruled, is provided by an organic cohesion in which feeling-passion becomes understanding and thence knowledge (not mechanically but in a way that is alive), then and only then is the relationship one of representation.

Antonio Gramsci, *Prison Notebooks*

CONTENTS

ACKNOWLEDGEMENTS

People whose names appear on the front pages of newspapers are rarely the sole authors of the actions they are credited with. And men who engage in 'their' work usually require the equally productive but invisible work of women in order to 'free' themselves for the task in hand. Those who actually produce the goods are relegated to the inside pages and supposedly 'non-productive' spheres – like the kitchen.

So it is with publishing. This book was cooked up between myself and, above all others, Carol Owen. It is my pleasure, then, to acknowledge her 'invisible' half of the work: most of the *jouissance* I've got out of this text comes from her part in it.

Thanks too to Roland Denning, of the Chapter Film Workshop, Cardiff, for valuable comments, and to Clare Richardson for more. To both her and Anna Patterson I owe thanks for permission to use extracts from their 'private collections' of old newspapers – I look forward to the next discoveries under the lino.

I have enjoyed benefiting from the tolerant company of Martin Montgomery and Garth Crandon of the Polytechnic of Wales, and from the technical assistance of Viv Cole and Malcolm Coundley. I am especially grateful to my General Editor, John Fiske, for his continuing support.

Much of the material I've used comes from the decisive contributions made in this field by the Centre for Contemporary Cultural Studies at the University of Birmingham; by the Centre for Mass

Communication Research at the University of Leicester; and, for me personally, by the Cardiff Critical Theory Seminar and *Rebecca* magazine.

My thanks also to the communication-studies students at the Polytechnic of Wales: of course, not much of this is news to them.

The publishers and I would like to thank the following for their permission to reproduce material which appears in the following pages (every effort has been made to trace the copyright holders; where this has not been possible we apologize to those concerned): Benn Publications for tables 3, 4 and 5; Macmillans for figure 2; Edward Arnold for figure 4; the BBC (and Rodney Foster, Jan Leeming and Angela Rippon) for pictures 1, 10 and 12; Syndication International for pictures 3 and 14; ITN, MCA and Thames TV for picture 4; ITN (and Alistair Burnet and Anna Ford) for pictures 6, 7, 8, 9 and 13; *Camerawork*, *The Leveller*, *Spare Rib* and *Undercurrents* (and Clifford Harper and the Minority Press Group) for picture 11; the *Daily Mail* for picture 14; the *Daily Star* (and David Willis and John Paul) and the *Sun* (and Roger Bamber) for picture 15; the *New Standard* and the *Daily Express* (and John Rogers) for picture 16; the Evening Standard (and Chris Moorhouse) and the Daily News (and Jack Smith) for picture 19.

J.H.

GENERAL EDITOR'S PREFACE

This series of books on different aspects of communication is designed to meet the needs of the growing number of students coming to study this subject for the first time. The authors are experienced teachers or lecturers who are committed to bridging the gap between the huge body of research available to the more advanced student, and what the new student actually needs to get him started on his studies.

Probably the most characteristic feature of communication is its diversity: it ranges from the mass media and popular culture, through language to individual and social behaviour. But it identifies links and a coherence within this diversity. The series will reflect the structure of its subject. Some books will be general, basic works that seek to establish theories and methods of study applicable to a wide range of material; others will apply these theories and methods to the study of one particular topic. But even these topic-centred books will relate to each other, as well as to the more general ones. One particular topic, such as advertising or news or language, can only be understood as an example of communication when it is related to, and differentiated from, all the other topics that go to make up this diverse subject.

The series, then, has two main aims, both closely connected. The first is to introduce readers to the most important results of contemporary research into communication together with the theories that seek to explain it. The second is to equip them with appropriate methods of study and investigation which they will be able to apply directly to their everyday experience of communication.

If readers can write better essays, produce better projects and pass more exams as a result of reading these books I shall be very satisfied; but if they gain a new insight into how communication shapes and informs our social life, how it articulates and creates our experience of industrial society, then I shall be delighted. Communication is too often taken for granted when it should be taken to pieces.

John Fiske

Read all about it

1 NEWS AS COMMUNICATION

But she only loves him because he's got a Cortina

The Lambrettas

In the beginning

When we learn to speak, we learn much more than words. From the very beginning we use language not just to name things, but, more importantly, to work out how to behave towards other people and the world 'out there'. For instance, together with the words 'biscuit' and 'dog' we may learn approval; similarly, together with the words 'hot' and 'dirty' we may learn not to touch the gas stove or that otherwise quite tempting object left behind by the cat. Even at this stage, we don't only rely on our own sensations but also on what we've learnt in language as the way of organizing the world around us into some semblance of order. So when a close and trusted grown-up says 'ah-hah, that's hot', we may well take our enquiring finger away from the teapot without actually feeling the heat. Likewise, we may not even notice many of the innumerable sensations that present themselves to our senses – preferring to concentrate on those we've learnt, or have been encouraged, to speak about.

Speech, then, is the means by which we select and organize our experiences, and it is the medium through which we learn how to behave, how to react, what to believe. Furthermore, speech isn't something over which we have individual control – it is supplied to us as a ready made tool by other people. We learn to find, explore and understand our own individuality within its terms. If you like, at the very moment when we begin to use language we enter the wider world of social relations – but at that same moment we have our first encounter with a form of social control. We learn to be what we are through a language-system whose rules and conventions we can neither alter nor ignore.

However, most of us are able and happy to take this impersonal and unavoidable social force of speech as we find it. It seems quite natural, and it is very much in our own interests to go along with the rules and constraints for the sake of the benefits we gain from successful communication. If, as often happens, we can't express our thoughts, feelings or desires adequately with the linguistic resources at our command, we generally blame ourselves and seek to find a way to improve our performance. It doesn't occur to us to say that because language has failed us this time it is no good and we'll henceforth either abandon it or make up a new one. Should we be tempted to take such measures, there are plenty of people around us who will do their best to 'cure' us and bring us back into the speech community. Hence our submission to the social control of the language-system is usually both voluntary and taken for granted. Having submitted to the range of possibilities offered by language (including, remember, both values and a structuring system by which we order the perceptions of the world and our own inner sensations), we are free to go on to make sense of our selves and our lives, and to act creatively in society. But even as we speak, language speaks us.

As time goes on, our command of language increases. But it doesn't just grow like a shopping list with the simple addition of more and more items. Instead, we learn whole new sub-languages, as it were, which we encounter as our experience and circumstances develop. In other words, whenever we enter a new field of experience, we find our way by a process which resembles not simply learning, but rather the first experience of learning language. We're immersed in a whole set of new terms, rules or codes, and the conventions which govern how this particular sub-set of language operates. As with all speech, these terms, codes and conventions are the bearers of a structure of meanings and values, which we construct out of the linguistic raw materials as we use them in context. Often we put a good deal of effort into getting it right and take a good deal of pleasure in 'playing' (often, as with puns, banter and verbal games, well beyond the bounds of rational 'sense') with the language sub-set associated with a field of activity that we value. We identify strongly with certain language-systems, and seek to present ourselves in their terms. And often we can communicate quite successfully within an area of language without necessarily having direct experience of its associated activities.

For instance, most people as they grow up are encouraged to get involved in activities which are somehow seen as appropriate to their gender. This process starts very early, with the differences between the kinds of toys seen as 'right' for boys and girls respectively; with the kinds of books, tastes and interests they are encouraged towards; and with the sorts of values and identifications they are expected to fulfil in themselves. By the time people reach their teens, this process has usually gone a long way, so there are quite specialized areas which separate still further the supposed distinctions between the sexes. Hence whilst it is apparently 'right' for boys to spend a lot of time learning about – and learning to *talk* about – cars, sport and the like, it is equally deemed 'right' for girls to learn the language of make-up, fashion, etc.

On the surface there's not much in common between cars and make-up. Indeed, the differences are often what is most valued by those who, respectively, enter 'cosmetics culture' and 'Cortina culture'. But the process by which these differences are achieved is much the same. Take the example of make-up. The skill required to choose, apply and combine the various types of skin care products and make-up is neither the first nor the most important thing to be learnt. There is a whole language or culture of cosmetics within which each person must find her own way of expressing her identity – as well as relating to others involved in the same culture. The language of cosmetics is learnt through the media of women's and girls' magazines, advertisements, the advice of parents or other older acquaintances, and by constant 'girl-talk' with school- or work-mates and friends. Along with ideas about colours, new products, and the relative merits of different lotions, there is an ordered world of meanings and values to which these practical activities give material expression. The 'symbolic order' offers an imaginative space for us to identify with – if we seem to fit that space, we'll take an interest in the products. More important, we'll be able to see and present our 'selves' with confidence in the recognized and accepted idiom of this linguistic system.

But while we are learning the specialized language-system of cosmetics culture (or Cortina culture), we are learning a lot more besides. For instance, it is obvious that much of this culture is promoted and directed by business and commercial interests – it is an industry. At the very moment we seek to express our real and innermost essence as individuals through the medium of make-up and its associated values and range of meanings, we are simultaneously entering into bargains with impersonal social institutions like cosmetics firms, magazine publishers and high street retailers. We learn how to live within the frameworks given by these institutions. Without losing our fascination for the products and for the culture by which both they and part of our own 'sense of self' is defined, we learn to accept as natural the existence and personal relevance of the industrial framework.

And so the effect, or function, of our individual involvement with cosmetics is two-fold. We unwittingly reproduce social structures and relationships and our identity is produced *by ourselves* to fit in with these structures and relations. It follows that we put a lot of personal effort into subjecting ourselves to subordinate, dependent positions in society.

The way in which we learn to accept the social forces and institutions around us as natural is primarily through the medium of language-systems like the one associated with cosmetics which I've just outlined. There is a two-way process involved with all of these cultural sub-systems. We literally create or produce our own individual identity by means of the various overlapping systems we learn to speak; and conversely the social forces and institutions are themselves maintained and transmitted over time by means of the active reproduction of their meanings, values and routines in the speech and habits of us, their bearers or carriers.

In a society as complex and industrialized as that of the West, there are innumerable specialized meaning-systems or 'discourses' that can be identified. Everyone's identity can be seen partly as a result of the selection and involvement to which s/he has been exposed or has chosen. However, not all of these discourses are esteemed as equally important. For instance, the world of public affairs, politics and current events seems to enjoy a higher prestige than the more private world of domestic life, personal relationships, sexuality and emotions. There seems to be a social process at work in which certain facets of our overall culture 'count' more than others.

News-discourse

And so we come to the news. It is a social and cultural institution among many others, and it shares their characteristics in important ways. It is, literally, made of words and pictures, so comprising a specially differentiated sub-system within language. Although many people don't take a detailed interest in it, especially until after they leave school, it nevertheless enjoys a privileged and prestigious position in our culture's hierarchy of values. And of course, the way we relate to it as individuals is actively to learn its particular language-system. We do this without needing to make any more or less of a deliberate effort than we expend on learning to speak for the first time. Just as learning ordinary language entails learning values and a range of selected and structured responses to what we see around us, so it is with news. News comes to us as the pre-existing discourse of an impersonal social institution which is also an industry. As we get used to its codes and conventions we will become 'news-literate' – not only able to follow the news and recognize its familiar cast of characters and events, but also spontaneously able to interpret the world at large in terms of the codes we have learnt from the news. Individually, we perceive and interpret the world in terms partly derived from classifications made familiar in the news; collectively, we make up 'reality' as we go along, perceiving it as meaningful to the extent that it can be made to resemble the expectations we bring to it from the ordered language-system of the news.

However, it must be said at once that the news, whether heard on radio, read in newspapers or seen on television, gains much of its 'shape' from the characteristics of the medium in which it appears. We shall explore later on in this book the extent to which TV news in particular promotes a similar view of the world as TV fiction, from soap opera to adventure series. In other words, the question arises as to how far news comprises an autonomous sub-system of language by itself, and how far it is merely one of the variations in a larger system.

In order to answer that question, we need to make a distinction between two of the terms I've been using almost interchangeably up till now. We must distinguish between a *language-system* and a *discourse*. A system is a structure of *elements* in a rule-governed set of *relations*. To understand it you have to be able to *identify* the different elements from each other, and show how they are selected and combined according to the rules or conventions appropriate to that system. In the case of language, for example, the system is the generative structure which enables us to produce actual speech in conditions of 'rule-governed creativity'. In other words, the system doesn't dictate *what* we say, it determines the *way* we can produce language that is understood as meaningful by ourselves and others.

Take, for example, Bernard Shaw's famous proposal for a spelling of the word *fish*, which he maintained could be justified by other examples of English spelling. His version is GHOTI. He arrived at this wonderful spelling by taking the pronunciation of three words, and using their established spelling to make up his fish. The three words are: enou*gh* (f); w*o*men (i); and na*ti*on (sh). But of course pronunciation is one thing, and spelling another. We know there is something fishy about ghoti because the elements *gh*, *o* and *ti* can only be used as *f*, *i* and *sh* in particular positions within words. The rules of combination dictate that if we want to ask for something to go with the chips we do as the language-system tells us: we have to use the conventional rules for combining the recognized elements.

Discourses, on the other hand, are perhaps best understood as the different kinds of *use* to which language is put. Hence in order to understand a discourse we need to look more closely at the social, political and historical conditions of its production and consumption, because these 'determinants' will shape what it says, the way it develops, the status it enjoys, the people who use it, the uses to which it is put and so on.

In discourses, language-systems and social conditions meet. Each individual person will have at her or his command a number of different discourses appropriate to various social relations and activities. Some discourses are more formal than others – for instance the discourse of the court of law is more formal than the discourse of the family. But the less formal (less consciously formal, at any rate) discourse of the family still has its particular forms, uses and effects. Certain terms become 'loaded' with significance, as for instance the whole galaxy of terms surrounding the concept of 'home', in which notions of housework, cleanliness, comfort, privacy, and so on come to *mean* the values associated with care, motherhood, refuge, etc. We come to live out our family roles through the discourse and its associated values.

Whether we then identify with the 'discourse of domesticity', and put our carpet-slippered feet up within it, or whether we resist it, preferring perhaps the discourse of the carpet-bagger, the city and the night, is another matter. What we cannot do is avoid it. Our everyday interactions are structured by our social/economic/political relations; these relations are experienced through various discourses, and discourses are structured by the generative system of language. Hence in order to live in the everyday situations that feel so natural, so familiar, we must make sense of them through the meanings which discourses have established as the taken-for-granted routine of 'reality'.

Returning to the question of whether or not TV news is an autonomous 'language' or whether it is merely a variant of a larger system, we can now answer more precisely. News is a discourse which is structured by the larger discourses of television. These larger discourses themselves are dependent upon the overall language-system for their elements (signs) and their rules and conventions (codes). News is a very specific example of 'language-in-use', of socially structured meaning. This is one of the reasons for studying it, of course. For language is a very big subject, and understanding its systematic nature does not always lead to an equal understanding of the uses to which it is put socially; the 'politics' of language. Studying a specific discourse, on the other hand, gives us accessible material which cannot be divorced from its social function.

However, once we have understood that news is a discourse generated by a general sign-system in relation to a social structure, we can move on to see that the particular way in which news discourse has developed and is used, is to some extent autonomous. That is to say, news develops in an active and even creative way – it doesn't simply 'reflect' its linguistic, social or historical determinants, it works on them. It transforms its raw materials into a recognizable product, which we accept as familiar.

Talking and writing about the news

One piece of evidence which suggests that the news is indeed an independent or autonomous discourse is the amount of attention and analysis it receives – the extent to which people talk about it. At the level of journalism itself, there is a wide range of journals, TV and radio programmes whose purpose is to comment on and interpret the news. News occupies a significant place in the informal talk of workplace, pub and street. And at the level of formal learning, there is a productive industry of articles, books and courses all seeking to understand what news is and how it can be related to other forces at work in society.

It is interesting to note that there is a specific and discernible pattern to the kinds of things which are regarded as important by those who talk and write about the news. In other words, as soon as we enter 'news culture' we're confronted by certain issues. High on the league-table of priorities is the question of impartiality – is the news biased towards one political position or not? Is the news more sympathetic to bosses than to trade unionists? Is the news sexist, racist and insensitive to the rights of minorities? Is the news a propaganda mouthpiece for mindless nationalism? In short, does the news report events which are meaningful in themselves, or does it 'translate' them, as it were, into its own meaning-system and scale of values? And if it does, then which social and political groups or forces benefit most from this translation of events into meanings?

Clearly a large proportion of the talk about the news will centre on its political role, since one of its prime purposes is to report on the world of politics and the economy. In addition, many researchers have followed the actual process of news-gathering and news-production, to see what influence the industrial and social organization of the news institutions has on the content of the output. Other researchers have concentrated on the social function of the news – why does a society like ours need it and invest such a large amount of money and prestige in it? What is the use of the news?

A different approach to these kinds of question is offered by historical research. Clearly the way news is produced, what it concentrates on, how its stories are put together and who takes an interest in it, all depend to some extent on the habits and conventions – not to mention technology – which were developed in a previous historical period. Although each new generation is free to break fresh ground and make the news fit its own needs, it has to start from what is already there. This applies to the inherited habits of thought, traditional styles of expression, well-established values, priorities, allegiances and subject areas as much as it does to the more tangible inheritance of machinery, offices and practical skills. In other words, the language of news culture is grounded in a historical process which makes certain choices easy, others much more difficult, as we shall see.

Similarly, the news is a social institution and a cultural discourse which exists and has meaning only in relation to other institutions and discourses operating at the same time. It cannot be understood in isolation from them, and the people involved in making the news have to fit their activities into a complex social network. Many of these other institutions are pursuing aims which are different and often hostile to those of the news-producers. The State, the law, their competitors, their audiences, and (not least) the people on whose activities they report all constrain the choices open to journalists and broadcasters.

Even so, there is a widespread unease about the 'press barons' ' and television's social and political power – sometimes wielded for the 'public good', sometimes irresponsibly. The corporations and capitalists who own the means of news production can mount campaigns, of exposure and investigation, or of war-mongering and witch-hunts, which help to alter the political or social direction of a country. Clearly such power leads to a dangerous imbalance between those who control that power and the rest of us. The news is, inevitably, largely what they say it is. Hence much of the critical attention given to news organizations concentrates on watching the watch-dog. Otherwise we would have no independent confirmation that what sounds so credible and natural in the news is actually right.

The purpose of this kind of critical attention is clear. Once you've exposed a problem in the way news is collected, put together, distributed, read or used, the next step is to put it right. It is at this point, of course, that your contribution to news-discourse collides with all its other elements. 'Putting things right' then becomes a process of negotiation, hard work, and struggle against opposing ways of seeing. Most of us have neither the time, nor the accredited social status, to engage in such struggles, or even to win access to the necessary positions of credibility and influence.

Thus, despite its value (to which we shall be indebted in this book), this kind of critical attention is limited in practice to relatively few people inside or near news organizations, or in academic, political and certain commercial contexts. For most people, then, there's little hope of changing things in news culture. But things can be changed.

If we can find out how the news works, what interests it serves, and analyse its meanings, we can use that understanding every time we see or read the news: our critical understanding of news-discourse and of the world constructed within it can change even if the news doesn't. As Umberto Eco has put it:

> In political activity it is not indispensable to change a given message: it would be enough (or perhaps better) to change the attitude of the audience, so as to induce a different decoding of the message – or in order to isolate the intentions of the transmitter and thus to criticise them. (1980, pp. 148–9)

This critical activity is something we can all perform. We need to know what role the news plays in the process I described earlier, whereby each individual puts so much work into learning social discourses which function to subject him or her to subordinate status. Armed with a little knowledge and a lot of suspicion, we can 'negotiate' with the apparently unarguable meanings of news-discourse on slightly more equal terms. This book is intended to provide some of the 'little knowledge' – the ensuing critical activity is up to you. But if you attempt it, you will be engaging in a crucial task for a society where news, among many other discourses, plays a part in determining how we see the world, how we act in it, and how we behave to other people. And you'll be engaged in a social as well as a personal activity: the struggle to demystify social meanings as part of the effort towards more equal relations between people.

2 READING THE NEWS

1 *Jan Leeming, BBC news reader*

What is news?

> Tidings; the report or account of recent events or occurrences, brought to or coming to one as new information; new occurrences as a subject of report or talk.
>
> (*Oxford English Dictionary*)

As the dictionary definition makes clear, news is not the newsworthy event itself, but rather the 'report' or 'account' of an event. It is a discourse made into a meaningful 'story' in the same way as speech is made up out of elements of language. Like speech, news is made largely of words, but (also like speech) there is more to it than that. Hence we need a broader term than language, with its implication of 'just words', to understand what news is made of.

Reality and relationships

News-discourse is made of *signs* (see p. 15) combined together by means of *codes*. There is an area of communication studies, called *semiotics*, which is the study of the social production of meaning. It is concerned with understanding the nature, features and social use of signs. A sign is any item which can produce a meaning, and thus semiotics has grown out of linguistics, taking language as the prime example of a *sign-system*. The emergence of semiotics and its current influence is based on an approach to the world that can be traced across the whole range of twentieth-century intellectual development, marking a radical break with 'Enlightenment' conceptions of reality. Stated at its most general, this approach sees 'reality' as a human construct. The natural and social world does not consist of objects, forces or events which exist, independently of the observer, in a state where their identity and characteristics are intrinsic to their nature and self-evident. Nor is the world 'ready-made', sitting quietly out there waiting to be discovered. Though we shall be pursuing this disquieting notion largely in the direction of social reality, it is worth pointing out that the same tendency towards abandoning any idea of the self-evident solidity of the real can be found at the heart of twentieth-century physics, where we might have expected to be on firmer ground. On the contrary, the closer physics has come to the 'particles' of 'matter' that make up the physical world, the less physical they appear. Sometimes the 'shattering implications' of modern physics are even deemed newsworthy. Here is a report from the *Guardian*:

> When the full impact of the new ideas sank in, physicists of the 1930s began a searching analysis of the nature of reality and the role of the observer (i.e. human beings) in the quantum universe. The inherent uncertainty within matter undermines our confidence in the concreteness of the external world. A magnified picture of the microcosmos does not simply reveal a scaled down version of the everyday world, but a shifting, insubstantial mêlée where all objects lose their individual identity. Indeed, it is not even possible to regard atoms as *things*, existing in a well-defined state independently of our perception of them.
>
> Niels Bohr, the originator of the quantum atom, argued that it is meaningless to regard the atom, or any other denizen of the microcosmos, as 'really' existing in a particular condition before we observe it. Only within the context of an actual experiment does a concrete reality appear. Change the experiment and you change the reality. (Professor Paul Davies, 'The Subatomic Anarchy Show', 1 May 1980)

As in physics, so in the study of social reality – the reality you observe depends on how you look at it. Unsettling as it is to find the familiar landmarks of the physical world now appear as a 'shifting, insubstantial mêlée where all objects lose their individual identity', it is perhaps even more profoundly disturbing to turn our attention to our own 'selves' and discover the same contending mêlée of forces where once we had 'individual identity'. It is interesting that our language ascribes exactly the same properties to people as to atoms – both are recognized as indivisible objects, as *individuals*. But in both cases the apparent identity of the individuals in question can be seen as a trick of the light that was shed upon them in the act of observation itself. If we change the focus of our attention, a different reality emerges – a reality which consists not in *things*, but in *relationships* within a system. Further, the notion of relationship requires us to think again about our habit of imputing intrinsic characteristics to individual objects – or individual people. Unlike a brick wall, a relationship is not 'there' in the sense that you can bang your head against it. If we are constituted by the relationships we maintain in systems ranging from the most immediately social – family, school, locality, friends etc. – to the large-scale systems of class, language, culture and historical 'moment', then it follows that these relationships only exist in so far as they are maintained in time and action, continuously produced out of the very difference between the various elements that the system differentiates. 'Accordingly', as Terence Hawkes argues,

> the *relationship* between observer and observed achieves a kind of primacy. It becomes the only thing that *can* be observed. Moreover the principle involved must invest the whole of reality. In consequence, the true nature of things may be said to lie not in things themselves, but in the relationships which we construct, and then perceive, *between* them. (1977, p. 17)

As in relationships, so in brick walls. Although you can bang your head against them, they are meaningless in themselves.

Clearly walls are not intended only or even primarily to communicate meaning, to act as sign-systems. But the fact that they do so, that they *signify*, and that they do it 'like a language', can help us to understand the extent to which the 'nature of the real' is a *result*, an *effect* of 'language' and not a source of our understanding of reality. In other words, the world is *realized* (in both senses of the word – made real and understood as such) in language. But of course language is itself real, and its workings are subject to analysis. However, once again we must remember those walls – their capacity for signification reminds us that 'language' is, in semiotics, a very broad, or 'stretched' concept, as Terence Hawkes has put it. He continues:

> Nobody just talks. Every speech-act includes the transmission of messages through the 'languages' of gesture, posture, clothing, hair-style, perfume, accent, social context etc. over and above, under and beneath, even at cross purposes with what words actually *say*. And even when we are not speaking or being spoken to, messages from other 'languages' crowd in upon us: horns toot, lights flash, laws restrain, hoardings proclaim, smells attract or repel, tastes delight or disgust, even the 'feel' of objects systematically communicates something meaningful to us. (ibid., p. 125)

If we seek to understand the news we will need to take account of two major determinants of what it means; (i) the language (*sign-system*) in which it is encoded, and (ii) the *social forces* which determine how its messages are both produced and 'read'. We shall begin by considering (i): news's semiotic determinants, and we shall return later on in more detail to (ii): the social forces relevant to its meaning. However, it should be remembered that the news, like all other discourses, is a social force in its own right.

Sign-systems

Although it is clear that the most mundane objects, like walls, are capable of producing meanings, and that this is part of their function, it is better to return to the model of spoken language to understand the formal properties and significant features of a sign-system. There is a wealth of published material on the subject, but it is worth summarizing some of the most important concepts and arguments in order to provide a basis for analysis. However, it must be said that the whole area is notoriously strewn with pitfalls, from the most technical (the meaning of terms) to the most profound (the nature of language, reality), and you are well advised to pursue the matter with the help of some of the readings recommended at the end of this book.

Of course it is not possible to speak of the news as a self-contained sign-system independent of the conventions and characteristics of language. And equally there are certain specific characteristics and conventions at work in the discourse of news which are unlike those of spoken language. But it is the combination of these general and specific characteristics of 'signification' that makes news meaningful.

It is not the *event* which is reported that determines the form, content, meaning or 'truth' of the news, but rather the *news* that determines what it is that the event means: its meaning results from the features of the sign-system and the context in which it is uttered and received.

Neither news nor language are transparent windows on the world. They are both more like maps of the world. A map differs from the terrain it indicates in very obvious ways, without ceasing to maintain a relationship which allows us to recognize the terrain through it. But in order to find our way about with a map we have to understand its own distinctive codes, conventions, signs and symbols. A map organizes, selects and renders coherent the innumerable sense impressions we might experience on the ground. It does not *depict* the land, since water is not blue, hills and fields are not brown and green, and neither natural contours nor social boundaries are visible in the way they are shown on a map. Clearly a map is an abstraction from reality, translating it into an autonomous system of signs and codes, proposing ways in which the various and contradictory phenomena of the land can be artificially categorized, classified and differentiated. Equally clearly, a map is dependent for its 'meanings' on being actually used, and different kinds of maps serve different purposes (rambling, driving, military exercises, geological or other specialist expeditions), just as different kinds of discourse serve different signifying purposes in social use.

The way news 'maps' the world and produces our sense of its reality depends very largely on the nature of the various signs it uses. But what is a sign? How is the selection and combination actually organized so that we 'recognise the terrain'?

Signs

It is important, in any attempt to analyse something, to look at the object in its relationships, and not to seek to explain its workings by reference to something completely different. Thus, although it is common practice, it is not much use trying to explain a work of literature by reference to the motives, intentions, literary genius, etc. of the author. This is because you haven't got the author there to interrogate – only the literary text. The text can work its magic without the author standing there telling you what s/he intended, and so it should be possible to do without the author to work the magic out. The habit (all too prevalent in teaching literature) of 'explaining' a text by appealing to data that cannot be recovered (as in 'What Shakespeare *really meant* was. . .') must lead away from analysis and towards the repetition of ideological opinions. You only succeed in explaining your text *away*.

So it is with signs. Signs cannot be understood by reference to the objects, notions, ideas, etc. that they seem so naturally and transparently to 'stand for'. In other words, the make-up of a sign, the way it relates to others, and the way it does its job of signifying are not determined by the external 'referent' of the sign. Instead they are determined by the internal structure of the sign-system, and *then* by the relationship which exists in use between that system and the reality it 'maps'. So what is a sign?

In the most influential terminology, that of Ferdinand de Saussure (1974), a sign is made up of two elements, just as a sheet of paper is made up of two sides which you can recognize as distinct, but you cannot divide from one another. The two 'sides' of a sign are called the *signifier* and the *signified*. The signifier in speech is the *sound-image*, and the signified is the *concept*. They are distinct because the relationship between any one signifier and its signified is *arbitrary*: the concept 'brown' and the sound-image 'brown' bear no necessary relation to one another. A language can signify the concept by whatever sound-image it likes, though you as a person can't – these relations are not under individual control. Any sound-image will do, as long as it is distinguished from others in the system. As Jonathan Culler puts it,

> Since I speak English I may use the signifier represented by *dog* to talk about an animal of a particular species, but this sequence of sounds is no better suited to that purpose than another sequence. *Lod, tet*, or *bloop* would serve equally well if they were accepted by members of my speech community. There is no intrinsic reason why one of these signifiers rather than another should be linked with the concept of a 'dog'. (1976, pp. 19–20)

Hence the signifier is always arbitrary in relation to its signified – they are distinct.

But you cannot divide them from one another because there is no pre-existing concept which is simply 'named' by a signifier. Concepts, or signifieds, are not natural, given entities corresponding to distinct parts of the world out there. Signifieds are just as much a part of language as signifiers – they perform the function of dividing up the natural and perceived continuum of sense-impressions into organized categories.

Take once again the concept (signified) 'brown'. There is nothing in nature to say exactly which segment of the colour spectrum is meant by 'brown'. The concept 'brown' depends not on the colour in nature, but on the way the spectrum is divided up in any particular language: 'in order to know the meaning of *brown*, one must understand *red*, *tan*, *grey*, *black*, etc.' (Culler, 1976, p. 25). In fact different languages do divide the colour spectrum differently: Welsh, for example, has no signified corresponding to English 'brown'. The perceived 'colour' is rendered in different contexts by *gwinau* (close to English *bay* or *auburn*), or by *cochddu* (literally *red-black*), or by *llwyd* (*grey* or *pale*), or even by the borrowed *brown* (just as English borrowed *brown* from preceding Germanic languages). Furthermore, the concept 'brown' is not even fixed in English. Originally, as the OED makes clear, it signified 'darkness', particularly the apparent 'darkening' of other colours in twilight. It was taken as very nearly synonymous with black (as in 'black' hair), except that in the languages from which it was borrowed, the concept included the notion of 'shining' (as in *burn*ished) as well as 'darkness'. Hence the modern concept, where the signified is 'yellow + black + red', is a development which itself demonstrates the arbitrary nature of both signifier and signified.

Notice that the arbitrariness we have been discussing is twofold: the signifier is arbitrary in relation to the signified; the signified is arbitrary in relation to the continuum of perceived sense-impressions of the world, or what Culler calls the 'conceptual field'.

From where then do the signifieds and signifiers get their capacity to do the job of meaning? Certainly not from simply 'reflecting' the intrinsic properties of the 'referents': as we have seen these do not have determinant properties that are recognized by language. Rather, *signs* (the combined signifier + signified) gain their capacity for meaning by the *differences* which they establish between one another. Brown only 'means' not-tan, not-buff, not-red, etc. As Saussure puts it,

> Instead of pre-existing ideas then, we find . . . *values* emanating from the system. When they are said to correspond to concepts, it is understood that the concepts are purely differential and

defined not by their positive content but negatively by their relations with the other terms of the system. Their most precise characteristic is in being what the others are not. (1974, p. 117)

The idea of linguistic *value* is a very useful one. It suggests that the apparently intrinsic meaning of particular signs is determined in fact by the existence or not of other signs within its conceptual field. The example given by Saussure is the value of the term *mutton* in English and of *mouton* in French. The two terms do not have the same value, because in France you can find *mouton* both on the table and in the field, whereas in English a distinction is made between *mutton* and *sheep*, and you'd be very surprised to see mutton in the field, or indeed sheep on the table.

In the context of our own 'conceptual field', it is interesting to discover that the value of the term *news* itself is equally dependent upon its relative position in a system of differences. First, the English *news* is not the 'same' as, for instance, the French *nouvelles*, which refers to tidings, novelty or novella (but not novel, which is *roman*). The French call their news *actualités*, but this does not hold the English sense of 'actually', existing in fact, for which the French is *réel*.

Second, the English sign *news* is historically recent, becoming common only after 1500 with the invention of printing. The older English term is *tidings*. In the OED the two terms are used to define each other, but in the historical examples the earliest uses of *news* all seem to refer to *written* 'tidings'. In other words, there is evidence that in English a technological distinction exists between (oral) tidings and (literate) news. And news has always included within its conceptual field the notion of both *public* (great affairs of state) and *published* (mediated by a social organization) accounts of events (see pic. 2). Hence the use of *news* (rather than *tidings* which is now archaic) to signify personal and private events is metaphorical; the term retains its public/published/technological conceptual value.

What determines the value of any sign, then, is not its degree of fit with some pre-existing entity or concept (whether of thought or of nature), since signs *themselves* define what is or is not a concept. The value of signs is determined wholly by their relationships with others in a system. Hence it follows that these values are *social*. Language is a 'social fact' and meaning is a product of socially *recognized* (conventional) differences.

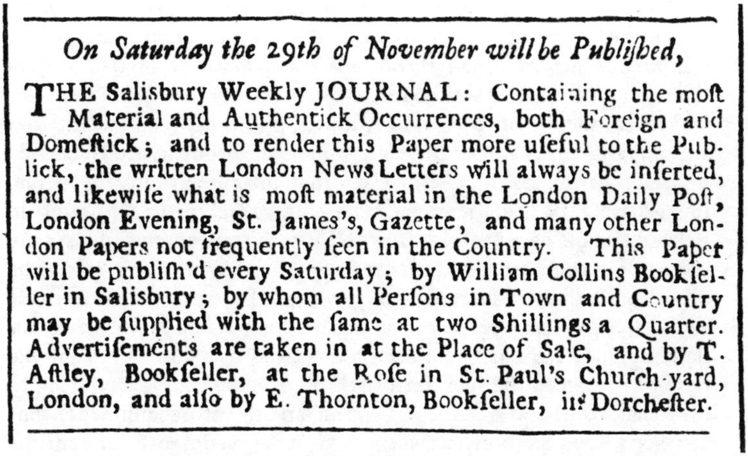

On Saturday the 29th of November will be Publiſhed,

THE Salisbury Weekly JOURNAL: Containing the moſt Material and Authentick Occurrences, both Foreign and Domeſtick; and to render this Paper more uſeful to the Publick, the written London News Letters will always be inſerted, and likewiſe what is moſt material in the London Daily Poſt, London Evening, St. James's, Gazette, and many other London Papers not frequently ſeen in the Country. This Paper will be publiſh'd every Saturday; by William Collins Bookſeller in Salisbury; by whom all Perſons in Town and Country may be ſupplied with the ſame at two Shillings a Quarter. Advertiſements are taken in at the Place of Sale, and by T. Aſtley, Bookſeller, at the Roſe in St. Paul's Church-yard, London, and alſo by E. Thornton, Bookſeller, in Dorcheſter.

2 *An eighteenth-century advertisement for a newspaper: notice that even at this early stage much of the news is borrowed from other publications – a major component of news to this day. (From Fog's Weekly Journal, 20 November 1736.)*

And so is the news. Take for example a report that might easily appear in tonight's national news programme. 'Terrorists today carried out an attack in Belfast.' Saying nothing for the moment about how we might *interpret* the sign 'terrorist', it is nevertheless clear that it is not directly determined by the intrinsic properties and 'nature' of the men and women who may have been involved in the conflict. Such meaning as the sign 'terrorist' is capable of generating in this context depends not on the external referent but on the place it occupies in a socially 'live' selection of signs in a rule-governed and conventionalized combination.

The sign 'terrorist' gains its meaning at the most basic level from the selection and combination of English-recognized sounds, or phonemes. Hence it *differs from*, for instance, 'theorist', or 'errorist', and in the recognition of phonemically distinct combinations of elements lies its capacity to signify at all. Likewise, 'terrorist' as a complete sign differs from others which could be chosen, as, for instance 'soldier', 'freedom-fighter', 'guerilla', 'volunteer', 'gunman', etc.

The sign 'terrorist' is the 'trace' of not one struggle but two. There is certainly a struggle in the streets of Belfast, but for the purposes of news-discourse the main issue is the choice of which sign to use to realize, to make sense of, that real event. The politico-military event is grasped through the discursive event (the re-production of it in news-discourse). Once chosen, the sign 'terrorist' still leaves plenty of room for argument, given that its interpretation will depend on the reader/hearer's ideological position on one side or other of the conflict. However, that interpretation will operate in the field of signification; since those real people fighting in Belfast could equally well suit all of the alternative signs (and others) instanced above, the struggle to signify them as 'terrorists' or otherwise is conducted wholly within the terms of a particular sign-system. Therefore, the meaning of the preferred term 'terrorist' derives not from their actions or identities as such, but from the relations between the sign 'terrorist' and others.

Social reality and its signification are therefore indivisible but distinct – the relation between signs and their real referents is arbitrary. Meaning is made possible by the relationship between sign and sign, and further by the social circumstances in which the signs are uttered.

Paradigm and syntagm

I have spent some time on the notion of signs in order to demonstrate that their apparently positive substance is only made possible negatively, by means of the absence or presence of related values. The way in which signs are selected and combined exploits this notion of absence/presence. The sequence of signs that makes up any act of communication involves relations in two dimensions, as shown in figure 1. There is the 'vertical' axis of choice, or selection, which is called the *paradigmatic* axis, and there is the 'horizontal' axis of chain, or combination, which is called the *syntagmatic* axis (see Fiske, 1982).

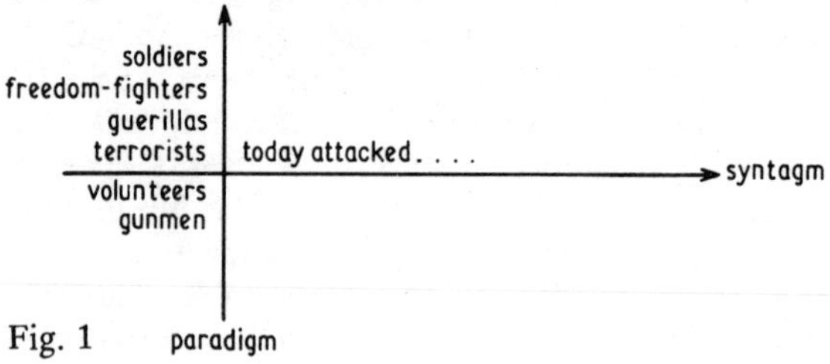

Fig. 1

Paradigmatic and syntagmatic relations work at all levels of language. Within words, phonemes are differentiated paradigmatically

f
b
pin
k
d
etc.

as well as syntagmatically: the phoneme /p/ in English can precede or follow any vowel, but in a syllable only the consonant /s/ can precede it, or /l/ and /r/ follow it (hence spin, plinth, prince, but not *tpin, *pdin, etc). Similarly, at a higher level, you can say 'terrorists attacked' but not 'terrorists renouned'. More importantly, the syntagm 'terrorists *liberated*' although 'grammatically correct' is unlikely. This is because, as Saussure puts it, 'the arbitrary nature of the sign explains in turn why the social fact alone can create a linguistic system. The community is necessary if values that owe their existence solely to usage and general acceptance are to be set up' (1974, p. 113). In other words the sign 'terrorist' and the sign 'liberated' belong to two opposing discourses in social use. To the extent that there is a 'general acceptance' of the value of 'terrorist', it precludes notions of approval. So, having selected 'terrorist' from the paradigm of possible signs, you would find it easier to combine it with 'captured', 'over-ran' or 'occupied' than with 'liberated'.

Multi-accentuality

Choosing not to combine a 'hooray' word (like *liberated*) with a 'boo' word (like *terrorist*) seems at first sight like a *linguistic* choice. We pick our way through contending discourses by choosing and combining signs whose linguistic values seem to fit well with each other. But of course the boo-value of *terrorist* is clearly not simply a linguistic value – it is at the same time an ideological one.

But just as the people signified as terrorists in the news have no intrinsic properties which require the use of that sign to describe them, so there are no intrinsic properties in the sign *terrorist* which require it to be used with a boo-value. In Saussure's phrase, values 'owe their existence solely to usage and general acceptance'. In other words, every sign is in principle capable of signifying different values; even when 'general acceptance' is established, signs still retain this capacity. There is, beyond the concept and sound-image of the sign, an *evaluative accent* which is exploited one way or the other in use. All signs have what Valentin Volosinov (1973) has called an 'inner dialectic quality' which he terms their *multi-accentuality*.

Multi-accentuality reminds us that signs do not have a fixed internal 'meaning', but only meaning-potentials, which are actualized in use. All signs can have their meaning potential 'accented', or directed towards a particular kind of meaning, depending on the context of the utterance, and on the speaker. For example, Dale Spender has suggested that terms which are used to qualify statements, like *perhaps*, or *maybe*, don't always appear as qualifiers:

> It seems to me that the use of the same term could be interpreted as a qualifier if used by females and an absolute if used by males; for example:
>
> '*Perhaps* you have misinterpreted me.'
> '*Maybe* you should do it again.'
>
> I think the determining factor is more often the sex of the speaker rather than the speech, so that when females use *perhaps* or *maybe* it is interpreted as a qualifier: when males use the same terms the interpretation is that they are using absolutes.
>
> (1980, p. 35)

In this case the grammatical function of the words is 'accented' towards different values depending on the speaker – the '*same*' words are *different* when uttered by men and by women. Multi-accentuality can be signified by intonation and stress in an utterance too. Consider how the 'meaning' of the statement 'she wants him' changes if you stress the different words in turn:

She wants him
She *wants* him
She wants *him*.

Multi-accentuality is a property of all signs, even those with apparently fixed and neutral meanings. For example, the word *democracy* is now 'generally accepted' to be a neutral descriptive term for a certain form of government, or a 'hooray' word in political rhetoric. But in its earliest uses in English, in the 1500s, it was virtually synonymous with 'mob' – very much a 'boo' word. The political pundits of the day worked hard to square the meaning of 'democracy' with the existing structure of politics. Sir Thomas Elyot (1531) saw democracy as a 'monster with many heads', which of all forms of government is 'most to be feared' (pp. 6–7). The French writer Jean Bodin (1576) wrote that a democracy 'is always the refuge of all disorderly spirits, rebels, traitors, outcasts, who encourage and help the lower orders to ruin the great' (pp. 192–3), whilst Thomas Hobbes (1651) saw democracy as the breeding ground for private vices – ever prey to 'a perfidious advice, a treacherous action, or a Civill Warre' (p. 242). Democracy is politically a threat to the monarchical *societies* of the sixteenth century. The monarchical *discourse* of Elyot, Bodin, Hobbes and others strives to 'naturalize' the sign democracy, making it seen intrinsically (by definition) endowed with the same negative evaluative accent as the terms they use to define it. In *Keywords* (1976), Raymond Williams lists a large number of terms like 'mass', 'industry', 'culture', 'ideology', etc., all of which have over the years been exploited in very different ways – their multi-accentuality being a site of struggle, as it were, in which contending social forces seek to 'fix' the meaning-potential of each sign with an evaluative accent conducive to their particular interests.

We can begin to see that signs don't command 'general acceptance' in privileged isolation from the contending forces which exist within any society. People struggle over what they should signify, and over what choice of accentuation for a given sign 'counts'. Even so, the 'inner dialectic quality' or multi-accentuality of signs is often suppressed in practice – the dominant accentuation seems natural and inevitable except, as Volosinov suggests, in times of 'social crises or revolutionary changes' (1973, p. 23). An example of the way an apparently inert or 'uni-accentual' sign has become an overt site of social (and therefore discursive) struggle is what Spender (1980, pp. 147 f.) calls 'he/man' language. When 'he' is used to denote not a male person but any person (male or female), it is aiding and abetting the patriarchal discourse which proposes male as the norm and female as secondary, derived, or just plain invisible. Many writers address their readers, or the generalized subject of their analysis, as 'he', or 'man'; as in (taken at random from one of the books I've been quoting in this chapter): 'a speaker of a language has a certain freedom in his choice of usage'. The choice to use 'man-made' language now appears as a *choice* rather than a 'grammatical usage' devoid of ideological value because, as Catherine Belsey puts it, 'we are aware of the connection between language and ideology in these instances because the position of women in the social structure and in ideology is currently in transition' (1980, p. 43). Walton and Davis have pointed out in this context that 'the news simply tends to assume that workers are men' (1977, p. 128), citing an example from ITN where a story about the 'determination of the men to save their jobs' is actually supported by reference to a named woman worker.

It is clear that news-discourse plays an important part in the struggle to affirm a single, uni-accentual value for signs. News-discourse is hostile to ambiguities and seeks to validate its suppression of the alternative possibilities intersecting its signs by reference either to 'the facts of the story' or to 'normal usage'. Many of the explicit 'values' of journalistic codes are concerned with unambiguity, clarity, etc. And, as we shall see, one of news-discourse's most consistent (self-imposed) tasks is to *prefer* particular meanings for events over against other possible meanings.

But since signs are necessarily multi-accentual, any discourse which seeks to 'close' their potential and to prefer one evaluative accent over another is ideological: such discourses present *evaluative* differences as differences in *fact*. Signs become an 'arena for the class struggle', and social forces which represent contending interests fight out their differences in discourse. However, we should remember that as with most struggles, there is at any one time a winner – certain potentialities within signs are conspicuous by their *absence* from what 'counts', or else by their apparent *error*. As Frank Parkin puts it:

> The characteristic speech patterns and linguistic usages of the dominant class are generally regarded as 'correct', or what counts as the grammar of the language; the usages of the subordinate class are often said to be 'incorrect' or ungrammatical where they differ from the former, even though such usages may represent the statistical norm. These examples serve to illustrate that what is essentially an evaluative matter can be transformed into an apparently factual one by virtue of the legitimating power of the dominant class. (1972, pp. 83–4)

Orientation

One of the implications of the notion of multi-accentuality is that signs don't have a fixed (dictionary) meaning, but rather that meaning is dependent on the realization of their possibilities in the process of socio-verbal interaction. The idea here is that all signs express not only a relationship between each other, and a relationship between the signifying system and its object or referent, but also a relationship between the addresser and addressee – the speaker and hearer, writer and reader.

When you speak, you listen to yourself. You organize each utterance to respond to what has been said before, you mentally take account of how your utterance will be heard, understood and reacted to by the other(s) involved, and you tailor what you say and the way you say it to the type of people you're with. In short, your utterances are oriented to the immediate social circumstances of the utterance, and through them to the wider social structure. All this and you still manage to talk *about* something.

It is clear, then, that just as individual signs are constituted by what they are not, so individual signs are inert (meaningless) until they are selected and combined in a 'live' social interaction. This applies not just to everyday conversation, but also to full-scale texts. Volosinov has made the point in respect of books, but his comments apply equally well to 'texts' like television programmes and newspapers. They too are *oriented*; their utterances are *dialogic* (structured as dialogue):

> A book, i.e., a *verbal performance in print*, is also an element of verbal communication. It is something discussable in actual, real-life dialogue, but aside from that, it is calculated for active perception, involving attentive reading and inner responsiveness, and for organized, *printed* reaction (book reviews, critical surveys, defining influence on subsequent works, and so on). . . . Thus the printed verbal performance engages, as it were, in ideological colloquy of large scale: it responds to something, objects to something, affirms something, anticipates possible responses and objections, seeks support, and so on. (1973, p. 95)

Hence it follows that meaning is never 'there' in the sign or in the text. Meaning is the product of the dialogic interaction that occurs between speaker (or text) and hearer (or reader/viewer). Therefore every utterance or text is incomplete – it is a 'moment' in the continuous generative process of language.

Equally, there is an orientation at work when we listen to or read other people's utterances. As Volosinov puts it:

> Each of the distinguishable significative elements of an utterance and the entire utterance as a whole entity are translated in our minds into another, active and responsive, context. *Any true understanding is dialogic in nature*. Understanding is to utterance as one line of dialogue is to the next. (ibid., p. 102)

It is important to remember this fundamentally interactive characteristic of language, because it gives the lie to any notion of 'passivity' in discussions of our responses to the media; it is impossible to understand 'passively'. All verbal interaction is an active *negotiation* between speaker/text and hearer/reader, an active *transformation* of the raw materials of signs into the product of meaning.

Connotation and myth

If meaning is a product of mutually oriented interaction, it follows that it is not a product of the individual person. Meaning is strictly a social phenomenon. This insight leads us on to one of the most important properties of language for any discussion of the public discourses of the media. It is this: meaning tends to be multiplied up from the particular sign or interactive utterance, until a single sign can be loaded with multiple meanings going far beyond what it seems actually to 'say'. This is a characteristic advertisers seek to exploit – after all, we all know what 'beanz' means.

There are a number of semiotic terms to describe ways in which the meanings of signs or sign-sequences are multiplied up. But whatever the terminology, the important thing to remember is that these meanings are not just 'added on', nor are they a matter of individual choice or opinion. They are an effect of the process of socially-oriented signification. The terminology I shall use derives largely from the influential work of Roland Barthes (1968, 1973). He describes two different ways in which signs are multiplied up into a 'second order' of signification: connotation and myth. Very broadly, connotation serves to signify emotion, feeling or 'subjective' values, whereas myth signifies conceptual, intellectual or 'objective' values.

1. *Connotation*

Very often connotation is described in opposition to another term, namely denotation. The idea is that a sign on its own simply denotes its distinctive features (i.e. those features that set it apart from other signs). Hence the sign *brown* (once again) *denotes* the colour brown. But it can be used to *connote* the qualities of, say, autumn, or of harvest-fare. In news-discourse the sign *moderate* may be used to denote a politician or union leader, but it also connotes approval of that status and therefore of that individual. Much of the media's attention is devoted to giving people labels that denote their job or status, but these also connote the attitude or value they attach to it. The trick is to make multi-accentual connotation look like uni-accentual denotation.

Connotation can work both syntagmatically and paradigmatically; it can result from the *cumulative* force of a sequence, or from implied comparison with *absent* alternative choices. An extreme example of a syntagmatic connotation is the famous line 'the horror, the horror' at the end of both Conrad's *Heart of Darkness* and Coppola's film-version of it, *Apocalypse Now*. In both, the cumulative build-up of the whole story is connoted in Kurtz's final utterance.

Paradigmatic connotation exploits our expectations of what might have been chosen, in order to compare it with what is there. A news-photo showing a male cabinet minister in an open-necked check shirt connotes relaxation, informality, and the home life he enjoys away from Westminster, largely because we expect to see him in a suit and tie. This thwarted expectation makes his informal get-up more significant.

Connotation is a product of signification – not of individual whim – though its possibilities can be exploited consciously, of course. An example of the way a paradigmatic connotation can work unwittingly is the verb *to have*. In English it is hard to avoid the *possessive* connotation of 'owning', a connotation not produced, for example in Welsh. Where in English one says, 'I have a book', the Welsh idiom is 'mae llyfr *gyda* fi' (there is a book *with* me); or 'I have a cold', the Welsh is 'mae peswch *arna*'i' (there is a cold *on* me). It is speculative, but interesting, to consider how much, in English culture, certain personal relationships are influenced by the multi-accentual connotation in male discourse of 'having' sex.

2. *Myth*

Where connotation signifies 'expressive' values, myth signifies values associated with concepts. The idea is that ordinary signs can serve to classify the world into conceptual categories, thus making it seem meaningful. Of course such classifications originate in the language, and so it is not the world that supplies meaning to the categories, but vice versa.

For example, take the front page of the *Sunday Mirror* of 28 December 1980 (pic. 3). The headline is 'SEXY ANNA TOPS POLL', which runs alongside a large photograph of the ITN 'News at Ten' newsreader Anna Ford. The report concerns a *Sunday Mirror* public opinion poll in which people were asked to name their 'new year honours' in various spheres. It begins: 'Lovely Anna Ford today wins the title she never wanted – Sex Symbol of 1980.' The sign in this case is Anna Ford – in both the picture and the report. But what is signified is not only the real historical individual, it is also two or three distinct but related *myths*. They include, first, the showbiz myths of glamour and celebrity – Anna Ford is 'known for being well-known'. The news as a whole is structured around the 'newsworthiness' of 'élite personalities', who are available to signify other myths. In this case the other myth is the sexist one in which a woman is, as Charlotte Brunsdon (1978) points out, defined 'through her procreative ability and her sexual attractiveness to men – a *definition through her body*' (p. 21). Or, as the *Sunday Mirror* puts it: 'Lovely Anna Ford'. She is made to signify the myth of female sexuality, even though the person Anna Ford explicitly objects to such myths, and is quoted as so doing in the report: 'My complaint is that women are always talked about on the basis of how they look. You get headlines like "Man and Blonde Die in Car", as though the only interesting thing about the woman is her hair, and it's sufficient to describe her as just "blonde".' But to no avail, it seems. Her social function as the signifier of sexist myths is something she can contest, but not by herself overcome.

Myths, then, are produced within signification. They are produced when signs are multiplied up so that their 'denotative' meaning includes (apparently intrinsically) signs of conceptual values. Hence it follows that myths are not ready-made, existing somewhere in a pre-formed state and waiting to be used. They are a product of the active generative process of language, formed and

Spain 90 pesetas. France 7 francs. Italy 800 lire. Malta 20 cents.

Sunday Mirror

Three days before the official list

20p December 28, 1980 No. 919

YOUR New Year Honours

SEXY ANNA TOPS POLL

By REVEL BARKER

LOVELY Anna Ford today wins the title she never wanted — Sex Symbol of 1980.

Britain's men rated the ITN beauty streets ahead of stunners like Sophia Loren, Bo Derek and Debbie Harry.

Anna, 36, has always preferred to be judged on the way she reads the News at Ten rather than her looks.

But was she furious at being voted the nation's favourite in an exclusive survey scientifically conducted for the Sunday Mirror? Happily, not a bit

"It's terribly touching, very sweet," said Anna when told the result. "I really am delighted."

Heroes

More than 1,000 men and women in all parts of Britain took part in the poll to compile *YOUR* New Year Honours List.

The survey (*see Pages* 10 *and* 11) included your top personalities and entertainers of 1980 and comes three days before the official Honours List.

Man of the Year is the Pope and your favourite heroes are the SAS and Pc Trevor Lock of the Iranian Embassy siege in London.

Anna also came third in the Women Of The Year vote—behind the Queen Mother and The Queen.

"I'm really flattered to be included in a list like that," she said.

The girl who faces millions of viewers each night was camera-shy yesterday.

"I'm on holiday, and just slopping about in jeans," she said. "I wouldn't want to be photographed like this."

The picture here is the one Anna said she would most like Sunday Mirror readers to see.

Anna explained her ideas on glamour. "There has always been a misunderstanding about my views," she said. "My complaint is that women are always talked about on the basis of how they look.

"You get headlines like 'Man and Blonde Die in Car', as though the only interesting thing about the woman is her hair, and it's sufficient to describe her as just 'blonde'.

"Women are a lot more interesting than that, and have lots of other facets.

"I'd like people to recognise it, that's all."

Here's what other personalities think of Anna's award.

Ex-colleague Reginald Bosanquet said: "I find her extremely attractive — physically, intellectually and professionally.

"I am not in the least surprised at the result of the poll. We get on well together and I would have voted for her."

TV star **Bruce Forsyth** said: "She is most attractive. I particularly like her when she has her hair up. She is a very lovely girl."

Actress **Diana Dors** said: "Many men who watch TV obviously sit there and fantasise about her."

Diana's husband, actor **Alan Lake**, said: "I think she appeals to men's primitive instincts."

Top fashion designer **Bill Gibb** said: "Anna is just terrific. I designed some clothes for her once and although she is not beautiful in the classical sense, she has a winning personality and charm. Anna reflects inner

Turn to Page 4.

Anna — her choice of picture

Happy New Year Anna—and to all our readers

CLIFF RICHARD A remarkable interview

WARNING TO PARENTS

BEWARE THESE DEADLY SNOWFLAKES

Sunday Mirror Reporter

A POLICE warning was issued to parents yesterday after a "magic" party trick pill almost poisoned

to produce a snowflake effect. But two-year-old Peter

ing. He began screaming and crying, and was taken to hospital, but was allowed to return to his home after treatment.

Doctors found the trick

We are warning every family to be on the lookout for them."

The packet that turned up in Peter's stocking was in a 75p Toy Sack bought by his

patches, a football album, a colouring book, and a memo pad. Police fear thousands of them could have found their way into children's Christmas stockings.

3 *Sunday Mirror, 28 December 1980*

reformed according to the relations between social groups and forces. Thus one of the primary functions of the news in any medium is continuously to signify myths through the everyday detail of 'newsworthy' events.

A word or two on the term 'myth' itself. In commonsense language a myth is usually signified as a story, and connotatively an untrue story. But that commonsense definition also implies a separation between the olden-days, or primitive societies (which 'have' myths), and our own modern world (which doesn't). However, the function performed by myth is, roughly, to allow a society to use factual or fictional characters and events to make sense of its environment, both physical and social. In short, 'primitive' myths do exactly the job I have described here – they endow the world with conceptual values which originate in their language. News is a myth-maker.

Icons

Most of the discussion of signification so far has concentrated on the model of verbal language. But much of the news is presented on television. Hence its way of producing meaning is visual as well as verbal. However, this is not an insuperable difficulty, since the way meaning is produced visually is fundamentally structured 'like a language'. Television, then, is a semiotic phenomenon. Its signifiers include visual images, but its signifieds are very close to those of verbal language (since they are borrowed wholesale), and its way of selecting and combining its signs by paradigmatic choice and syntagmatic chain is similar. Signs on television are, if possible, even more multi-accentual than verbal signs, and television multiplies meanings by connotation and myth. Its meanings are a product of its social orientations, and not complete until 'negotiated' by the viewer.

However, there are some differences. The first is that, unlike the verbal signifier, the visual image *resembles* its signified in some way. A picture of Anna Ford looks like Anna Ford, where the sound-image or written name does not. This characteristic of visual signs is called *motivation*. A motivated sign is one where the arbitrariness so characteristic of language is limited, curtailed. *Planned* resemblance to 'the real' is introduced.

Motivated signs like photographs and television pictures are the least arbitrary ones, but there is a sliding scale, as it were, in which degrees of motivation can be discerned. Road signs which depict cars are motivated, but there is an arbitrary element in the conventionalized 'abstract' shape of the car. Some verbal signs are motivated: the sign *box-office*, for example, is motivated by the existing signification of *box* and *office*. Over time such motivated signs can themselves become arbitrary and radically change their signified. For instance, who would know that *rehearse* once signified 'plough again'? But the metaphorical use of the term to signify 'going over the same (verbal) ground' was enough to capture it for play rehearsals long after its ploughing association had withered away.

However, motivated verbal signs and motivated visual signs – known as *iconic signs* – are still signs. Their resemblance to their referent paradoxically blinds us to their essential origin in signification. Their equivalence to their object is carefully constructed, and established by convention. The determinant of 'realistic' iconic signs is not the 'real', but the same process of differentiation of recognized elements in a systematic relation to one another. For as Belsey has argued, 'Realism is plausible not because it reflects the world, but because it is constructed out of what is (discursively) familiar' (1980, p. 47). A newsphoto or video image of Anna Ford is not 'really' Anna Ford, it is Anna Ford captured, imprisoned in and made to serve as a signifier. Anna Ford does not 'mean' what the signifier 'Anna Ford' 'says'. But the result is, as James Monaco puts it, that 'the power of language systems is that there is a very great difference between the signifier and the signified; the power of film is that there is not' (1977, p. 128).

Simultaneous signifiers

A further difference between news discourse and verbal language is that the television screen and the newspaper page present signifiers simultaneously, whereas in speech signifiers are presented one at a time, in a linear sequence. Hence in both television and the newspapers – especially the popular tabloids – there is as much attention given to, and signification in, the spatial composition as the sequence of verbal/written signs. The composition within the TV screen puts different iconic signs together so that they modify or reinforce each other's signification. The same is true of the combination of headline + picture + story in newspapers. We read them simultaneously, and this is where a picture can indeed be worth a thousand ideological words. Pictures, whether moving or still, tell us the 'truth' imperatively: that is Anna Ford, therefore that is what Anna Ford is *like* (means). Her picture thus validates the headline and story with which it is simultaneously printed.

Codes and conventions

We have seen how the signs of a language are combined syntagmatically to form a sequence. There are 'rules' of combination that tell us which paradigmatic elements can go together. These rules are not prior to the act of combination – you don't normally think about which phonemes can coexist peacefully and which can't when you utter a word. You just do it. Hence the idea of a code is descriptive, analytical – it describes a particular system, or the conventions at work in producing meaning in a particular system.

Thus there are all sorts of codes, from the English language to codes of dress, codes of practice, codes of logic, etc. What they all share is the social agreement of their users – the 'encoder' of a message puts it together in a way calculated to be recognized by the 'decoder'. Codes are discernible not only in what a message says, but in its style, or mode of address. In other words, codes are a cultural phenomenon, expressing the relations between people and groups.

The term convention is often used as a synonym of the term code; you can equally well speak of the 'code' or the 'convention' of realism, for example. In television there are 'codes' of composition of the picture, and codes of movement in the picture. All of them are established by convention, but some of them originate in the culture at large, some in other media (cinema for example) and some are specific to television. Codes of composition include the way a subject is framed, coloured and lit; codes of movement include movement of both the subject and the camera. Codification in studio news presentation is rigid: the static, eye-level camera, the neutral lighting, the medium-close-up framing of the newsreader, etc. In news-films from outside the studio the code appears to be that of television location filming in general – the shots are composed to 'look like television'. However, there are certain subcodes at work which have in their turn influenced other genres of film and television. In particular, 'realism' somehow seems more naturally conveyed by a hand-held camera down there in the thick of the action and by the grainy appearance of news film shot in inconvenient lighting. Hence grainy shots and hand-held cameras have been exploited in aesthetic codes of filmmaking to express the gritty, unorganized subjective reality required: compare the shots in pic. 4.

Codes and conventions, then, intersect and organize the various processes of signification. But they are at best informal. When you learn a new code – for instance a foreign language – you don't feel confident in using it until that moment arrives when you can break the 'rules', and work creatively within the conventions. Similarly, recognition of the existence of a code does not require slavish adherence to it: there are journalistic and television codes at work in the production of news, and it is helpful to recognize them. But they are not Holy Writ. Their 'conventional' element implies not only agreement but also *choice*: that is to say, agreement between alternatives. It follows that the way the agreement is reached, and whose interests it represents, is of crucial interest to us. Simply noting the agreement embedded in what is then taken for a somehow 'necessary' code is a sure route to mystification.

Discourses and referents

> I open the newspaper for information on the news; how can you maintain that I myself created the news by opening the paper? (Bernardino Varisco, cited in Gramsci, 1971, p. 443)

Semiotics (among other intellectual enterprises) discloses the constructed quality of 'the real' – the extent to which every thing and every idea that we 'know' is known through sign-systems. And sign-systems have properties which 'speak us' even as we create meaningful utterances. Hence, for news, what makes it meaningful is not the world it reports but the sign-system in which it is encoded.

However, this valuable notion can get out of hand. The word 'mountain' is a sign, meaning what it does in the fact of its difference from other signs in its system, like hummock/hillock/hill/cliff/slope/escarpment, etc. But there are also mountains 'out there'. Is semiotics suggesting that there are only mountains out there when we say there are? As a matter of fact there are two just up the road from my house – Caerphilly Mountain and The Garth. Do they exist?

Funnily enough quite a few visitors deny it. They come to Wales armed with the concept of 'mountain-ness', which seems to produce twin visions: those Victorian-gothic, picturesque illustrations of landscapes with snow-capped pinnacles; and the model of Snowdon as a 'Welsh' variant. But Caerphilly Mountain is neither very high, nor very pinnacled; hence, for the unsuspecting visitor, it's not a 'real' mountain, even though it is 'really there'.

In other words, there is a distinction between signs and the objects/activities/notions they refer to – their *referents*. The sign-system determines the way in which we will see the referent, and referents are not pre-given entities with fixed determinate properties. This is not to say that the referent doesn't exist independently of its realization in a discourse. What is clear, though, is that both sign and referent are merely *potential* when it comes to meaning.

What makes a *sign* potential are the qualities I have described already – its arbitrariness, multi-accentuality, orientation, and its capacity for connotation and myth.

What makes a *referent* potential is that the things/ideas referred to have properties and qualities, or behaviour, which are selected by signs, for emphasis, but which may escape attention entirely or be interpreted differently in different contexts (what does 'woman' refer to?). Thus the argument about whether Caerphilly Mountain is 'real' or not is conducted by appealing to both the sign-system and the referent at once. The English language sign-system differentiates mountains from hills, and Caerphilly Mountain (the referent) *looks* pretty much like a hill. In fact, Welsh divides up the altitude continuum differently: mountain/mynydd and hill/bryn are not equivalent terms. So Mynydd Caerffili makes more 'sense' than Caerphilly Mountain.

Socially-structured discourse

The idea that both signs and their referents 'go live' only in particular discourses, and that we only know various things about reality through discourse, takes us on to new considerations. We

4.1

4.2

4.3

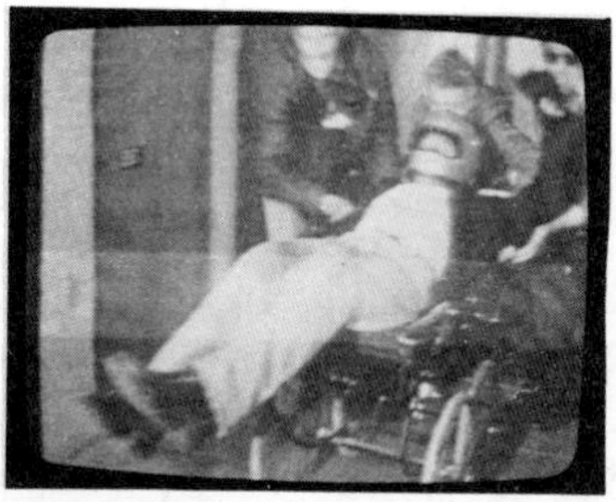

4.4

4.5

4.6

4.7

4.8

4 *Fact or fiction? How can you tell the real from the realistic?**

**All the shots on the left are from 'News at Ten', 7 January 1976; those on the right are from 'The Sweeney' (4.2, 4.4, 4.6) and 'A Man called Ironside' (4.8).*

need to know what the various forces are that shape a particular discourse, and we need to know how those forces are effective through it.

We have already seen that language is fundamentally social – its meanings are dependent on 'social agreement', or more properly on social interaction in which certain alternative choices prevail. Further, language is a continuous generative process – all utterances are but moments, pauses, in a continuing dialogic to-and-fro between speakers, groups, classes.

Thus we move on to two related determinants of the meaning of news-discourse. First, news communicates more than just inert information. Within news-discourse we need to consider the shaping forces that determine *how* the potential of sign/referent is going to be realized in a particular context. Part of the meaning of the news, and part of the ability of news to mean at all, is derived from the social structure in which it is 'uttered'.

Second, meaning is a product of interaction. Hence news means nothing at all at the time it is broadcast or printed. It has to be 'read' – and the same social-structural determinants that are at work in news itself will be at work when you read it. So there is a 'social context' which makes some meanings easy to 'read', others hard. You cannot 'read' a story about football hooligans as being about breadmaking (very easily), and you cannot escape the construction put upon the event in the news. This construction (what it 'means') cannot escape the shaping force of socially-produced ideas about hooliganism, the young, authority, etc. But you can 'read' the story differently, all the same. Either you agree with its construction (that event was hooliganism and that is what hooliganism means); or you can go along with it some of the way (that was hooliganism, but I don't like the way they've interpreted it); or you can refuse it altogether (that event took place, but calling it hooliganism is wrong, and anyway it didn't happen the way they show it). However, both your response and the original news-construction of the event into 'meaning' are unlikely to be unaffected by the circumstances in which you and the news find yourselves: both the encoding and the decoding of the message are socially determined in some way. There are patterns of response, patterns of 'preferred' meanings. We cannot speak simply of something being 'just a matter of opinion', since opinion comes from somewhere, and is maintained or changed somehow.

But it is important not to suggest that the social structure simply reaches through the news and grabs hold of you, making you an offer you can't refuse. It does reach through the news, and through you too, but what happens then is not pre-determined. For the social structure, as you can imagine, is a complicated one, with contradictory as well as coherent tendencies. Furthermore, the social structure doesn't exist anywhere outside the interaction of people involved in the continuous generative process of language. As Halliday puts it: 'The social structure is not just an ornamental background to linguistic interaction. . . . It is an essential element' (1978, p. 114).

3 NEWS AND SOCIETY

Well that's all the news and all the fairy tales tonight.
(Alastair Burnet 'News at Ten', 1980)

Topics

You might think that since news is about society, then watching the news will tell you about society. What in fact does the news tell us about? What are its referents? Although news is supposed to be about new, unexpected things, it is quite easy to outline its main preoccupations. They are grouped around and within six major topics.

1. *Politics* Defined as government (Whitehall/White House), parliament (Westminster/Capitol Hill) and the policies, personalities and disputes that make up the context of decision-making.
2. *The economy* Defined as (a) companies and the City – their performance, their figures and their management; (b) 'government figures out tonight' – the economy as a statistical model of trade figures, imports and exports, unemployment, wages, inflation, prices, etc.
3. *Foreign affairs* Usually the relations between governments and especially those involved in an issue concerning 'us' (i.e. the British Government); also reports on wars, coups, earthquakes, etc.
4. *Domestic news* Here the range of referents is wide, but the organization of them is quite tight. They fall into '*hard*' and '*soft*' stories. Hard stories are characterized by *conflict* (violence). Soft stories include *humour* and *human interest* (often defined as having a 'woman's angle'). The major areas of 'hard' news are:

Northern Ireland, industrial relations (strikes), race relations, crime, 'single-issue' campaigns (nuclear power, abortion, vivisection, conservation, etc.), social welfare (education, housing and the NHS), etc. 'Soft' news often occupies the tailpiece of news bulletins, where the newsreader settles more comfortably, smiles, softens his or her tone and perhaps even goes so far as to make a joke. We're then treated to champion one-armed shepherds and fairy stories by Prince Charles.

5. *Occasional stories* Stories about disasters, celebrities, the Royal Family and topical talking points of the day (like 'who shot JR?' – BBC news showed the clip of 'Dallas' in which he was shot).
6. *Sport* Accented towards male, professional, competitive sport; football in winter, cricket in summer, with a league-table of 'other' sport in season.

But what is missing? The Annan Committee on the Future of Broadcasting (1977, p. 275) received a number of suggestions for stories about neglected areas. They were: more European (EEC) and foreign affairs; more regional news (including the other British nations, Scotland, Ireland and Wales); more coverage of local government; and demands that the news should 'anticipate problems' (rather than simply reflect them) and that it should include more good news. Apart from the last two items here, these demands seem plausible because they simply seek to extend what is already offered and make it more comprehensive.

However, even these additions don't include vast areas of social life. There's an overwhelming 'bias' towards 'public' as opposed to 'private' life, and towards men rather than women. Little is said about the lives of ordinary people – only about the decisions made in politics, the economy, etc. which are taken to affect those lives (usually in the wallet); and only what is said by 'representative' personalities. Personal relations, sexuality, family and working conditions, and the more or less coherent voices which sound a different note to that of the familiar 'spokesman' – all these are invisible in news. The question arises: are the events that get so much coverage there because they already 'affect our lives', or do they affect our lives largely because they are constantly reported in the news?

It is interesting that the kind of topics I've outlined are by no means confined to British news in British society. Although the USA is composed over over fifty states with their own governments, two hundred million people, and a cultural, ethnic and geographical diversity quite unlike that experienced in Britain, little of this gets into their national news programmes. The same topics seem to operate. Here is a running order of items included in an NBC national news broadcast (6 p.m., 15 September 1980).

1. *2 minutes 08 seconds* Statement from President Carter on the American hostages in Iran, leading to film coverage of his presidential campaign tour of Texas. This occupied most of the item, with two filmed quotations from Carter, including a comment on the 'leave of absence' taken by his campaign manager to face drugs charges.
2. *2 minutes 01 seconds* Film report from Capitol Hill where Governor Reagan had assembled his 'team'; interview with Reagan on his policies, including attacks on the 'divisions' in the Democratic party.
3. *1 minute 51 seconds* Recap on Carter's hopes for a 'resolution' of the hostage issue, leading to a news conference by the Secretary of State, Edmund Muskie, whose comments seem to contradict his president's optimism.
4. *25 seconds* Studio report on the forthcoming debate in the Iranian parliament on the hostage issue.

Commercial break

5. *1 minute 53 seconds* A film report from the business correspondent in Vienna on the OPEC oil ministers' summit meeting, concentrating on the likelihood of oil price rises and their effect on business.
6. *1 minute 25 seconds* A film report from Turkey in the wake of the military coup. The film shows people returning to work as ordered by the military; the reporter quotes 'people' who approve of the coup, calling it a 'course correction for democracy', calling the military rulers benevolent and claiming that people are obeying them because they respect them.

Commercial break

7. *1 minute 24 seconds* A domestic story from Wisconsin, where a Cuban refugee is charged with murdering his 'sponsor', a fifty-year-old woman. Filmed vox-pops voice the fears of the residents, their determination not to sponsor any of the four thousand

Cubans waiting in centres in Wisconsin. Interview with person in charge of the centre – bad publicity hinders his work.

8. *1 minute 57 seconds* Domestic story on forthcoming Food and Drug Administration decision on whether to ban drug used for easing morning sickness in pregnancy. Interview with mother who is sueing manufacturer; short history of drug, statement of the pros and cons of the possible ban.
9. *20 seconds* A marine pleading insanity to charges of collaborating with 'the enemy' in Indo-China over fourteen-year period. Symptoms described.
10. *15 seconds* Abbie Hoffman (a 'celebrity' radical of the 1960s) faces further charges (jumping bail) after returning from exile in Canada.

Commercial break

11. *5 minutes 20 seconds* A 'special segment' on the background to the forthcoming debate between presidential candidates Reagan and Anderson. Describes the first debate (1860) involving Abraham Lincoln; goes on to the Kennedy–Nixon (1960) and Ford–Carter (1976) debates, concentrating on the impact of television: giving numbers of viewers, and interviewing Nixon on the significance of his sweaty look. Film of high-school debate, showing how it should be done, with experts criticizing the format. Filmed extracts of other political debates in which things went wrong for one candidate.

Commercial break

12. *2 minutes 10 seconds* Coverage of 'tomorrow's' Massachusetts primary, in which the Catholic Church is involved, and abortion a major issue. Closing music with preview of next morning's 'Today' programme – Henry Kissinger interviewed on the hostage issue (15 seconds).

Commercial break

It is clear from this bulletin that the stories covered are not just strung together haphazardly. They are clustered into topics, each one roughly coinciding with a segment of the programme between commercial breaks. Thus there are five segments of unequal length (between 6 minutes 25 seconds and 2 minutes 25 seconds). They are structured as follows:

1. National *politics* (presidential campaign) + *foreign affairs* (hostages in Iran).
2. *Foreign affairs* (Vienna/OPEC and Turkey) + the *economy* (oil prices) + *politics* (a 'course correction for democracy').
3. *Domestic news* – all 'hard': crime, single-issue conflict, and two fillers on 'national interest' court cases involving *occasional* stories about treason and celebrity.
4. The '*special segment*' is not currently a regular feature on British news (although 'extended programmes' are set up when Prime Ministers resign or celebrities are murdered): background detail to national *politics*.
5. *Politics*: national and 'local' at once in the form of a State primary, but also foregrounding the twin *domestic* issues of Church–State relations and abortion.

It is noteworthy that sport is entirely missing from this bulletin, but it did occupy a complete segment in the preceding 'local' programme, concentrating on sport in the State where this news was taped (California).

Apart from this difference, the NBC news is remarkably similar to British TV news in topic and length, and in the weighting given to the topics. It is also similar in the way the different topics are knitted together in each story, so that all five segments refer in one way or another to politics, for example.

Treatment

Quite apart from the six categories of coverage, which simply give us an absent/present paradigm of topics, there are two other categories of choice involved which shape the subject matter of news. They are the way a topic (once chosen) is *treated*, and the way it is *told*.

The treatment of a topic includes choosing whose comments, opinions and 'definitions' of the topic are to be sought and 'accessed' (see p. 111 for an explanation of this term). Typically, the 'accessed' voices belong to representatives of 'both' sides of a dispute, and to an 'expert' commentator.

But there is more to treatment than that. Again there is a paradigm of choice, in which certain aspects of a topic are included, others not. Take for instance one of the staple fillers of local newspapers – crime stories, or more exactly, stories from the magistrates' courts. These are a familiar sight down among the display ads, and their treatment of crime is familiar too. They concentrate on drunks, drivers, fines and magistrates' comments. The headlines to the crime stories in the *South Wales Echo* of 8 November 1979 are listed in table 1.

Table 1.

Page	*Headline*	*Length (in column inches)*
3	£20 FINE FOR THEFT ATTEMPT	7½
7	£1000 FINE FOR 'CRIMINAL FOLLY'	9½
7	DRIVER COLLIDED WITH GARDEN WALL	6
9	SIMPLY CONFORM, GUITARIST IS TOLD	12
9	CHARGES DROPPED	3½
11	DRIVER RAN AWAY AFTER CAR CHASE (pic. 5)	18¼
11	MAN IN CUSTODY ON CANNABIS CHARGE	2
11	BUS FIRM FINED	1½
19	DRIVER CAN KEEP LICENCE	3½
22	DRIVER REMEMBERS NOTHING	4¾
23	BRICKS SMASHED AFTER NIGHT OUT	9¼

Clearly such stories are useful to a local paper. There is a guaranteed supply of copy, day after day, and the magistrates' courts make 'safe' places for trainee reporters to learn the skills of their craft (in the conventional wisdom). In addition, some of the stories told in court are fascinating, even funny, and court reports often include elements of the 'invisible' areas of social life, if only in the form of marital disputes and scandals. They are sources of human interest, and magistrates often supply a moral or authoritarian quote. As a spectacular example of the latter, Cohen (1980, pp. 108–10) cites the comments of a Margate magistrate who sentenced some of the Mods and Rockers in 1964. These comments were amplified and used to justify their own readings of the events by most national newspapers: '"Sawdust Caesars hunt in pack" says magistrate'; '"Clamp down on Mods and Rockers – a Vicious Virus" says JP'; 'Town hits back on Rat Pack Hooligans'; etc.

(a)

OPENEYE

SECOND CLASS JUSTICE

ELY: the sprawling housing estates on the outskirts of Cardiff provide the capital city's magistrates courts with one out of every six defendants. But only one magistrate actually lives there.

PENYLAN: Cyncoed Avenue boasts no less than 10 magistrates. It is part of the Penylan ward where more than a third of Cardiff's JPs live. Less than four per cent of the defendants came from this ward.

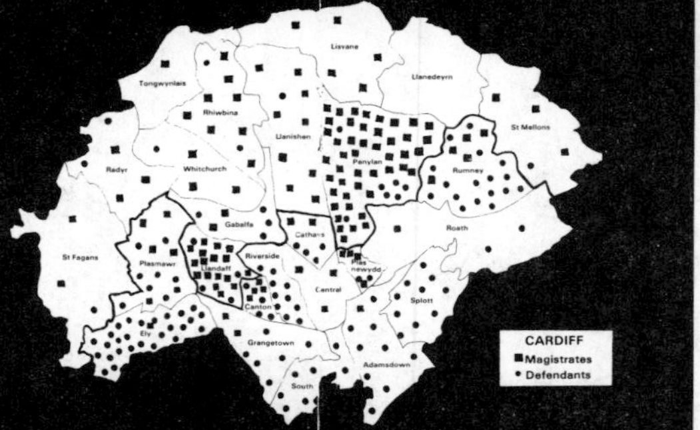

THE DIVIDED CITY: the thick black line running through Cardiff divides the affluent middle and upper class areas of the north from the poorer working class sections of the south. The overwhelming majority of the city's 128 magistrates – shown in red – live in the prosperous north. But the bulk of the 128 defendants in the OPENEYE survey – shown in black – lived south of the line.

Welsh magistrates are powerful people. In 1977 they found nearly 24,000 defendants – most of them from working class communities – guilty of criminal offences and sent more than 700 of them to prison. This OPENEYE presents evidence that magistrates are not, as is often claimed, drawn from all sections of society but mainly from the ranks of the middle and upper classes. They are selected by a bizarre process that is totally secret and completely undemocratic. Many of them are so prejudiced against working people that often the only justice available in their courts is second class justice.

On August 22 Alan Wright, a 22-year-old unemployed labourer from Adamsdown in Cardiff, appeared before the city magistrates to answer motoring charges.

There was no need for him to have appeared in person. He had written pleading guilty but was advised to attend because he might lose his licence.

After a brief appearance before two magistrates in Court No. 2 he kept his licence — but had lost his liberty. There are two versions of what happened. Court records show that he was fined £400, given no time to pay and promptly gaoled for three months. Wright only remembers being imprisoned.

Either way he should not have been gaoled. The charges he faced did not carry prison sentences and it is illegal not to give time for the payment of fines.

After 37 days in prison, Wright was freed by Judge John Rutter at Cardiff Crown Court on September 7. The judge gave him an absolute discharge, quashed the fines — and ordered an inquiry into the strange circumstances surrounding the case (see 'Wright — And Wrong' in the Mixed Morsels section of the Supplement).

Five weeks later another man was unlawfully imprisoned, this time by Cardiff's stipendiary magistrate, Sir Lincoln Hallinan. On September 28 he sent slaughterman Mark Oliver, aged 28, to prison for seven days after finding him guilty of being drunk and disorderly.

There was just one snag — the 1978 Criminal Law Amendment Act had removed the power to imprison for this offence. On October 1 Hallinan, who is paid £16,202 a year for duties that include keeping abreast of legal developments, brought Oliver back to court and publicly apologised to him.

Both Wright and Oliver were among the more unfortunate victims of the social prejudice of Welsh magistrates. But heavy sentences, out of all proportion to the offences committed, are commonplace in the 87 Welsh magistrates courts.

When Saleh Said, a regular but incompetent Cardiff shoplifter, appeared before Hallinan on November 1 he was found guilty of stealing goods worth £8.85.

Hallinan sent this harmless old age pensioner — he is 69-years old — to prison for no less than six months. The sentence works out at one day in gaol for every 4.8p worth of stolen property.

None of these people would have been gaoled had they been 'respectable' people like Hallinan or the city's lay magistrates. They would have been able to afford decent legal advice and would have been treated with more compassion.

Take the case of Midland Bank cashier Bernard John Wilkins who came up before Hallinan in July 1977. He was found guilty of stealing £350 from his employers but, although the amount involved was nearly 40 times greater than Said's haul, his three month prison sentence was suspended.

Many 'professional' crimes are too serious to be dealt with by the magistrates. But sentences in the higher Crown Courts are often far more lenient than those handed down by the magistrates.

In February 1979 Vernon Hopkins, Ogwr Borough Council's £11,500-a-year housing officer, pleaded guilty at Cardiff Crown Court to charges of defrauding insurance companies of more than £2,000. He was gaoled for 18 months but, again, the sentence was suspended.

These differences in the sentencing of defendants — recognised by most professionals involved with the courts and approved of by the majority — is due to the simple fact that defendants come from one class and magistrates from another.

Because a substantial slice of English law is designed to protect property, theft and burglary are the two most common criminal offences. Of the 130,000 crimes reported in

SWEET AND SOUR PORRIDGE

THEY CALL it porridge because that's what you get — almost every day you're there. But, just as there are different forms of justice, so there are different types of porridge.

This morning, for example, the 396 prisoners in Cardiff Prison forced down a putty like porridge made of water with a little milk for colouring.

But over the border in Gloucestershire, the 316 inmates of Leyhill Open Prison — many of them from South Wales — enjoyed a classier porridge made almost entirely with milk.

The difference is no accident. Leyhill, a former US army hospital, was taken over by the prison service after the end of the last war. The first of a new breed of open prisons, it cast aside the service's grim Victorian traditions and placed its emphasis on 'rehabilitation'.

In stark contrast, Cardiff was built even before Queen Victoria came to the throne. It was designed to 'punish' people and, even today, overcrowding and other problems mean that 'rehabilitation' comes a long way down the list of priorities.

The two prisons take completely different types of prisoners. Cardiff's prison population is made up mainly of working class men gaoled for theft, criminal damage, violence and burglary.

☐ Leyhill Open Prison: sweet . . . .

Leyhill, although it does have a substantial number of 'lifers' — murderers and others serving life sentences — is basically reserved for the better class of criminal. Mainly professional people such as bank managers, estate agents, solicitors, accountants, policemen and politicians like Gerald Murphy from Swansea and Ernest Westwood from the Rhondda.

Bridgend businessman John Williams, whose story is told in the *Corruption Supplement*, sampled both institutions in 1977.

'Leyhill was just like you would expect a health farm to be', he recalls. 'Cardiff was completely different, a terrible place. I wouldn't mind going back to Leyhill but the thought of returning to Cardiff makes my blood run cold'.

'You're a pig in Cardiff', says Alan Wright, the labourer wrongfully imprisoned there for five weeks in August. "It's impossible to describe. The food, the cells, the facilities — everything's hell'.

CARDIFF IS badly overcrowded. The 150-year-old prison has 125 more prisoners than its 'certified normal accommodation' of 271. Swansea, the only other prison for adults in Wales, has 40 more inmates than its 'normal' level of 266.

Cardiff and Swansea took many of the 1,538 men gaoled by Welsh courts in 1977. (The 100 women imprisoned went to gaols in England — there are none in Wales).

The report of the May Committee of inquiry into the state of the prison service, published in September, found that many of these people should not have been gaoled in the first place.

The mentally ill, alcoholics, maintenance and fine defaultors as well as persistent but harmless petty offenders — most of these should be dealt with in a more humane way, according to the committee.

The report also recommended the 'progressive replacement or effective rebuilding' of older local prisons like Cardiff and the 120-year-old Swansea goal.

The committee also pointed to disturbing evidence that Britain's prison population of 42,300 in June — probably the largest in Europe — may have little impact on crime figures.

Britain's general population is only four times greater than Holland's but its prison population is no less than 12 times larger. Yet the crime rates in the two countries are very similar.

Whatever the conditions in the Welsh prisons, there were no problems at Leyhill. At the time of the OPENEYE survey in August, the prison was actually four men short of its normal accommodation of 320 . . .

☐ . . . and sour: Cardiff Prison.

8 – Spring 1980 – **Rebecca**

Rebecca – Spring 1980 – **9**

5 *Treatment: two ways of treating the same crime in the same city ((a) Rebecca No. 11 1980 (b) South Wales Echo, 8 November 1979)*

(b) **YOUR ECHO — BIG VALUE EVERY DAY**

Driver ran away after car chase

A DINAS POWIS MAN and his wife were said in court to have run off after stopping their van following a high-speed chase by police.

By Echo Reporter

Alan Charles Stephenson, aged 27, of Heol-y-Frenhines, jumped a wooden gate and was climbing over the back wall of a house when police caught him, Barry magistrates heard.

His wife, Yvonne, who had been screaming at him to stop the van when police took up the chase, also ran away.

Signalled

Stephenson, a self-employed grocer with premises in Cardiff, was found guilty of driving recklessly, fined £100 and given an endorsement.

For failing to stop when required by police he was fined £40 and for failing to conform to an access only sign, £20. He admitted both these charges and was ordered to pay £10 costs.

No evidence was offered on a charge that he obstructed Police-constable Susan Fontaine, and it was dismissed.

Prosecuting, Mr. Nicholas Candler said two officers in a Panda car noticed a white van go up Andrew Road, Cogan, an access-only route, in the early hours.

The vehicle was signalled to stop in Cardiff Road, and the driver wound down the window but he said he could not stop, and accelerated away.

Stopped

The police car followed, and at the Swan Inn bend the van crossed to the other side of the road and overtook several vehicles, travelling at 60 m.p.h., said Mr. Candler.

"The driver showed a total disregard for the other vehicles. He overtook some and caused both them and oncoming cars to pull in to avoid a collision," he said.

"He turned right across oncoming vehicles into St. David's Avenue, skidded and slid towards the pavement.

"The driver almost lost control when turning into Dennis Close, stopped the vehicle and ran into a garden."

Police-constable Nigel Case, the police driver, said the van overtook moving vehicles at about 65 m.p.h.

"When it eventually stopped the driver threw himself over a wooden gate and I caught him as he was trying to get over the garden wall," he said.

"The only time I saw the vehicle's brake lights come on was when it finally stopped," said Police-constable Case.

Stephenson told the court it was fear of the breathalyser test that made him drive off. He was given two tests; the first proved positive, and the second, in Barry police station, was negative.

No danger

"I was in complete control of the van and there were no vehicles approaching," he said.

"My speed was between 40 m.p.h. and 50 m.p.h. and I overtook only one vehicle. I caused no danger to anyone else. My wife was screaming at me to stop but I said it was too late," he said.

Mr. Candler asked him why he had left his wife to "face the music", but Stephenson said she had run off too.

Mr. Martin Olden, defending, said Stephenson had admitted that he did a stupid thing in driving off.

He had panicked and had pleaded guilty to failing to stop but felt he was in control of the vehicle and did not cause any danger to the general public, he said.

Council to give up land after rent rise

GWENT County Council are to give up a piece of land after 80 years—because the rent is to go up dramatically.

Since September, 1901, the authority have rented a small area of land near West Monmouth School at Pontypool for a rent of 25p a year.

Now, British Rail, who own the land, have checked on all rents paid to them and have told the authority that from this year the rental is to be increased—by 4,000 per cent. to £10 per year.

The increase has forced Gwent to take a look at the land and they say it serves no useful purpose as far as they can see.

They believe it was originally rented so that a fence could be erected but they are not certain of that.

Now they are to tell British Rail they can have their land back.

Man in custody on cannabis charge

Vernon Kenneth Orchard, aged 18, of Osprey Court, Barry, pleaded guilty at Barry Magistrates' Court to possessing cannabis and to stealing a car radio worth £9·95.

He was remanded in custody until November 19 so that social reports could be prepared. No evidence was offered on a charge that he war found drunk and it was dismissed.

Bus firm fined

EDMUNDS OMNIBUS SERVICES of Ebbw Vale, were fined £25 with £2 costs by Barry magistrates after they admitted permitting a motor vehicle to be used by Victor Adishead in Barry although he did not hold a public service vehicle licence.

But there is more to crime than the endless succession of petty thieves, drivers and drunks that are indicated by the *Echo* headlines above. An example of the way in which a different treatment of the same topic in the same city produces utterly different stories can be offered by comparing these *Echo* stories with one published in the investigative news magazine for Wales, *Rebecca* (No. 11, 1980). *Rebecca* took the number of magistrates in Cardiff, and followed the fate of an equal number of defendants who appeared in front of them during one week (pic. 5). It found that whereas the overwhelming majority of magistrates came from middle-class districts of the city, the bulk of the defendants were from working-class areas. *Rebecca* was interested in the claim that magistrates are drawn from 'all sections of society' and in the counter-claim that people are not tried by their 'peers', but on a class-divided basis. The evidence that in Cardiff there are clear class differences in the two sides of justice may be news to its citizens, but it never enters the treatment of crime in the *Echo.*

Telling

Exactly what or who the *Echo* is 'echoing', then, remains an open question. But news is not made by echoing anything; it is made in the *telling*. Returning to the NBC news (p. 40), consider the first section, in which the stories of the latest developments in the hostage issue, the Carter campaign and the Reagan campaign are covered together. Here there is a clear 'sub-plot' in the way the story is told. It concerns the 'divisions' in the Democratic party, which follow President Carter through all the first three items. First a word he uses in one of his own speeches, 'embarrassment', is picked up by the reporter to describe Carter's own position with the drugs charges against his campaign manager; then in the next item Reagan's 'team' is contrasted with Carter's inability to get legislation through his own Congress; then the item on Secretary of State Muskie shows one member of the Administration contradicting another. The 'divisions' are allowed to 'arise' in the speeches or topics themselves, but they are made explicit and amplified in the way these topics are placed in the sequence and linked in the telling. This bulletin becomes a microcosm of the campaign in general – Carter lost it.

An interesting characteristic of the telling of news is its *entertaining* quality. In this respect, news is in a contradictory position in relation to the rest of the medium in which it appears – especially television. Writing about the way in which television tells history, Colin McArthur suggests that *all* television, factual as well as fictional, aspires towards 'the condition of entertainment'. But, he adds, there is also

> the apparently paradoxical impulse to signal the *difference* of television history from the comedy show which precedes it and the police series which comes after it, to signal its *seriousness*. (1978, pp. 22–3)

As McArthur points out, the paradox is resolved in the '*rhetoric* of narration' – the dramatic way history is told, in which the seriousness of the narrator's tone adds to the drama. The code of television news shows a similar characteristic. It signals by the formal, static 'impersonal' semiotic of the newsreader and the studio that it is serious. But on the other hand the stories are told in entertaining language, and film is used where possible to brighten things up. There are quite subtle ways in which the serious tone is undermined: certain male newsreaders compensate for the soberness of their dress by the loudness of their ties. Whether this also undermines the stories themselves is speculative, but certainly television news is competing with the 'semiotic context' that surrounds it. No matter how terrible the event, broadcasters must still exploit the semiotic and discursive arsenal at their disposal. Otherwise there might be no viewers to tell it to.

News in society

Clearly, then, television news doesn't really tell us about society. It tells us quite a lot about certain aspects of society, and it tells us quite a lot about television. But why are only certain topics included in the news? Why are they treated only in particular ways? And why are they told in ways which can transform a speech by the President of the United States into a tale that damns him?

To answer these questions we have to understand the news not as a separate force, outside the social relations it seeks to report, but very much a part of them. Part of what determines the discourse of the news is the way the news-makers themselves act within the constraints, pressures, structures and norms that bring the larger world of social relations to bear on their work. News is just one *social agency* among many – news organizations are themselves determined by the relationships that develop between them and other agencies. Like signs, news organizations are largely defined by what they are not.

In societies like ours, the two most important 'agencies' likely to have a say in the news are capital and the State – commerce and government.

Capital

The relations between news and capital take three main forms. First, news media may be owned by private corporations. This applies to newspapers in Britain, and to ITN, which is a non-profit-making company owned by the other Independent Television companies. The exception is the publicly financed BBC. Second, news media, whether privately owned or not, operate in a commercial climate. Thus, for example, the BBC has to compete with ITV for large audiences in order to justify its licence fee, and it has to avoid making a loss by the same criteria of 'cost-effective' production as are used in private companies. Thus, as Murdock and Golding point out, 'as with any public corporation operating in a capitalist economy, the BBC behaves in many ways as though it were itself a commercial undertaking' (1977, p. 21). Third, news media interact on a daily basis within the norms of commercial life. The management–worker hierarchy, for example, is the same. There is a constant exchange of personnel between them and commerce in general, and much of the information they seek is provided by commercial organizations, rather than disinterested individuals. Small wonder then, that the information often simply assumes the commercial context.

However, it would be wrong for us to assume that because of the commercial context, the news media simply reproduce the ideas and ideologies of those who own them, or of those who 'count' in the commercial world at large. We have seen that not all news media have one owner, and even among the newspapers which do have a continuous history of private ownership, often by a single 'press baron', his ideas and ideology play second fiddle to a more imperative commercial dictate, namely financial survival. As one of the most famous of the old press barons, Lord Beaverbrook (then owner of the *Daily Express*), put it in 1948:

> My purpose originally was to set up a propaganda paper, and I have never departed from that purpose through all the years. But in order to make the propaganda effective the paper had to be successful. No paper is any good at all for propaganda unless it has a thoroughly good financial position. So we worked very hard to build up a commercial position. (Murdock and Golding 1978, p. 142)

In short, in a competitive capitalist environment, the news is seen as both a commercial undertaking in its own right and as a desirable vehicle for disseminating particular views – but these two criteria can be mutually exclusive.

As commercial undertakings, the national daily and Sunday newspapers in Britain seem increasingly risky propositions. Some of them make long-term losses, others stagger from crisis to crisis. Titles merge and disappear. Nevertheless, there is little sign that the owners of the means of production are abandoning the field. There have been three long-term tendencies in the developing pattern of press and media ownership whereby capitalist control is intensified rather than relaxed. They are *concentration, diversification* and *multinationalization*. These tendencies are not confined to media corporations – they mark the current phase of business development in general, and have been especially significant since the Second World War.

1. *Concentration* This is the trend towards ownership in what Murdock and Golding (1978, p. 147) call 'fewer and richer hands'. In all sectors of media production, the market is dominated by a small number of big corporations. Thus, according to Murdock and Golding (1977, p. 25), by the beginning of the 1970s the top five firms in each sector accounted for between 65 per cent and 80 per cent of sales in newspapers, cinema admissions, paperbacks and records. And of course commercial television production is almost entirely in the hands of the five network companies (ATV (now Central), Granada, Yorkshire, LWT and Thames).

2. *Diversification* The practice of keeping one's eggs in several baskets. In the 'culture industry', this has produced a bewildering network of interlocking interests ultimately owned by the same firm. Thorn-EMI own the largest record company in the UK, the

ABC cinema chain, half of Thames Television, the companies that make Ferguson/Ultra radios and televisions, and many others. Reed International own IPC, the biggest magazine publisher in the UK, and Mirror Group Newspapers, as well as having shares in ATV. Reed International itself is a paper and paint concern. S. Pearson controls the *Financial Times*, the Westminster Press (a leading local newspaper group), Penguin Books and a merchant bank (Lazards), and has interests in commercial radio (BRMB, Clyde and Metro) and television (ATV and LWT). (For many further examples, see Murdock and Golding 1977, 1978.) Many newspapers have diversified into oil holdings.

3. *Multi-nationalization* A number of diversified conglomerates operate on a world basis, not confining their activities to one country. The last of the press barons – Lord Thomson and Rupert Murdoch – bought themselves into the British press from bases in Canada and Australia respectively; the American oil corporation Atlantic Richfield owned the *Observer* until the spring of 1981, when an offer by the multi-national firm Lonhro to buy it was referred to the Monopolies Commission. Of course the process works the other way around as well, with British conglomerates buying into overseas companies. For example, although newspapers are not its main interest, Lonhro owns the *Glasgow Times* and *Evening Herald*, together with the *Kenya Standard* and the *Zambia Times*. And even though Lonhro succeeded in its bid to buy the *Observer*, the original deal included a provision for Atlantic Richfield Oil to retain a 40 per cent stake in the company.

Newspapers in particular, then, are prey to the varying fortunes of commercial ownership. These strategies, adopted to maximize profits in periods of declining circulation and generally squeezed profit-margins, have had their effect in the boardrooms of newspapers. But of course that does not prove that boardroom criteria necessarily reappear on the page as 'the owner's opinion'. However, it does suggest that certain choices facing editorial staff are constrained. They cannot overstep the commercial mark in the allocation of resources, in the appeal to mass rather than minority markets, and in the broad limits of 'acceptable' opinion.

The State

'Broadcasting', as Tony Benn says, is 'too important to be left to the broadcasters'. Television news is subject to State control in the sense that both the BBC and IBA are directed to maintain impartiality by their respective charters. The definition of impartiality given in the Annan Report (1977) is interesting, coming as it does from so august a body (the biggest ever government-sponsored inquiry into broadcasting). The report (pp. 267–9) considers the requirement of impartiality in contrast to the notions of balance and neutrality. *Balance* is the 'first the Tories said and then Labour said' approach, often accompanied by a stop-watch to balance not what, but how much, each says. *Neutrality* is not to be shown to those who oppose parliamentary democracy, says Annan:

> The broadcasters are operating within a system of parliamentary democracy and must share its assumptions. They should not be expected to give equal weight or show an impartiality which cannot be due to those who seek to destroy it by violent, unparliamentary or illegal means. (ibid., p. 268)

In place of 'mathematical' balance and 'indifferent' neutrality Annan proposes 'due impartiality', which comprises three elements. First, the broadcasters should allow a full *range* of views and opinion; second, they should take account of the *weight* of opinion ('While it is right that the accepted orthodoxies should be challenged, equally it is essential that the established view should be fully and clearly put. . .'); third, they should recognize that the range and weight of opinion constantly *changes* (p. 269).

What is interesting about the Annan definition of impartiality is that in it, 'impartiality' disappears. It is not to be extended to the very groups whose challenge to the orthodoxies it is supposed to protect. As Bennett comments, 'tolerance is exercised only within the sphere of the tolerable – which is no virtue at all' (1977, p. 38).

Despite the criticisms which may be levelled against this semi-official definition of impartiality, it remains a bulwark against direct control or intervention by the State itself. The benefits of this arms-length relationship between the State and broadcast news work both ways. For both parties, legal separation and the requirement of impartiality guarantee a credibility for what is said. And for the State, this credibility is more important in the long run than any short-term setbacks caused by a particular piece of adverse publicity or a damaging revelation. But for the broadcasters, of course, it is precisely on such occasions when they need the protection of their autonomy.

The proof of this pudding is in the arguments that occasionally erupt between news editors and the government of the day. Here the evidence points both to autonomy and influence. Clearly there is autonomy from government viewpoints if an item is covered in a way that arouses government fury. But on the other hand a full-scale public row is damaging to the news organization's reputation – it has often been argued that as a result, editors-in-charge practice 'self-censorship' in sensitive areas. That is, they tailor their comments or coverage to keep within the limit of what is believed to be tolerable to the government.

A further possibility for indirect influence by government on broadcasters is the 'old boy network'. Here the idea is that the State doesn't need the instruments of direct control because it can rely on behind-the-scenes contact to keep news to its liking. Evidence for this is by definition hard to come by. And in any case, *any* kind of interference represents not the norm, but a breakdown in the normal routines of news gathering and reporting. So the 'old boy network', if it exists, operates as a last, desperate resort.

However, there are one or two examples of how it has played a part in the 'management' of news in the past. For example, the Munich crisis of 1938 was covered, not of course by television, but by its predecessor in the field, cinema newsreel. The British Paramount newsreel of 22 September 1938 included an item on 'Europe's Fateful Hour', which showed scenes from Czechoslovakia and elsewhere as the British Prime Minister, Neville Chamberlain, met Hitler to decide that country's fate. British Paramount also included an 'expert' discussion of the kind familiar in current affairs television today but relatively unusual then. The participants were Wickham Steed, former editor of *The Times* and friend of Czechoslovak President Masaryk; A.J. Cummings, a well-known foreign affairs journalist; and a popular man-in-the-street broadcaster, Herbert Hodge. Their comments were sharply critical of the Anglo-French handling of the crisis. Here is a sample of what they said:

Steed Our government, together with that of France, is trying to make a present to Hitler, for use against us when he may think the time has come, of the three million men and thousands of aeroplanes he would need to overcome Czechoslovak resistance. . .

Hodge . . .What worries me about it all, Mr Cummings, is whether we've simply postponed war for another year or two, against a much stronger Hitler of the future.

Cummings I'm afraid we've only postponed war and, frankly, I am very fearful about what is yet in store for millions of young men of military age in all the countries of Europe.

These comments were all cut from the newsreel after only one day's release. Cinema newsreels were not subject to official censorship, and when questioned in Parliament about the cuts, the government denied direct involvement. But Tony Aldgate (1977, p.156) suggests that the roundabout route which resulted in the cuts may have been as follows: the British Foreign Secretary speaks to the American Ambassador (Joseph Kennedy). He contacts the Hays office in the USA (the US equivalent of the British Board of Film Censors). That office contacts American Paramount, the parent company. American Paramount contact British Paramount and the cuts are made.

In their place, British Paramount put in a new story called 'Premier Flies For Peace', in which Chamberlain speaks of 'understanding' and 'peace' between Britain and Germany.

Striking as such incidents are, they do not constitute an everyday threat to broadcasters. Rather, they define the limits within which the State is likely to allow 'free' comment: it isn't very interested in areas apart from those it defines as affecting 'national security'.

However, when the State does spot a journalist wandering too close to 'national security', the results can be startling. The best known recent example, perhaps, is that of the notorious 'ABC' trial (see State Research, 1978–9). In May 1976 the London weekly *Time Out* published a story by Mark Hosenball and Duncan Campbell called 'The Eavesdroppers', which referred to the Government Communications Headquarters at Cheltenham, and to its functions in intelligence gathering. Around that time, and separately, ex-CIA agent, Philip Agee, published an exposé of the CIA's clandestine operations (1975). The government decided that Agee and Hosenball should be deported, since both were American citizens, for 'disseminating information harmful to the security of the UK'.

A defence committee was set up to oppose the deportations

(which eventually went ahead), and the committee itself attracted the attention of the internal security agency, MI5. Out of this surveillance emerged the ABC trial: so called because of the defendants' names – Crispin Aubry, John Berry and Duncan Campbell (who co-wrote the original *Time Out* article). They were charged on nine counts under the Official Secrets Act, but the judge eventually stopped the trial in September 1978.

However, before it was over the trial led to further charges. These followed from the appearance for the prosecution of a mysterious witness, named only as Colonel 'B'. *Peace News* traced his real name, H.A. Johnson, from the Signals Association magazine *Wire*. But for printing it *Peace News* was fined £500.

The State's failure to secure more substantial convictions no doubt had something to do with the public availability of all the information the various defendants and deportees had gathered. But this case suggests that journalists – especially from papers operating outside the established press – can only go so far in matters concerning national security without attracting legal pressure from the State.

The main mechanism of State control of the media on a day-to-day basis is the law. The media are not singled out in law for attention, but certain specific laws have specific effects on media coverage of events. One of the most important for investigative journalism is the law of libel. It is not simply the law's existence that fosters caution, but more its ill-defined potential. All news media keep specialist lawyers to 'read for libel' on sensitive issues like the exposure of corruption or malpractice, but it has been pointed out that 'press lawyers are inevitably more repressive than press laws because they will always err on the safe side where they cannot be proved wrong' (see Minority Press Group 1980a, p. 24). Even when they give the go-ahead, a major piece of investigation can be halted by a court injunction – the most famous case here being the injunction obtained by the Distillers Company to stop the *Sunday Times* revealing what it had unearthed about the effects of the thalidomide drug.

The armoury of law also contains the Official Secrets Act, and there are a number of laws which periodically denude newsagents' shelves of what are designated obscene publications. In fact the obscenity laws are open to wide interpretation, and often the deciding factor is the attitude of local police forces. In all cases, even in the case of the Official Secrets Act, there is a pattern of uneven application: the law is there if needed, but whether it is invoked is dependent on the individual case.

What is interesting about this discussion of the State and the law is that both share with television news the mantle of 'impartiality'. Neither the State, nor the law, nor the news can work if they appear openly to serve a particular class or group; their credibility in each case is dependent on their being identified not with class or sectional interests, but with the 'general' or 'public' interest. But credibility is one thing, and power another. The 'public' is not made up of a mass of equal individuals, but of groups with unequal sources of power. The 'neutral' State, law and news are the means by which power interests are *translated* into 'general' or 'national' interests with a claim on everybody.

Relative autonomy and ideology

What emerges from our discussion of the relations between news media and the agencies of State and capital is that in both cases there are direct constraints operating in a climate of routine autonomy. The 'relative autonomy' of the news media is an important element in their relations with society. But does it follow that the preservation by news editors of their autonomy, and the exercise within that space of 'due impartiality', will then lead to the making of news stories that are ideologically inert? Far from it. As Connell (1978 and 1979) and Hall *et al*. (1976) argue, the relative autonomy of the news media, and their commitment to impartiality, are the necessary conditions for the production of *dominant* ideological meanings.

The forces within society are not equally balanced and the relationship between capital and labour is at root an exploitative one, hence potentially antagonistic. But the unequal relationship is rarely experienced as directly antagonistic or exploitative: at the workplace, the point of production and source of the imbalance, it is 'neutralized', as it were, in the form of wages. In short, a society which is structurally fractured into necessarily opposed fragments is actually experienced as something quite different. We rarely think of ourselves in class terms, and when we do, we more often refer to cultural status than to the stark opposition between capital and labour.

I have neither the space nor the specialism to analyse fully the implications of a class analysis of social relations. But the role of the media in society, and in particular the role of 'impartial' television news, is difficult to understand without some reference to it. Fortunately, you do not need to accept as an act of faith the notion of what Westergaard (1977b) has called 'principled inequity' – the distribution of unequal 'life chances' on the principles of a particular 'mode' of production. You can follow the arguments in some of the reading I've suggested at the end.

Meanwhile, we can show how the concept of potentially antagonistic class inequality does have considerable explanatory power when used in an analysis of the 'impartial' news. More than that, an analysis of the news in these terms will begin to show why, although we live in a society where the capitalist mode of production leads necessarily to class-divided social relations, the 'lived reality' of everyday life often looks and feels very different. It is 'made sense of' in terms that leave the fundamental fractures out of account.

The social function of the news emerges from this analysis as very different from its everyday, obvious function of providing information, entertainment and the like. Along with other social agencies which also perform more than their 'stated' functions, the news contributes to the 'climate of opinion', to the horizons of possibility, and to the process of marking the limits of acceptable thought and action. In other words, it functions to produce social knowledge and cultural values. But knowledge and values are themselves actively productive, contributing to the process whereby people's submission to the 'prevailing climate' – including the continuity within this climate of class inequality – is secured.

Given that the capitalist mode of production continuously generates potential antagonism between classes, the acceptance of or submission to capitalist social relations is contingent upon the 'neutralization' of this antagonism. Capitalist societies are characterized by agencies such as the media, the family, education, the law and the State which, without removing the fundamental causes of potential class antagonism, translate it into other forms. None of these agencies could be effective on its own, but equally none of them can be understood adequately unless this aspect of their social function is analysed.

However, the agency that concerns us – the news – is like its fellows in performing what looks like its more 'obvious' function.

Like them, it is also characterized by various fractures (in this case, for example, the distinctions between broadcast and press news, between quality and tabloid papers, and between left- and right-wing editorial stances) which obscure the unified social function that collectively, despite such differences, the news media perform.

In order to 'neutralize' potentially antagonistic class relations a number of translations are necessary. They include translations

from	condition	*to*	appearance
	class subject		individual personality
	productive labour		earnings
	class antagonism		'natural' differences
	power		authority
	class		culture

The significance of these terms will be discussed in the sections that follow. I have listed them here to show some of the forms which translations can take. As far as the news is concerned, they are achieved by means of routine professional assumptions about, first, what the overall map of social relations looks like (see chapters 5 and 6), and second, how to make the regular diet of news both intelligible and 'relevant' to the 'average' viewer or reader. Hence it is in the practical workaday context of newsmaking that ideology is produced. In seeking to make sense of the world according to the terms listed on the right, news organizations can be seen as one of what Althusser (1971) calls the ideological 'apparatuses' of the State. In ignoring or suppressing the terms listed on the left, they contribute to a situation in which our submission to capitalist social relations is rendered more likely simply because those relations are not clearly seen. However, neither the news nor any of the other agencies I've mentioned could perform their ideological function if they were merely mouthpieces for the dominant economic class. In order to perform their social function at all, they must be relatively autonomous – acting as self-motivating and regulating organizations free from direct control by any one 'interest group'.

In practice, then, the news sees people as individuals with personal attributes, not as individuals whose condition is determined by their class relations. When people are considered as members of groups, they are always allocated to groups like the family, the nation, or the public. Where class enters the picture, which is rarely, it refers more often to lifestyle than to the formal relations generated by the mode of production. Newsworthy issues are assessed on the basis of their relevance to the individual viewer or reader (and his or her family), and their importance is assessed by reference to the national or public 'interest'. That this interest coincides with the interests of the dominant economic and political forces is a function of their power. The frequent discrepancy between what is claimed as the national interest and the needs of people living in that nation (as in 'It's in the national interest to beat inflation – but meanwhile you lose your job') is made sense of as either a consequence of a particular government (not class) action, or even as a natural and inevitable 'fact of life'.

Winning consent: hegemony

One of the facts of life is that the dominant economic and political forces do not 'rule' in their own persons, and cannot rule by themselves. Power is translated into authority, and authority is exercised in the 'general' interest by 'neutral' agencies such as the State, the law, etc. The exercise of power in the interests of those who 'rule' and who benefit from it is achieved not by direct coercion (a last resort), but routinely by seeking to win the consent of subordinate and powerless groups.

However, it is not a simple matter of 'the ruling class' winning the consent of 'the working class' to its rule. This is partly because neither of these fundamental groups acts in the self-conscious co-ordinated way that such labels suggest: the competition between groups of workers, professionals, managers and members of the public/nation is currently more 'obvious'. And it is partly because the dominant economic class does not and cannot rule on its own. The situation is more like an often uneasy alliance of classes and 'class factions'.

The consent of both allies and subordinates has to be won continuously and in the face of the continuing fundamental 'principled inequity'. By economic and political concessions and by constantly representing its long-term interests as the only reality, the dominant economic class seeks to win legitimacy for its wider authority. It follows that dominance is not justified by reference to power; rather it is justified by appeals to the apparently neutral and all-inclusive authority of government, law and ideology which 'represent' the general public and the nation. As Hall *et al.* argue:

> The State is required as a neutral and objective sphere, precisely in order that the long-term interests of capital can be 'represented' as a general interest. It is through the 'relative neutrality' of the State – not in spite of it – that conflicts are settled "to the profit of the ruling classes", but in ways which, because they appear as neutral and general, command the assent of the nation as a whole. (1976, p. 88)

Or at least, in ways which *seek* to command the assent of the nation. The process by which consent is sought and won is called *hegemony*.

Consent is not won by convincing people that noughts are in fact crosses – it is won by taking the real conditions in which people live their daily lives and representing them in ways which *do* 'make sense'. One of the real conditions most people experience is powerlessness. Hegemony is not in business to *remove* this powerlessness. On the contrary, it is achieved when people ascribe their powerlessness not to its source in economic and social relations, but to eternal forces of nature. For most practical purposes such an explanation is not only plausible, but actually helpful in coming to terms with the very limited gains to be had within the practical horizons of 'realistic' demands.

In order to achieve hegemonic consent, not only must the real conditions of the subordinate and allied classes be taken into account, but they must be 'represented' in neutral terms, on neutral terrain. This is largely achieved as an effect of the process of *translation*. As I've argued, it occurs when specific conditions are granted the status of eternal verities. Class divisions are transformed or displaced into cultural/personal differences. Clearly such a translation cannot be achieved by one agency alone.

From class to culture

It is part of the condition for successful hegemony that translation from class to culture is achieved in as many spheres as possible. The same message must be delivered on all channels.

In the translation from class to culture we can begin to see how it is that the fundamental divisions generated in the mode of production can be experienced as differences apparently so distant from this source that it seems irrelevant to any understanding of them. Even so, it is in the economic sphere itself that the translation of class relations into cultural 'facts' begins. Instead of inequality being attributed to the relation between those who own the means of production and those who don't, it is attributed to personal differences between individuals. Earnings, which are seen as what a person can command by the expenditure of his or her personal attributes of skill, hard work, talent, aptitude and the like, are the yardstick by which people are differentiated – the division capital:labour is replaced by the difference high earnings:low earnings.

These 'differences' are produced and reproduced in the cultural sphere. They emerge as differences in taste, competence, status and personal preference:

high culture	popular culture
serious art	mass art
creative genius	commercial consumption
high IQ	low IQ
middle class	working class
etc.	etc.

The point about these differences is not that they *reflect* any 'natural' differences between people, but rather that they are *produced* as apparently natural distinctions not connected with social relations as such. Indeed, it hardly matters what the intrinsic properties of, for example, a piece of writing may be. Its allocation to the category of high or popular culture respectively will largely determine how it is published, how it is read, and how it is assessed. Further, the distinction between these opposites is valued as much as the items which are said to comprise them; people who are committed to serious art will take an interest in, and associate themselves with, the products of that sector partly in order to locate themselves in a particular social group. In short, culture is the sphere in which social hierarchies can be maintained without any apparent reference to class.

The three major institutions for achieving the cultural translation are *family, school* and *the media*. In all of them, socially-originated divisions are converted into 'natural' differences validated by appeals to timeless criteria. In the family, the differences are experienced as gender and generation oppositions, which can result in the conversion of women into sex/mother beings. Of course one of the main 'differences' proposed by dominant ideology is the difference between home (being where the heart is) and work (being somehow 'outside' the self). Hence the home's role in the transmission of culture (language/values) is itself seen as a timeless, non-political, natural process.

However, the family plays its part in naturalizing power inequalities, so that the *condition* of individuals is translated into *personal attributes*. This process is taken up and amplified in the school. The idea here is that the pupil's 'cultural competence' – a product of class/family and 'encoded' in her/his discourses – is differentially assessed by criteria which are 'neutral' but nevertheless favour the already-favoured. In other words, and as Kennett puts it, the teacher functions to separate the sheep from the goats in perfect impartiality, but:

> 'All are equal before the examination' it appears, but in fact the existing structure in its inter-relations with the dominant culture has already picked the winners. . . . 'All are equal before the examination' is a 'produced' fact regarded as a fact by dominant and subordinate alike, and its consequence is that order is maintained in the school and on the streets. (1973, p. 244)

In short, beyond the unequal ownership of capital as such, there is an unequal distribution of 'cultural capital'. The linguistic and cultural competences that are recognized and accredited as 'better' than others tend to correspond with favoured class positions. Indeed, the argument has been taken a stage further in the work of Basil Bernstein (1973), whose notions of a *restricted* and *elaborated* code (see p. 149) suggest that our position in the social structure is not one of static 'belonging', but a constantly re-created and 'lived' process; this we experience through the mechanisms of the discourses into which we have been socialized. Bernstein's work suggests that the unequal distribution of power is, literally, realized in the distribution of speech forms. As Halliday comments, 'It is a theory of society in which language plays a central part, both as a determiner and as determined: language is controlled by the social structure, and the social structure is maintained and transmitted through language' (1978, p. 89).

Small wonder, then, that the social structure is also maintained and transmitted through the media and, in particular, through the 'impartial' news.

What are the implications of these relations within the social structure for the meaning and status of news? First, the impartiality, objectivity, neutrality and balance which form the bedrock of editorial ideology are no sham. They are required if news is to act alongside the other agencies in naturalizing dominant ideology and winning consent for hegemony.

Next, the mutual confirmation of ideological meanings between news and agencies like the family and the school is no deliberate conspiracy to 'dupe' the public. It is the product of a complex historical process and is deeply embedded in the discourses through which we learn to interact with the world, and in which we make sense of it. This goes just as much for news-people as for anyone else. It suggests, further, that news is not a *producer* of ideological meanings in the sense that they are originated here and nowhere else. News re-produces dominant ideological discourses in its special areas of competence.

Finally, the ideology of the news is not a 'partisan' ideology. On the contrary, the purpose of news ideology is to translate and generalize, not to choose this opinion or that. In other words, news naturalizes the (fairly narrow) terrain on which different sectional ideologies *can* contend – it constantly maps the limits of controversy.

Those limits cannot be crossed with impunity though. As we have seen elsewhere (p. 53), the acceptable limits are defined not only by what is inside, but also by what is excluded. Non-parliamentary dissent, for example, is characterized as deviant and deviancy is defined as irrational or criminal. And the parliamentary form of the state is generalized to a 'universal' status – 'beyond the power of history and time to modify or dismantle' (Hall *et al.* 1976, p. 91).

4 THOSE WHO THREATEN DISORDER

Preferred readings and ideological closure

In the daily routine of newsmaking, the ideological determinants of news-discourse gain practical expression. What happens is that the multi-accentual 'potential for meaning' of the chosen signs (verbal and visual), and their capacity for connotation and myth, are filled in until the signs are 'closed', apparently uni-accentual.

In order to effect ideological closure, the event is put together with signs that indicate how it should be understood – what it 'means'. There is, in other words, a 'preferred reading' (Hall 1977, pp. 341 ff.) encoded into the way a story is told. To dig out the preferred reading whilst watching the news can sometimes be hard, in the sense that what an event 'means' so often seems to flow smoothly from the event itself, having nothing to do with the way it is told. To separate the event (referent) from the preferred reading you need to look at its news-construction in some detail.

Here, then, is a complete news item broadcast on ITN's 'News at Ten' on 11 December 1980. It is the lead story, and falls into three sections. In the first (section I) the newsreader, Alastair Burnet, describes the event from the studio. He shares the screen with a still photograph of the Prime Minister (taken from stock, i.e. not from the event Burnet is describing). In the second (section II) there is a film-report from the location itself, which includes an on-the-spot interview (section IIa) with a nominated, accessed voice (see pp. 108 and 111 for these terms). The third section (III) is also shot on location, but it doesn't look like it, as we shall see.

'News at Ten'

Headlines

Twenty five arrests as the Prime Minister goes to Cardiff
(bong!)
She says tonight's demo harms Wales
(bong!)

I

Mrs Thatcher is in Cardiff tonight on the eve of the announcement expected from the British Steel Corporation that thousands more jobs are to go. The Prime Minister was met by demonstrators as she arrived at Cardiff City Hall to speak to the Welsh CBI. Twenty-five people were arrested when a flare and other missiles were thrown. A policeman was injured. The CBI's Director General, Sir Terence Beckett, and six other guests, had to squash into a police van to get through the crowd. In her speech Mrs Thatcher attacked the demonstrators, saying their actions didn't help the unemployed. She said Britain had created some of its own problems, and, the time had to come when all this had to stop. On the steel industry, so important to South Wales, she said, by all commercial criteria it was bankrupt. But she said there were hopeful signs, with a lot of investment interest in Wales being shown in America. Our Political Correspondent, David Rose, is in Cardiff:

6.1

6.1a

II

(*singing on soundtrack*)
Come and join the working class
(*then fade to inaudible*)

Zoom-out

6.2

(*Voice-over commentary begins*)

The Welsh TUC and Labour Party had threatened a campaign of civil disobedience, and Plaid Cymru had said Mrs Thatcher should be exceedingly worried about coming here tonight

6.2a

if a Welsh steel plant was to be closed. Perhaps

6.3

because of the Prime Minister's visit

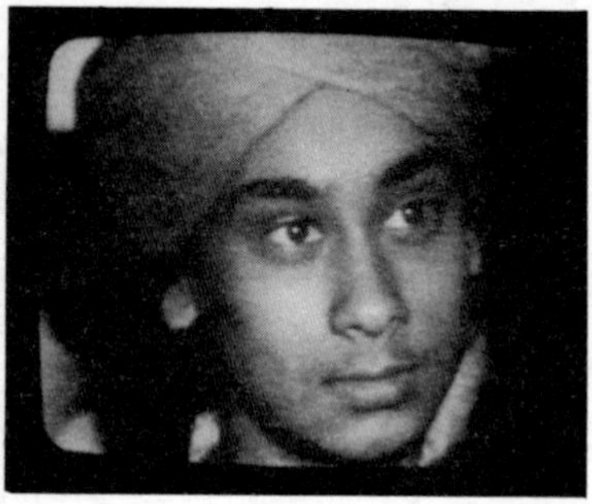

6.4

it still wasn't known whether Llanwern or Port Talbot will go, and the political parties must have been disappointed that no more than 1500 people were waiting for her.

6.5

Zoom-in and follow police action: shot held on close-up framing. The close-up part of this shot has already been seen in the news headline sequence.

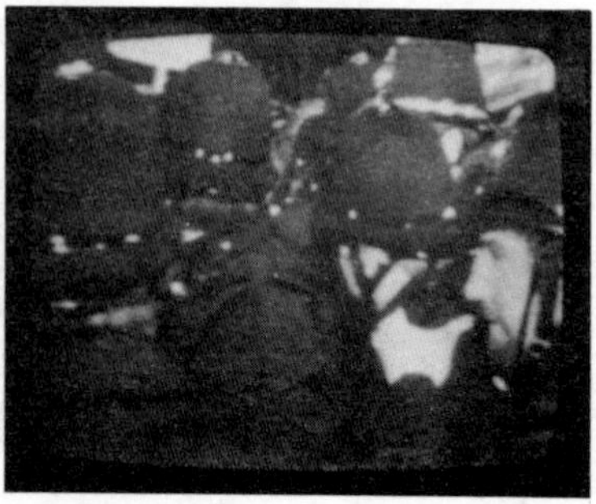

6.5a

IIa
(*on-the-spot interview with 'Mr Hubert Morgan: Welsh Labour Party'*)
(*Morgan's words on soundtrack*)
'What they're trying to say to Mrs Thatcher is for goodness sake change your policy; that she's killing Wales; the industrial and community-communal life of Wales is being destroyed completely by the action which this government are taking. And what we're trying to do is: asking her to listen to us; this is what democracy's all about, and unless she listens at this particular stage, well goodness knows

6.6

6.6a

what could happen in the future.'
(*Voice-over commentary resumes*)
Taking no chances the Prime Minister arrived very early for this dinner, and an egg hit the bonnet just before she was hustled into the City Hall.

6.7

Most of the demonstrators hadn't

6.8

even seen her, and the mood outside got much tougher for an hour

6.9

though twelve-hundred police – more than half the South Wales force – ringed the City Hall.

Shot held to show two policemen clambering over obstacles into the crowd.

6.10

One policeman was injured after a struggle deep in the crowd.

Camera follows movement in close-up framing.

6.11

After the eggs, several flares flamed out of the crowd, but no-one was hit.

6.12

Hand-held camera is walked to better position: police and photographers mill about, silhouetted by flares and smoke.

6.12a

Then the arrests started. Altogether there were over twenty. One or two resisted but most went quietly. Among those arrested was the Treasurer of Plaid Cymru. Despite the few demonstrators, they were giving police a tough time

6.13

Camera holds on action of arrest and struggle: close-up of dramatic movement (this is the longest single shot in the sequence).

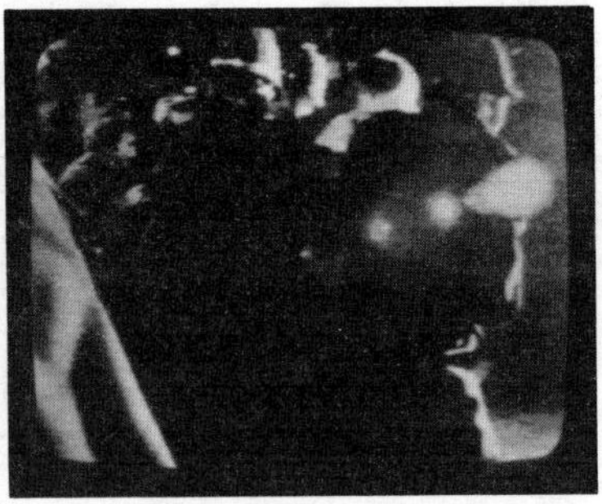

6.13a

and there are fears here of real civil disorder if one of the steel plants is closed. Tonight

Hand-held pan follows arrest: as suspect is bundled against police-van an audible voice in the crowd asks 'What happened, John?'

6.14

police had the situation well under control

6.15

while inside Mrs Thatcher spoke to those who threaten disorder.

Zoom-out from close-up on policeman in 'guarding' pose to long-shot framing police through portal of City Hall.

6.16

III
(*Mrs Thatcher's words*)
'Demonstrations don't provide solutions, and those who threaten disruption or law-breaking do not help the unemployed.'

Tripod-held camera in bright interior light. No camera movement.

6.17

(*applause*) 'They don't present a

Cutaway shot – Slow pan across assembled diners, showing applause.

6.18

true or an attractive picture of Wales, and I believe that people who act in this way sell Wales short (hear hear). 'N they make it that much more difficult to attract new investors and new industries to Wales, and they obstruct the arrival of new jobs, which are so badly needed here.'

Repeat of previous shot of Mrs Thatcher. 6.17a

6 *'News at Ten', 11 December 1980*

Trial by semiotics

The first way in which a particular 'reading' for this story is preferred is by simple repetition. The shot of policemen shoving against crowds is used in the headline (6.5a), and several of the film-report shots take up this aspect of the story. So it *looks like* a story about police and demonstrators – a very familiar sight on television. The theme is reiterated in the verbal part of the story – there are numerous references to 'tonight's demo' and to 'the demonstrators', and in particular to 'civil disobedience', 'resisting arrest', giving the police a 'tough time', 'real civil disorder' and 'those who threaten disorder'. So it *sounds like* a story about threatened disruption and law-breaking – which is exactly what Mrs Thatcher calls it in her speech.

However, the opposing point of view is put by a member of the Welsh Labour Party (6.6). Far from law-breaking, he appeals to 'what democracy is all about' – namely the obligation of politicians to 'listen to us'.

But it is not the arguments between the factions themselves that concern us here so much as the way these are presented in the impartial news. And the most obvious thing about them is that they are not *presented* impartially. Whereas Mrs Thatcher's interpretation of the event (threatened law-breaking) is taken up and used to define the whole event, the opposing view is put in the visual context of police action and arrests. It is not my point that because the Labour party is by far the majority party in Wales, their view should have been preferred to Mrs Thatcher's. The point is that *political opposition* has been translated by 'News at Ten' into *violent disorder.*

The translation is partly achieved by 'silent' visual means. The Prime Minister is seen in a prepared context (6.17) and without the 'helpful' voice-over explaining exactly what the threats to civil order are. She speaks authoritatively for herself and the camera defers to her: it is 'neutral' in framing her at the optimum mid-shot, and is held still on a tripod. Opposing voices, on the other hand, are seen in a series of snappily-edited, hand-held shots, as if the camera is down there in the thick of the action. Hence 'opposition' and 'authority' appear as two quite different 'facts' – opposition is action, shouting, disorder and an appropriate context for police, while authority is statement, reason, order and an appropriate context for applause.

Within this semiotic, it makes little difference what the opposition voices actually say. Their statements are brought to us by the 'authoritative' voice-over: the Labour party says this, Plaid Cymru says that. Even the accessed voice of Hubert Morgan (relatively unknown to ITN viewers) has to compete with the shouting. His final comment ('goodness knows what could happen in the future') is semiotically 'stolen' by a deftly placed picture-cut (6.6a and 6.7) which makes it into a voice-over lead-in to the pictures of an egg hitting Mrs Thatcher's car and the subsequent arrests.

Notice in this context the ideological productivity of the arrests (shots 6.13 and 14). The preferred reading is anchored on them, since they retrospectively validate both the police action itself and ITN's translation of the event into a story about disorder. The voice-over commentary does not indicate whether the police presence was justified by the event 'despite the few demonstrators'. The 'threat of disorder' theme is partly vindicated simply by giving certain facts; if 'twelve hundred police – more than half the South Wales force – ringed the City Hall', then there must have been a considerable threat. But the arrests themselves clinch the matter. If there were arrests, it follows there was law-breaking. And if there was law-breaking, then the threat was real.

The result of this logic is to make 'factual' a proposal which is actually rhetorical. When Mrs Thatcher speaks of 'those who threaten disruption or law-breaking' there is no necessary connection between them – disruption is one thing, law-breaking another. However, despite the political context of the protest, which is not outside the sacred terrain of party-and-parliament but firmly inside it, its *form* is one which the impartial news finds easy to assign to a very familiar place in the chamber of horrors. A street demonstration is arguably a disruption, but when it is signified by means of the arrests which are shown in big close-up within the two longest shots of the sequence, it quickly becomes law-breaking. The whole protest is tarred with the same semiotic brush.

5 SELECTION AND CONSTRUCTION

News values

Imagine a football game. The players are on the field going about the business of football. Their behaviour is full of purpose (to contain the initiatives of the other side and to gain the advantage for their own), and it is ordered, with shared rules, conventions and styles governing the unpredictable immediacy of the run of play. The spectators, for whom all this energy is expended, are absorbed in watching.

But on the sideline, player number twelve wants to get on to the pitch to take part, and to be seen by the spectators. How is the substitution to be done? If he leaps about, gesticulating wildly, his frantic antics might be noticed as a distraction and an amusement, but they won't get him on. To succeed he needs, first, to be known and recognized as a bona fide player. Second, he (or his accredited 'representative', the manager or coach) must go through an established routine to catch the referee's eye. And finally, some other player has to be displaced from the field to make room for him. Only then will he make his mark and, if he's lucky, gain the attention of the spectators.

Events don't get into the news simply by happening, no matter how frantically. They too must fit in with what is already there (just as a circus clown would find it hard to succeed as a sub for a football team, whatever the opposing fans may say). Events need to be known and recognized, coming from a known and trusted – and preferably a 'representative' – source. To win inclusion in any particular news, they must fulfil a certain number of criteria; in short, they must be seen as newsworthy. Finally, newsworthy events themselves must jostle for inclusion in the limited number of slots available.

In order to pick out newsworthy events from the jostling crowd of clowns on the sidelines of their game, journalists use an informal paradigm of news values. In a famous study, Galtang and Ruge (1973) isolated a series of conditions which have to be fulfilled before an event is selected for attention. Some of these are general conditions, applicable not just to news, but to the perception of events at large. They apply to news-selection the world over. The others are more 'culture-bound'; these are the news values underlying selection in news media in the 'north-western corner of the world'. Here is their list of *general news values*:

1. *Frequency* The time-span taken by an event. Murders take very little time and their meaning is quickly arrived at. Hence their frequency fits that of daily newspapers and programmes. On the other hand, economic, social or cultural trends take very much longer to unfold and to be made meaningful: they are outside the frequency of daily papers. Thus they have to be 'marked' (if they are reported at all) by means of devices like the release of reports or statistics on a particular day.

2. *Threshold* The size of an event. There is a threshold below which an event will not be reported at all (varying in intensity between, for instance, local and national news). And once reported, there is a further threshold of drama: the bigger the story, the more added drama is needed to keep it going. War reporting is an example of this. Already very big news, its coverage is unlikely to increase unless an especially cataclysmic event happens. But of course the added drama does not have to originate in the event. After the murder of John Lennon, for example, events which in themselves would normally not reach the threshold of newsworthiness were made into dramatic stories in order to keep the pot boiling. Thus we read in the *Sun*

> Heart-broken John Lennon fans in America are getting a helping hand with 'grief therapy'.
> Special 'Grief Clinics' have been set up in New York to aid those who cannot cope with his death.

Hundreds of Beatle fans, ranging in age from 14 to 41, have called to join the groups. (etc.) (19 December 1980)

The same story appeared in that day's *Daily Express* – under the headline of 'Grief Clinics'.

3. *Unambiguity* The clarity of an event. Events don't have to be simple, necessarily (though that helps), but the range of possible meanings must be limited. In this way news-discourse differs radically from literary discourse. In news, the intrinsic *polysemic* (ambiguous – capable of generating many meanings) nature of both events and accounts of them is reduced as much as possible; in literature it is celebrated and exploited.

4. *Meaningfulness* (a) Cultural proximity: events that accord with the cultural background of the news-gatherers will be seen as more meaningful than others, and so more liable to be selected. This works in two ways. First, Islamic, third-world and oriental events may not be seen as self-evidently meaningful to Western reporters unlike European, American or even Russian events. Second, within 'our' culture, events connected with underprivileged or ethnic groups, with regions remote from the centralized bases of news organizations, or with specifically working-class culture, will be seen as less intrinsically meaningful than those associated with central, official, literate culture.

(b) Relevance: events in far-off cultures, classes or regions will nevertheless become newsworthy if they impinge on the news-gatherer's 'home' culture – usually in the form of a threat; as with OPEC and the (mostly Arab) countries with oil – their lifestyles, customs and beliefs are suddenly fascinating for Western journalists.

5. *Consonance* The predictability of, or desire for, an event. If the media expect something to happen, then it will. The classic case-study of this phenomenon is by Halloran *et al.* (1970) (summarized in Murdock 1973), where it was found that the news coverage of the anti-Vietnam war demonstration in Grosvenor Square, London, in 1968, concentrated almost exclusively on what was expected – namely violence. Very little occurred, but it was massively reported, whereas the issues at stake in the demonstration were ignored.

6. *Unexpectedness* The unpredictability, or rarity, of an event.

Of course it is within the *meaningful* (4) and the *consonant* (5) that the unexpected is to be found. Hence the 'newness' of unexpected events usually gets discovered in thoroughly familiar, expected contexts.

7. *Continuity* The 'running story'. If an event is covered, it will continue to be covered for some time.

8. *Composition* The mixture of different kinds of event. If a newspaper or TV bulletin is packed with major foreign stories, a relatively insignificant domestic story will be included to balance the mixture. Alternatively, if a major story is running, other similar events may be selected for inclusion in a 'round-up' of stories on that subject.

In addition to these eight general news values, Galtang and Ruge propose a further four which are of prime importance in western media. They are:

9. *Reference to élite nations* Stories about wars, elections and disasters are good examples of this tendency. Wars involving the USA, USSR, or forces explicitly allied to one or the other, will be reported, whereas others go virtually unnoticed – like the Indonesia/East Timor conflict, the Chad civil war and the Nicaraguan revolution. Elections in France, Germany and Italy will receive more coverage than those in Latin America, Africa, etc. And of course there is the famous head-count equation for disasters: disasters in Bangladesh, for example, need thousands or hundreds killed to reach the newsworthiness threshold, whereas those in 'élite' countries will be newsworthy with progressively lower body-counts.

10. *Reference to élite persons* Firstly because it is assumed their actions are more consequential than the daily activities of ordinary people – they 'affect our lives'. Secondly, the social activities of élite people can serve as representative actions – their weddings, opinions, nights out and domestic habits are taken to be of interest to us all, since we too engage in these things. But who cares how I wipe my nose, if we can watch Rod Stewart doing it?

11. *Personalization* Events are seen as the actions of people as individuals. Individual people are easier to identify – and to identify with – than structures, forces or institutions: hence 'the government' is often personalized as 'Mrs Thatcher', etc.

12. *Negativity* Bad news is good news. It is generally *unexpected* (6), *unambiguous* (3), it *happens quickly* (1), it is *consonant* (5) with general expectations about the state of the world, and hence its *threshold* (2) is lower than that for positive news.

These basic news values give a good idea of the kind of event that will survive the selection process. The list also provides clues as to the priority different stories will be given – the more of these conditions a given story fulfils, the bigger it will be. Take the murder of John Lennon. Its *frequency* was right (although it happened after the British dailies had 'gone to bed', so it was already a running story by the time they caught up on the following day); its *threshold* was no problem (although I heard one complaint on the radio that news editors are older than the generation for whom Lennon was significant, resulting in coverage which was deemed inadequate); it was certainly *unambiguous* and *meaningful* (everyone has heard of the Beatles); it was *consonant* in several ways – rock stars die young, New York is a violent city (much of the coverage centred on the twin themes of mugging and gun control), and modern society is characterized by the assassination of élite people by fame-seeking nutters; it was *unexpected*; it concerned two *élite nations* (Britain and the US); John Lennon is a prime *élite person*, whose place in the cult of *personality* (the 'star system') was of the first order; and it was *negative*. Hence its *continuity* was assured, and other killings were *composed* with it to form part of the same story. It had the lot.

However, there are certain stories which at first sight seem to achieve wide coverage without fulfilling any of these news values in an obvious way. An interesting recent example is one that concerns the theoretical perspective I've relied on in this book, that is, structuralism and semiotics. On the face of it an unlikely topic for full-page articles in the news pages of the national and Sunday papers, but suddenly in January-February 1981 they blossomed with bluffers' guides to structuralism. It was an attempt to clarify a dispute in the University of Cambridge, where a lecturer associated with structuralist writings, Colin MacCabe, was refused a permanent post. The way the dispute was reported did exploit a number of our news values (like personalization, negativity, reference to élite persons and institutions), but the news values themselves give little clue as to why the story was deemed newsworthy in the first place.

In fact the 'MacCabe Affair' provides us with a useful reminder.

News values can actually disguise the more important ideological determinants of a story. It might seem implausible to link the Cambridge dispute with a recently shown television drama series (*The History Man*), and to link both of these with the twin themes of government economic policy and public sector spending cuts. But it is noteworthy that this unusual conjuncture of fact, fiction and political economy did not go unnoticed at the time. Colin MacCabe was explicitly compared with Howard Kirk, the fictional character of *The History Man* (*Sunday Times*, 25 January 1981, p. 13) and within weeks the papers were giving prominent coverage to various plans for savings among universities and polytechnics, plans which included letting some go bankrupt. It may be that the 'newsworthiness' of the MacCabe Affair consisted in *making* the link between fiction and fact – by the time Cambridge itself has been tarred with *The History Man*'s brush, the credibility of any opposition to the cuts is seriously undermined. As Terence Hawkes reported in *Time Out*;

> Significantly it was *The Listener* which overtly imprinted the model onto the real world by roguishly placing a still from The History Man's credits on the cover of the issue in which Noel Annan was recently advocating health-giving university cuts. The political implications of those cuts were thus easily masked and objections to them stifled. (*Time Out*, 20 March 1981, p. 54).

Of course news values are neither natural nor neutral. They form a code which sees the world in a very particular (even peculiar) way. News values are, in fact, an ideological code – as we shall soon see. Meanwhile, one of their ideological implications can be stated here, interestingly in the words of a working journalist who uses them every day. Writing in the *New Statesman*, the journalist Anna Coote outlines what news values are, and how they are ranked. She goes on to suggest they are fundamentally sexist:

> We concur in decisions about what is a 'good story' and what is not, what is central and what is peripheral, what is 'hard' news and what is 'soft'. . . . These [news values] have been developed, of course, by white, middle-class men, generation upon generation of them, forming opinions, imposing them, learning them and passing them on as Holy Writ. We have inherited a *hierarchy* of news values. What are the major stories of the day? The

> economy, industry, politics (of Whitehall and Westminster), foreign affairs, and so on, down the scale. A 'hard' story is generally deemed to be one based on facts, on something precise which has happened, in a particular sphere already labelled 'Important'. A story based on description, individual experience, nuance – a 'human interest' story, perhaps, or something which has happened in a sphere *not* labelled 'Important' – may be considered 'good', but is nevertheless 'soft' or 'offbeat'. Why? Where did these ideas come from? Are they objective, universal, or simply man-made? (*New Statesman*, 2 January 1981, p. 11)

Clearly news values are man-made, in both the generic and the gender sense of 'man'. But it seems an individual journalist, whether male or female, is unable to escape their institutionalized force (presented as the *right* way of doing journalism), even when s/he contests their ideology.

Mapping reality: consensus and dissent

While news values are crucial in the paradigmatic *selection* of events, they play only a part in the syntagmatic *construction* of those events into stories. Just as our football player, once selected, must play by the rules and in the spirit of the game (so he can't suddenly decide to pick up the ball, trade blows with an opponent, or join the opposing team), so news events are assigned to their 'proper' place in the order of things. As Hall *et al*. point out,

> If newsmen did not have available – in however routine a way – such cultural 'maps' of the social world, they could not 'make sense' for their audiences of the unusual, unexpected and unpredicted events which form the basic content of what is 'newsworthy'. (1978, p. 54)

At the most general level, these maps assume society to be:

1. *Fragmented* into distinct spheres – sport, politics, family life, etc.
2. Composed of *individual persons* who are in control of their destiny, so that actions are the result of their personal intentions, motives and choices. 'Newsworthy' people are usually associated with only one sphere of society.
3. *Hierarchical* by nature: some people, events, spheres are more

than others. And the hierarchy is *centralized* both
ıd regionally.

al by nature. The notion of 'the consensus' is a basic
ıg principle in news production. It is worth looking at in
tail.

Consensus

First, consensus requires the notion of unity: one nation, one people, one society, often simply translated into 'ours' – 'our' industry, 'our' economy, 'our' nuclear deterrent, police force, balance of payments, etc. Within the notion of unity goes the notion of diversity, plurality, fragmentation. The different spheres of society interlock in institutions, organizations and personnel, each with its own special interests, idiosyncracies and fund of stories. Within the notion of fragmentation goes the notion of hierarchy, with all the spheres ranked in order of importance and all, of course, represented by their associated personalizations. Hence, as Hall argues,

> Newspapers are full of the actions, situations and attributes of 'elite persons'. The prestigious are part of the necessary spectacle of news production – they people and stabilize its environment. But the very notion of 'elite persons' has the 'routine knowledge of social structures' inscribed within it. . . . 'Elite persons' make the news because power, status and celebrity are monopolies in the institutional life of our society. In C. Wright Mill's phrase, 'elite persons' have colonized 'the means of history making' in our society. (1973, p. 183)

Of course there are major contradictions within the consensual model. It requires both unity and fragmentation, both the notion of 'élite persons' and the 'assumption that we also all have roughly the same *interests* in the society, and that we all roughly have an equal share of power in the society' (Hall *et al.* 1978, p. 55). This 'equal share' is of course institutionalized in 'our parliamentary system', 'our democratic institutions', and in the guaranteed 'freedoms' of speech, of access to wealth in the 'free market economy', and so on. Disputes have 'normal channels' in which reconciliation can be effected, whether those disputes are personal (the law), commercial (the law), industrial (ACAS as a last resort after institutionalized 'free collective bargaining'), or political (parliamentary or local politics).

We are left with a closed societal circle, with everyone inside. In the consensual model, there are no dissidents, since everybody has access to the expression and resolution of their grievances in the official establishment of social institutions.

Hall *et al.* see this 'background assumption' as crucial, going far beyond the recognition of shared language and knowledge:

> In recent years, however, this basic cultural fact about society has been raised to an extreme ideological level. Because we occupy the same society and belong to roughly the same 'culture', it is assumed that there is, basically, only *one* perspective on events: that provided by what is sometimes called *the* culture, or . . . *the* 'central value system'. (ibid.)

Hence 'this view denies any major structural discrepancies between different groups, or between the very different maps of meaning in a society' (ibid., p. 55), and so it takes on political significance. Groups outside the consensus are seen as deviant and marginal, be they skinheads or strikers. The bread and butter of news is conflict, violence, rivalry and disagreement. But for all these negatives to be newsworthy, a prior assumption of the 'underlying' consensus to which they are a threat must be at work.

Here one of the consensus model's contradictions becomes crucial. If 'we' *are* characterized by a consensus, then how is *dissent* to be understood?

Mapping the outsiders: dissent

First it should be made clear that the often rough handling of dissent and alternative views of social structures is not the result of personal animosity on the part of individual broadcasters and journalists towards those views. On the contrary, the way dissent is made sense of, made to mean, in the media is determined by the impersonal social process of newsmaking itself, as a professional practice. In other words, the assumptions we have been discussing are not 'personal opinions' in the usual sense, they are the routine mental orientations shared in a necessarily unreflecting way by busy people; their efforts are directed not towards criticizing and making explicit their own model of society, but towards recording and making sense of the doings and sayings of others. Hence, the political consequences of the consensual model of society are just that: political consequences not political intentions.

However, the consequences are quite striking. For instance, since journalists are in business to make sense of social events, it falls to the media to *make sense of* dissent; it is not enough simply to *report* its manifestations, they must be assigned a place in the mental map. If we look at an alternative to the consensus which *is* given wide publicity in the media, the ways in which dissidence and dissent are made sense of will become clearer.

The major alternative model to the consensual that can be seen regularly in British media does reserve a vital and important role for dissidents. This is the model of society used to make sense of events in the USSR and other 'soviet bloc' countries. Here there is said to be no institutional place for conflict – all such countries are seen as, above all, 'one-party states'. They are characterized as such – and as different from ours – by the existence of (the word looks familiar now) 'dissidents', whose only recourse is to act *outside* the 'official' channels of their society.

Of course there are groups and individuals in 'our' society who also act outside the official channels. But they are not seen as dissidents: they are seen as deviants. This characterization is an effect of the consensual model and, conversely, of the association of dissidence with totalitarian régimes. The terms used to characterize strikes, direct action and other expressions of dissent concentrate on notions of irresponsibility, irrationality, and either mindlessness or bloody-mindedness; there is always the implication of violence. This is, according to Hall, 'the most salient, operational "news value" in the domain of political news', because, he argues,

> at the level of 'deep structure', political violence is 'unusual' – though it regularly happens – because it signifies the world of politics *as it ought not to be*. It shows conflict in the system at its most extreme point. And this 'breaches expectations' precisely because in our society conflict is supposed to be regulated, and politics is exactly 'the continuation of social conflict without resort to violence': a society, that is, where the legitimacy of the social order rests on the absolute inviolability of 'the rule of law'. (1973, p. 184)

Hence manifestations of dissent are seen as containing the 'threat of violence', and the threat of violence is 'anti-social' in the profoundest sense. Exactly *whose* 'society' is being so threatened is not an open question, since the consensual model requires 'society' to be everyone. Dissidents, then, are mad or malicious.

We can see what happens to dissent by making use of a diagram (fig. 2). If we think of the consensual model in spatial terms, it looks like a set of concentric circles, with 'civilized society', complete with all its various spheres of activity, personalities and media coverage, at the centre. Beyond its boundaries matters get progressively less easy for this central system to tolerate.

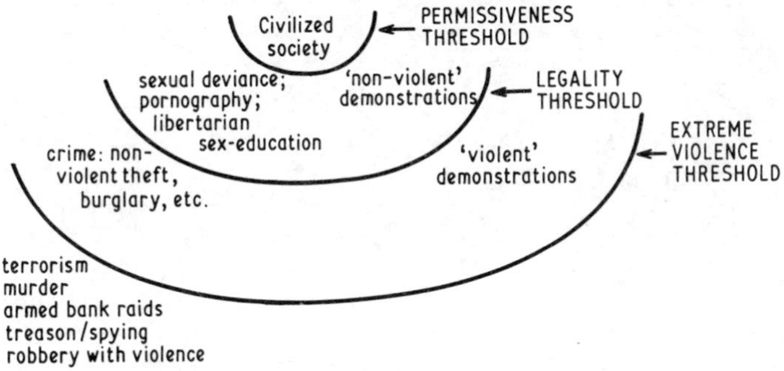

Fig. 2 *(From Hall et al., 1978, p. 226)*

Several forces can be seen at work here. First there are the thresholds themselves. Beyond the bounds of 'civilized' society, but within the law, is the area of *moral* disapproval, which can be applied to dissent as well as to non-family sexuality. The further the acts are from the centre, the more likely it is that they will be seen as either violent in themselves, or leading to violence. Second is the phenomenon called '*convergence*' by Hall *et al.* In figure 2 political dissent is listed alongside more traditional crime: to the extent that an association between the two can be established, it is possible to see 'political dissent' *as* 'crime', as in the notion of 'student hooliganism' applied to the protest movements of the 1960s. As Hall *et al.* comment,

> The public might be reluctant to see the strong arm of the law arbitrarily exercised against legitimate political protesters. But who will stand between the law and a 'bunch of hooligans'? Imaginary convergences therefore serve an ideological function – and that ideological function has real consequences, especially in provoking and legitimating a coercive reaction by both the public and the state. (ibid., pp. 224–5)

Perhaps 'the public' is not now thought to be so squeamish – see for example the 'News at Ten' in Chapter 4. Finally there is the notion of *escalation*. Reading into the centre from the periphery of the diagram, it is easy to see the 'milder' dissidence as causally connected to more 'extreme' kinds of violence. Hence 'non-violent demonstrations' can be seen as the 'thin end of the wedge' – and be dealt with accordingly.

6 HAIL FELLOW WELL MET

Mode of address

Having looked at news values and the associated 'mapping' processes at work in making events into news, it is time to consider the ways in which these events are *made meaningful* in news-discourse. In order to make anything meaningful, the initiator of a message must not only have an orientation towards the event itself, but also an orientation towards the receiver of the message. For example, how would you describe a simple event in which you were personally involved – say a night out to see a band at your local rock venue? Clearly much depends on *who* you are talking to. You will foreground different aspects of the event for different addressees, but the *way* you recount the stories of the event will also differ. Not only will your tone, choice of words, and the degree of interaction you expect from the hearer all differ, depending on whether you are talking to, for instance, a close friend of the same sex or an authoritative figure, but in addition, these elements of your account will be organized by the expectation you have of the hearer's attitude to the event and to you. In short, your tale will bear within it your awareness of a 'triangular' relationship between the event (X), yourself (A) and your friend (B). Such a relationship has been schematized in communication theory by Newcomb (see Fiske 1982, p. 32) as shown in figure 3.

Because this model proposes the interdependent relationship of the elements in the conversation, it follows that if you change one of the elements – substituting parent or boss for friend at B – the *whole* relationship changes, and the event is 'made to mean' something different.

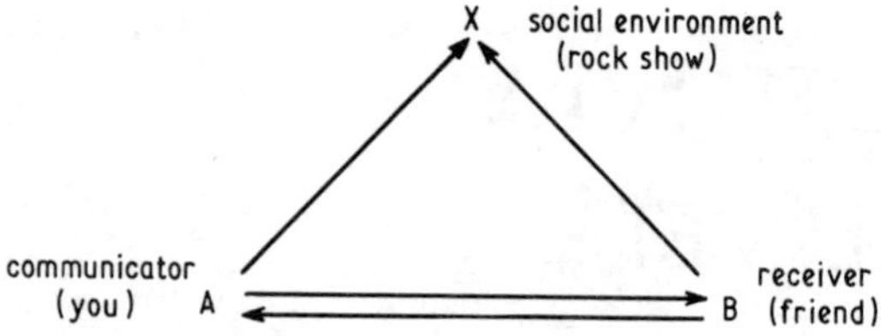

Fig. 3

The point not made clear by this model is that the mutual orientations of A and B towards each other and towards X are manifested in, and carried forward through, the conversation itself, i.e. in language. This point has been put clearly by Volosinov:

> Orientation of the word toward the addressee has an extremely high significance. In point of fact, *word is a two-sided act.* It is determined equally by *whose* word it is and *for whom* it is meant. As word, it is precisely *the product of the reciprocal relationship between speaker and listener, addresser and addressee.* Each and every word expresses the 'one' in relation to the 'other'. (1973, p. 86)

When we turn from personal relationships to the relationships between newspapers or TV and their audiences, we are faced with a problem. They too must include an orientation to their addressees as part of the message, but except in the most general and abstract of ways they don't know who the addressee is. It is a problem the media cannot escape. They *must* develop a practical 'mode of address' which expresses not only the content of the events they relate but also their orientation towards the viewer or reader, since this orientation is an unavoidable constituent element of all language. However, it cannot be just any old orientation, for it is the 'mode of address', the 'tone' of a newspaper or broadcast, that distinguishes it from its competitors and provides much of its 'appeal' to us as viewers and readers.

There are different solutions to this problem. Perhaps the best known alternative to modern practice (which I shall discuss in a minute) is the mode of address developed by the BBC in its early, radio days. Conceived as public service broadcasting, the BBC's public orientation to its listeners was paternalist, élite, of high moral tone and very formal. Its founder, John Reith, had decided views not only on the BBC's mode of address, but on the alternative, to which he objected. As Burns notes:

> In the view of people like Reith and the conservative party politicians and civil servants who made the crucial decisions, the products of the newspaper industry, no less than those of the film industry, represented the consequences of 'giving the public what it wants' and were consequently silly, vulgar, false and contemptible. Broadcasting, if they were to have anything to do with it, had somehow to be developed in the completely opposite direction. (1977, p. 52)

And it was. Some of the decisions taken look bizarre now; the patronizing moral tone of the Corporation led it to be dubbed 'Auntie'. Under pressure from Radio Luxembourg, then ITV and the pirate radio stations of the 1960s, together with social changes and the slow defeat of the 'Reithian ethic' within the Corporation, it has progressively abandoned its high-culture stance and its lofty attitude to its listeners and viewers. Only echoes remain in such notions as 'BBC English', or 'education by stealth'.

But even within the Reithian BBC, the alternative which was eventually to prevail gained a foothold as early as 1952. Connell (1978) has traced the historical development of the fight within broadcasting to challenge 'the existing traditions in order to connect with what had come to be identified as the "mass" audience'. He cites the example of a programme called 'Special Enquiry' (modelled on an American programme, 'See it Now') broadcast in 1952 and produced by Norman Swallow, who comments:

> it seemed to those of us who were concerned with the birth of *Special Enquiry* that one of the most exciting merits of *See it Now* was the way in which Ed Murrow had seemed to place himself *on the side of the audience*. His approach was that of the hardened reporter whose concern it was to find out the facts on behalf of the viewer, and to let nothing and nobody stand in his way. (Connell 1978, p. 81)

The idea that a programme should identify with its audience, and invite the popular audience to identify with it, was reproduced in the British programme. The presenter had a 'slight northern accent' which was taken to add to his 'earthy, no-nonsense approach', and for Swallow 'this was clearly no routine spokesman for the Establishment, but a man to be trusted – one of "us" rather than one of "them"' (Connell 1978). Connell goes on to trace three innovations which were introduced, eventually to transform the presentation of news and current affairs on television. They are:

1. *The mediator* The professional broadcaster who acts as a link between ordinary viewers and the newsworthy worlds beyond their immediate experience. This notion is now thoroughly familiar in the current affairs field, in which 'figures who personify characteristics which are taken to be typical of the "target" audience' anchor the various different kinds of programme: David Dimbleby for 'Panorama', Peter Snow for 'Newsnight' and the team currently including Sue Lawley for 'Nationwide', and so on.

2. *The 'vox pop'* The term comes from the Latin for 'voice of the people' and refers to 'wo/man-in-the-street' interviews which are used to give flavour, reaction, or mood to issues that have been raised in the news. Hence their function is twofold. They *authenticate* the coverage given to particular events by showing the concern of ordinary people in the issue; and they serve as potential *points of identification* for the audience, who are presumed to share the style and 'widely held opinions' voiced in the vox pop.

3. *The probing/tough interview* With disagreement inside the consensual range so evident, and with disillusionment – if not outright dissent – as features of contemporary public life that the media recognize, there is little room for *one* point of view to prevail. Not only does this lead to 'balanced' reports of both parties in a dispute, but to probing interviews which are intended to get behind the public image of official representatives and politicians. The stronger variant of this development, the tough interview, has the same purpose. As Connell puts it,

> the 'hard', 'tough' style of interviewing, the leading exponent of which is still Robin Day, was legitimized as an attempt 'to get at the facts' on behalf of the public. This adoption of a 'watchdog' role on behalf of the ordinary voters also led to the attempted identifications with 'us', and the attempts to articulate the kinds

of questions that 'we' would ask of 'our' powerful representatives if 'we' only could. (ibid., p. 83)

There is evidence that the interview performed by the mediator is spilling over into the hitherto more formal realm of TV news itself. ITN's lunchtime bulletin, 'News at One', is usually read by Peter Sissons. But he does not simply read the news. Here is a report by Godfrey Smith in *The Sunday Times* on what happens:

> When the news involves a famous politician or tycoon, Peter invariably turns aside in midstream to reveal that he [sic] is in the studio so that Peter can ask him just the questions you had in mind. He does 500 such interviews a year. . . . His own hero: Robin Day. (21 December 1980)

Compare this development with the role of the original BBC radio newsreaders, such as Alvar Liddell and John Snagge, who were 'announcers' as well as newsreaders, and whose names were not released to the public until 1940 (and only then for fear of the possibility of fake enemy bulletins being broadcast). Kumar notes the Reithian logic of newsreaders' anonymity:

> It is striking that from the very start Reith and his senior staff adopted a deliberate policy of using the announcers to create 'the public image' of the BBC. The very decision to make announcers anonymous followed from this policy, as did the sedulous cultivation of their formality. Both were intended to create a particular style by which the BBC could be identified in the public mind, and which more than any other device was to be used to establish its claim to a special moral and cultural authoritativeness. (1977, p. 239)

It is interesting to note that the analysis by Kumar suggests that the eventual abandonment by the BBC of its 'aloof, well-bred style' was not done to pull its practice into line with that of other media, but rather to preserve its identity and, crucially, its autonomy from the conflicting pressures to which it has been increasingly subjected since the 1960s. But the strategy still revolves around the public image of the presenters or mediators – the orientation of the Corporation towards its addressees – and remains as the attempt to hold the middle ground via the 'professional', 'non-partisan' mediator, who according to Kumar,

> must not stand, certainly must not seem to stand, for Left or Right, organized capital or organized labour, the professional 'moralist' or the professional 'libertarian'. One marked expression of this position in recent years has been the way in which the professional broadcaster has taken to 'identifying' with 'us' – that is, 'taking the role' of 'us' as 'the unrepresented', 'the consumers', 'the suffering public', the victims of planners and public servants of all kinds, as well as of large industrialists, selfish trade unions, property speculators and the like. This involves taking something of a 'populist' stance as well as style. Ministers are questioned as aggressively as trade unionists, environmentalist pressure groups as much as planning agencies, along the lines of, 'what are the gains and losses in all this for us, the public?'. More generally there is displayed an attitude of faint cynicism and scepticism towards almost all 'official' sources, whether in governmental or private organizations. (ibid., p. 247)

This development is very crucial. What it represents is a recognition within the BBC that 'the consensus', if it ever existed in fact, is being increasingly broken up. At the same time, however, the policy has been to develop an explicit identification with the 'commonsense' viewer, and to appeal to a consensus located not in the relations between Corporation and State but in the relations between the 'commonsense' presenter-mediator and the 'commonsense' family. As Kumar puts it,

> The BBC is trying to hold 'the middle ground' on a terrain that is treacherous and unstable. It cannot afford identification with any organized section of the community, however large. It can no longer ignore political issues, since 'politics' has penetrated so many areas – the family, school, even entertainment and sport – hitherto regarded and treated as non-political. Its solution has been to choose a certain kind of broadcaster, promote him [sic] and diffuse him throughout the medium, so that broadcasting can give the appearance of allowing expression to every tendency, every movement in British society – while at the same time ensuring that basic control is still in trained and trusted hands. But it is a precarious balancing act. (ibid., p. 248)

Connell also notes the awareness among senior TV spokesmen that the national 'faith' in parliamentary democracy, the law, the family and Christian morality are no longer consensual assumptions but 'issues of contention and debate'. But as he (sardonically) points out:

> As a consequence, broadcasting's quest for explanations consistent with these faiths, what 'most people' used to think, has proved an increasingly difficult one, but not one on which it has turned its back. Throughout the entire period this task has been pursued with vigour and diligence. (1978, p. 85)

In short, the BBC is a case study in the more widespread phenomenon of the media's response to the break-up of political consensus. Precisely in order to maintain some independence, 'objectivity' and autonomy, media organizations are driven towards a mode of address to their recipients which appeals to the supposedly 'non-political' common sense shared by the mediator and 'us', the public.

Common sense and images of the audience: conversation

The mode of address we have been discussing, then, seems closely bound up with assumptions about who and what the audience is. These assumptions require the construction of an image of the audience to which the journalist and broadcaster can work on an everyday basis. There are many clues to suggest what kind of image this is, and most of them point to its being grounded in the notion of common sense. According to Westergaard,

> broadcasters work to a highly nonvariegated image of their audience: to a conception of their viewers and listeners as a mass of ordinary people of 'ordinary common sense', men and women with their feet on the ground who take the world as it is and for whom the natural interpretation of affairs involves asking, in simplified form, much the same sorts of questions which those actively involved in matters of state put to each other's activity. (1977a, p. 108)

It seems clear that this image is one that is not only noticed by observers of the media, but also held quite explicitly by the broadcasters themselves. Thus Gilbert reports on the conceptions of the audience he found whilst working as a freelance producer within the BBC:

> The audience, then, is perceived in domestic, in familial terms. The viewers are husbands with their wives and (sometimes) their children, breadwinners and housewives; they are not, be it noted, workers; they are not a great many things that, as individuals, they might be. They are, rather, relaxing at home; they require to be, in the venerable Reithian axiom, 'educated, informed and entertained'. Television implicitly seeks to reinforce their familial situation or to advocate it to those viewers who have yet to attain it. (1980, p. 39)

The image of the audience as made up of families derives, in part, from the broadcasters' wish to stand apart from the hurly-burly of contending parties in the field of traditional (parliamentary) politics – especially in the light of their uncertainty as to whether or not there is any longer a consensus in this area. Quite apart from their legal requirement to maintain political impartiality, broadcasters are unwilling to 'take sides' in issues that they have to present to an audience which is itself 'sectionalised, fragmented, making contradictory demands, and less willing to be submissive if these demands were not met' (Kumar 1977, p. 246). The escape route has been to construct an image of the audience as non-political *families* – appealing to a consensus deemed to be ultimately more lasting and strong than any politics. This particular consensus is the focus of all categories of television output, not just news and current affairs, so that the appeal to the family audience is, as Gilbert argues,

> at its most naked in the kind of television which actually funds independent programmes and which is therefore the most rigorously tailored to the imagined audience – the commercials. The commercials illustrate two major themes – the responsibility of the woman to consume wisely on behalf of her husband and children (and, indeed, even news bulletins and current affairs programmes constantly characterise the consumer as 'the housewife'); and the association of inessentials with the opposite sex. In the latter case, the models are always young as well as glamorous (and white), on the assumption that this appeal is a prelude to marriage. (1980, p. 39)

In the field of current affairs, the appeal to the family is often made over the heads of politicians, exploiting the 'well-founded fact that audiences tend to identify with the presenter as against contending parties' (Kumar, 1977, p. 247). This leads to the populist perspective adopted by current affairs programmes like 'Nationwide'. In their analysis of 'Nationwide', Brunsdon and Morley show how the effect of this populist perspective gives a very privileged position to the mediator (who in the period they cover was Michael Barratt) and tends to 'translate' political issues into apparently 'a-political' comments grounded in common sense.

> Barratt presents himself as the embodiment of this 'populist' perspective: a no-nonsense man of the people, stressing down-to-earth common sense, not only by asking the questions he thinks the public would want to ask but also, unlike many other current affairs presenters, by adding comments ('Well, they do seem rather daft reasons for going on strike. . .' *Nationwide* 14/3/73) he assumes the public might make, or at least agree with. (1978, p. 8)

As Brunsdon and Morley point out, these comments are directed to an image of the audience as somehow 'outside' politics, 'in' the family:

> The comments are not seen to transgress the requirements of balance and impartiality. They rest on an image of 'the people' *outside* the structures of politics and government. Precisely because they are made from a perspective at odds with that of parliamentary politics – 'the politicians' as such are suspect from this perspective – these comments do not favour the position of one party against another within that framework. This 'common-sense' critique of 'politics' presents itself as a-political, despite the obviously political content of common-sense wisdom about what 'we all know. . .'. (ibid., p. 8)

In short, the 'Nationwide' appeal is based on a 'set of assumptions about "what everybody thinks"', and it 'poses "ordinary people" as its source' (ibid.).

The kind of process I have just outlined for television, whereby an image of the audience in the routine practices of the broadcasters is used to construct a mode of address deemed appropriate for that audience, is at work just as powerfully in newspapers. As Hall *et al.* put it,

> Of special importance in determining the particular mode of

address adopted will be the particular part of the readership spectrum the paper sees itself as customarily addressing: its target audience. The language employed will thus be the *newspaper's own version of the language of the public to whom it is principally addressed: its* version of the rhetoric, imagery and underlying common stock of knowledge which it assumes its audience shares and which thus forms the basis of the reciprocity of producer/reader. (1978, p. 61)

The idea of appealing to common sense, to what 'most of us' think, and to the 'common stock of knowledge' might seem at first glance to be a good one. Not only does it seem to avoid the pitfalls of politics, but it seems to ensure that the media don't get too far out of line with the 'real interests' of their viewers and readers. However, things are unfortunately not so simple. John Westergaard sounds the warning note:

My point is not that this image of 'the public' is totally false; but that it is a caricature which sacrifices the diverse and ambiguous reality of popular outlooks on the world – a contradictory mixture of dissent, disgruntlement, resentment and suspicion with conformity and acquiescent 'common sense' – for a picture of 'mass' opinion and taste which singles out only the safe 'common denominators' of orientation that square with the practical order of things as they are. In this respect, broadcasters' images of their audience are much the same as newspaper producers' images of their readers, and to much the same effect. (1977, p. 108)

That effect, says Westergaard, is 'a down-to-earth, everyday interpretation of the world to a collective "man in the street", who has a uniform common sense attributed to him consonant with the conventional wisdom on public affairs' (ibid., p. 108).

How does it come about, then, that the very attempt to escape the political, and to base broadcasting and journalism in the 'real concerns' of the people, lands the media straight back into the laps of those who are the current beneficiaries of the way power and rewards are unequally distributed? Part of the answer to this question lies in the way common sense itself is viewed and used. Recently there has been an increase in the critical attention being given to the whole idea of common sense, which has, in the words of Catherine Belsey,

> put in question not only some of the specific assumptions of common sense, some of the beliefs which appear obvious and natural, but the authority of the concept of common sense itself, the collective and timeless wisdom whose unquestioned presence seems to be the source and guarantee of everything we take for granted. (1980, p. 3)

The drift of this critical attention has been to show that

> what seems obvious and natural is not necessarily so, but that on the contrary the 'obvious' and the 'natural' are not *given* but *produced* in a specific society by the ways in which that society talks and thinks about itself and its experience. (ibid.)

The ways in which a society 'talks and thinks about itself' are obviously complex. But they are concentrated in the chief mechanism available to us for what Berger and Luckmann call 'reality-maintenance', namely conversation. But, as they go on to point out,

> it is important to stress, however, that the greater part of reality-maintenance in conversation is implicit, not explicit. Most conversation does not in so many words define the nature of the world. Rather, it takes place against the background of a world that is silently taken for granted. (1966, p. 172)

The 'taken-for-granted' reality of the world is maintained in turn by three very important characteristics of conversation.

1. It is *casual* – and as Berger and Luckmann argue it 'can *afford to be casual* precisely because it refers to the routine of a taken-for-granted world' (ibid.).
2. It is *cumulative* – it requires continuous reinforcement in everyday interaction.
3. It is *situated* in the observed and experienced surface phenomena of everyday life.

As the linguist M.A.K. Halliday suggests, one of the formal features of conversation in linguistic terms is its setting, since

> it is in such contexts that reality is constructed, in the micro-semiotic encounters of daily life. The reason why this is so, why the culture is transmitted to, or recreated by, the individual in the first instance through conversation rather than through other acts of meaning, is that conversation typically relates to the

environment in a way that is perceptible and concrete, whereas other genres tend to depend on intermediate levels of symbolic interpretation . . . Conversation . . . is structured in such a way as to make explicit its relationship to its setting. (1978, p. 140)

These characteristics of conversation are important in any consideration of the notion of common sense and of the media's exploitation of it; firstly, because, as part of their conception of their audience as a mass of commonsensical ordinary people, the media expect their products to be treated casually, as part of everyday experience. John Westergaard sees this as part of the reason why the 'popular' daily newspapers, the *Sun* and the *Daily Mirror*, restrict their coverage of politics and societal affairs:

> Personalia, sport, sex, snippets of this and that – with much space devoted to pictures and, of course, to advertisements – loom far larger, in a package designed to appeal to what are taken to be the common denominators of casual interest among a 'mass' wage-earning public. (1977, p. 103)

But it is not just among the tabloids that the threshold of casual interest is seen as a problem. Both ITN and the BBC gave evidence to the recent Annan Committee on the Future of Broadcasting on their reactions to demands for more analysis and explanation in news programmes. The Director General of the BBC told the committee that 'it's no good if you put the explanation after the audience has switched off', and ITN suggested there was a danger of 'boring them to death' (Annan Report 1977, p. 285).

Perhaps just as important, however, is the way the media 'colonize' that taken-for-granted world in which conversation achieves coherence and order. Media output is not the same as conversation; it is itself part of the environment that we relate to, as Halliday puts it, in conversation. Nevertheless, a lot of media output is modelled on the casual, cumulative, situated structure of conversation. Take 'Nationwide' for example:

> *Nationwide* adopts the language of popular speech – the language is always concrete, direct and punchy, with an assumption of and a reference to always pre-existing 'knowledge'. This populist vocabulary is the language of 'common sense' which the programme adopts and transforms, picking up popular terms of speech (much in the style of the *Daily Mirror's* 'Come off it

> Harold . . .'), mimicking phrases and clichés, and putting them to new uses, making them carry the weight of a political message. (Brunsdon and Morley 1978, p. 8)

Here the ideological use to which commonsense language is put becomes apparent. As we have noted, the staple diet of news is the sayings and doings of the 'élite persons' who not only wield institutional power, but also act as 'representatives' of large social groups – MPs, Ministers, trade-unionists, industrialists, experts, campaigners and the like. The media's colonization of commonsense language serves to 'translate' the sayings and doings of these people and institutions into a familiar idiom. Hall *et al.* argue from this that

> this translation of official viewpoints into a public idiom not only makes the former more 'available' to the uninitiated; it invests them with popular force and resonance, naturalising them within the horizon of understandings of the various publics. (1978, p. 61)

A striking example of this work of translation is discussed in an analysis John Fiske and I undertook, in *Reading Television* (1978), of a 'News at Ten' story about Northern Ireland, broadcast in January 1976. Reporting on the aftermath of what was termed the 'Bessbrook massacre', in particular a government decision to use the SAS (Special Air Service) in South Armagh, the ITN discourse performed two remarkable pieces of translation.

The first was to create a public identity for the then relatively unknown SAS (in the context of post-Watergate public disquiet about 'undercover operations'). ITN's defence correspondent, Peter Snow, mobilized a full repertoire of commonsense idioms to 'naturalize' the SAS. He began, of course, by personalizing the government decision – it is 'Mr Wilson' (then Prime Minister) who is the initiator of action:

> Mr Wilson's taking a carefully calculated risk. He's putting into South Armagh the men who have the reputation, earned behind enemy lines in Indonesia, Malaya and other recent wars, for individual toughness, resourcefulness, and endurance. They've been, not entirely of their own choosing, the undercover men. The men whose presence has struck fear into the heart of the enemy. (Fiske and Hartley 1978, p. 92)

The effect is to take the alien, unknown and very probably unpleasant SAS, and signify them in the heroic language of the popular mythology of commandos.

The second piece of translation performed in this same bulletin concerned the adversaries into whose hearts the SAS were about to strike fear. However, by the time the story had moved on to the hunt for the perpetrators of the so-called Bessbrook massacre, the SAS had completely disappeared. Their place was taken by a more familiar figure:

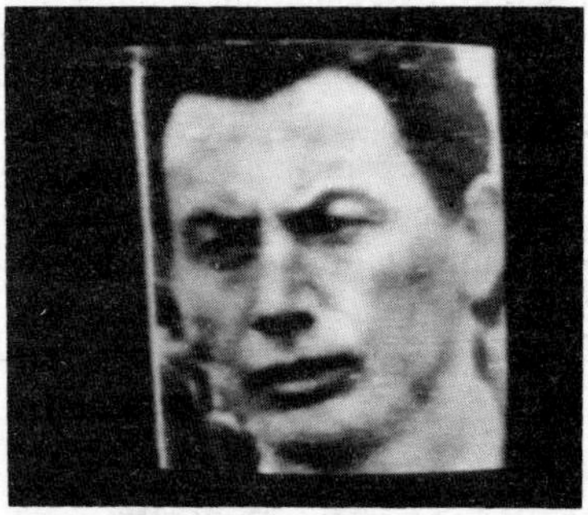

7 *The suspect: this mugshot (in black-and-white) is held for 41 seconds on screen, whilst the 'Troubles' become part of the discourse of crime. 'News at Ten', 7 January 1976.*

> The new troops and police who have been sent to South Armagh to track down the gang who shot dead ten Protestants on Monday night have been issued with this photograph of B– S– [named in bulletin and shown in mugshot], born in Bessbrook where the murdered men came from and now living south of the border in County Louth. S–, aged 31 and dark-haired, has long been wanted for questioning by detectives in Northern Ireland investigating what they classify as serious terrorist crimes in the area. S– has never been in custody in the North, but he appeared three years ago in the Dublin Special Criminal Court on arms charges, and spent two years in prison after conviction. He appealed against the sentence, thereby breaking IRA conventions in recognizing the court, and was reported to have been thrown out of the movement. But shortly after his release he was back again on the

> wanted list compiled by military intelligence officers operating in South Armagh. (Fiske and Hartley 1978, p. 113)

Here we can discern the collision of two discourses, one of which is decisively victorious. The complex military-political affairs of Northern Ireland are translated into the language of cops and robbers. It is much easier to understand this discursive idiom, but (quite apart from the questionable ethics of 'trial by semiotics') we should note how uneasily the affairs of Northern Ireland fit into it. The 'commando' myth of 'behind enemy lines' is ridiculous in the Irish context – where are the 'enemy'; where are their 'lines'? Similarly, the notion of detectives, and the catalogue of police-court nomenclature that supports it, leads to a mystification of the troubles. Given its placing at the end of the story the weight of this translation is to offer an alibi to the watching millions: the troubles in Ireland (like the 'massacre') are criminal acts caused by criminals; this man is the criminal.

It seems that politics has nothing to do with it – except that the British government in 1976 instituted a policy of 'criminalization' with respect to the troubles. ITN's cops and robbers discourse happens to fit well with a policy that set up the 'Diplock Courts' (which sit without juries and have special rules of evidence), and removed the special category status for prisoners which had operated in Longkesh since the time of internment without trial.

How much of what the 'News at Ten' discourse 'naturalized' into commonsense language was official government policy is impossible to judge, but it is clear that the public idiom that was used did little to enlighten the public. And of course this bulletin does not stand alone; as Eamonn McCann wrote as early as 1971,

> the great majority of the British people, dependent on the press to tell them what is happening in the North of Ireland, are by now *incapable* of forming a judgement about it, so one-sided has the reporting been. (McCann 1971, p. 4)

The important point about the translation into a commonsense public idiom of British military-political policy in Northern Ireland (SAS = commandos; Irish dissidence = IRA; IRA = criminals) is not that it is meaningless. On the contrary, the main purpose of both news in particular and common sense in general is to *make* the world meaningful. As Stuart Hall has argued:

> What passes for 'common sense' in our society – the residue of absolutely basic and commonly agreed, consensual wisdoms – helps us to classify out the world in simple but meaningful terms. Precisely, common sense does not require reasoning, argument, logic, thought: it is spontaneously available, thoroughly recognizable, widely shared. It *feels*, indeed, as if it has always been there, the sedimented, bedrock wisdom of 'the race', a form of 'natural' wisdom. (1977, p. 325)

As a result, and as we have seen in reference to the 'News at Ten' bulletin on Northern Ireland, 'you cannot learn, through common sense, *how things are*: you can only discover *where they fit* into the existing scheme of things' (ibid.).

Common sense and 'understanding': the bardic function

Just as conversation is *structured by* the situation in which it is produced, so common sense seems to derive its meaning from the 'given' 'facts' of the 'natural' situations in which people find themselves from day to day. However, it is not the 'facts' themselves (apart from their classification as such) that concerns common sense. Rather, it is the relations between them – the construction of the fragmented elements of knowledge, derived from the immediate social and physical environment, into a coherent, comprehensible order. Common sense's function as a producer of *understanding* has led it to be dubbed the 'philosophy of non-philosophers' by Antonio Gramsci, who is the writer to whom we owe much of recent theory on the subject. Gramsci outlines the main characteristics of historically-produced common sense: it is

> the conception of the world which is uncritically absorbed by the various social and cultural environments in which the moral individuality of the average man [sic] is developed. Common sense is not a single unique conception, identical in time and space. It is the 'folklore' of philosophy, and, like folklore, it takes countless different forms. Its most fundamental characteristic is that it is a conception which, even in the brain of one individual, is fragmentary, incoherent and inconsequential, in conformity with the social and cultural position of the masses whose philosophy it is. (1971, p. 419)

Hence one of the important consequences for the use of commonsense conceptions in the media is that 'common sense is a chaotic aggregate of disparate conceptions, and one can find there anything that one likes' (ibid., p. 422). It is rather like proverbial wisdom (and of course proverbs *are* commonsensical): you can always find one proverb to contradict another. Hence 'many hands make light work', but 'too many cooks spoil the broth'. It depends on the situation in which – and the purpose for which – the conceptions are used.

For Gramsci the elements out of which common sense are constructed are provided by a number of sources. In the context within which he was writing, that is, Italy in the 1920s and 1930s, the most important source is popular 'religion' – not only formal religious doctrine as promulgated by the priesthood, but also informal moral codes and precepts of behaviour. For the kind of rural community with which Gramsci was faced in parts of Italy (and in the midst of which he himself grew up), the origin of this kind of common sense is in 'the "intellectual activity" of the local priest or ageing patriarch whose wisdom is law, or in the little old woman who has inherited the lore of the witches or the minor intellectual soured by his own stupidity and inability to act' (ibid., p. 323). Despite his jaundiced view of rural common sense, Gramsci is well aware that these figures in themselves are a minor and declining force in the modern world. For as the anthropologist Claude Lévi-Strauss notes, 'we are no longer linked to our past by an oral tradition which implies direct contact with others (storytellers, priests, wise men, or elders), but by books amassed in libraries' (1968, p. 366). Hence the function performed by these figures is taken over by other, newer, social institutions. Gramsci points, for instance, to

> the importance and significance which, in the modern world, political parties have in the elaboration and diffusion of conceptions of the world, because essentially what they do is to work out the ethics and the politics corresponding to these conceptions and act as it were as their historical 'laboratory'. (Gramsci 1971, p. 335)

However, even political parties are not the current champions. This role has been taken over by the media and the schools (ibid., p. 342). Stuart Hall analyses the media's leadership and its function:

> Quantitatively and qualitatively, in twentieth-century advanced

> capitalism, the media have established a decisive and fundamental leadership in the cultural sphere. Simply in terms of economic, technical, social and cultural resources, the mass media command a qualitatively greater slice than all the older, more traditional cultural channels which survive. Far more important is the manner in which the whole gigantic complex sphere of public information, intercommunication and exchange – the production and consumption of 'social knowledge' in societies of this type – depends upon the mediation of the modern means of communication. They have progressively *colonized* the cultural and ideological sphere. As social groups and classes live, if not in their productive then in their 'social' relations, increasingly fragmented and sectionally differentiated lives, the mass media are more and more responsible (a) for providing the basis on which groups and classes construct an 'image' of the lives, meanings, practices and values of *other* groups and classes; (b) for providing the images, representations and ideas around which the social totality, composed of all these separate and fragmented pieces, can be coherently grasped as *a 'whole'*. This is the first of the great cultural functions of the modern media: the provision and the selective construction of social knowledge. (Hall 1977, pp. 340–1)

In other words, and as Fiske and I argue in *Reading Television*, the media have not simply supplanted the priest, the patriarch, the little old woman and the minor intellectual: they have, in both fictional and factual output, taken them over, and have *used* them in a mediating role to construct cohesion out of the fragmented 'facts' of life. In our literate culture, then, the media offer 'us' a mediated

> 'contact with others', in which all Lévi-Strauss's lost storytellers, priests, wise men and elders are restored to cultural visibility and to oral primacy: often indeed in the convincing guise of highly literate specialists, from newsreaders to scientific and artistic experts. (Fiske and Hartley 1978, pp. 125–6)

Fiske and I have proposed that in this respect the role of the media in modern society is not unlike that of the maker and teller of tales in oral cultures – television in particular performs a 'bardic function' (Fiske and Hartley 1978, p. 85 ff.).

More recently, Raymond Williams has put our notion of the bardic function back into the historical context of traditional Celtic societies, where he notes that

> There is then an immediate problem in interpreting their actual social relations. It has been said, on the one hand, that in this situation the bard is accountable to society, and is its spokesman; on the other hand, that it is his duty to serve the past and present glory of the ruling class. (1981, p. 37)

Clearly the same 'problem' applies to television. Indeed, the value of comparing television with the original bardic role is to point out the extent to which modern capitalism has 'moved towards a situation in which it could again be said (but with the qualitative difference of an epochal change) that cultural institutions are integral parts of the general social organization' (Williams, 1981 p. 54). In other words, both the original bardic order and the modern media constitute distinct and internally coherent social organizations, but they both occupy the very centre of the cultural stage – their position is not that of the alienated artist, and their 'message' is at once the source and the result of pervasive, common meanings – 'common' sense.

The implication of the notion that the media perform a 'bardic function' is that their role is active and productive. Common sense is not just there, waiting to be used. While the media are appealing to our common sense to explain all manner of different subjects, they are at the same time constantly 'reminding' us of what the explanations are based on. Like conversation, which achieves 'reality-maintenance' by cumulative reinforcement in everyday interaction (see p. 97), common sense has to be *produced* continuously. But unlike conversation, the media's commonsense explanations are not produced spontaneously in the situated 'lived experience' of everyday casual interaction. They are produced by the corporate production routines of the mass media. In other words, the media don't so much remind us of commonsense notions and classifications that we already 'have', rather they *produce and reproduce* them out of 'raw materials' selected from the cultural and linguistic environment.

In fact this active and creative work of the news media is their distinctive feature – their special job among the various institutions in society. They themselves originate neither the factual stories, nor the commonsense categories, nor the public idiom into which they translate those stories. They take their stories (and some of the ways of making sense of them) from the groups, institutions and people with power and 'representative' status. They take their commonsense stance and their public idiom from both these sources and from their image of what their audience thinks and says. Hence, as a result, when they translate the doings of the mighty into the language of the rest of us, they implicate us in the thinking and policies of our elders and betters.

Thus, as Connell has claimed, 'dominant' definitions of the world are *granted* 'the status of what "many" or "most" people think' (1979, p. 88), and this *actively contributes* to the continuing dominance of those definitions and of the groups whose interests are thereby made accessible, 'natural' and 'the same' as our own.

The practical effect of this process is not inconsiderable. Take for instance the Northern Ireland story discussed earlier. Translating the political-military affairs of Northern Ireland into the popular mythology of commandos, and into the commonsense discourse of cops and robbers, 'News at Ten' produces a way of understanding which proposes that not only is it possible for the events be made sense of in this accessible, commonsense way, but that this is *necessarily* what they mean, of themselves. From this 'insight' it is perhaps only a short step towards 'our' uncritical acquiescence in the government policy of 'criminalization' – which is never discussed as such in this bulletin. On the contrary, it hardly needs to be seen as a policy, since its rationale appears to arise 'naturally' from the 'facts' of the situation. If there is a bunch of ruthless criminals on the loose (like B– S–), then 'naturally' the government must do its best to catch them. Meanwhile, of course, the troubles continue and the policy of 'criminalization' results in H-Block protests and hunger strikes.

The news, then, works hard to preserve its autonomy from the contending groups in society, and it works hard to report events in an accessible but impartial way. However, the strategies it has evolved to do this, and the language it takes from out of 'our' mouths to make sense of the world *for* us, do not secure it from other social forces. The impartiality and autonomy of news production are real and are actively struggled for by newspeople. The function of that hard-won space is to guarantee that the meanings constructed there are not mere propaganda, either for the government, the 'establishment' or anyone else. In the process the sense that is made of the world turns out to be much more ideologically active and productive for the maintenance of one particular (dominant) 'reality' than 'mere' propaganda would be. For propaganda is contestable, whereas, as common sense tells us, 'nature' is not.

7 A WINTER OF DISCONTENT

> A good journalist – by training and instinct – has a gut feeling about objectivity and can find a way, via common sense rather than tortured hair-splitting semantics, through the objectivity-commitment minefield. One thing is certain: if he [sic] cannot, propaganda will soon take the place of genuine information.
>
> Arnold Hadwin, editor of the *Bradford Telegraph & Argus* (Hadwin 1980, p. 30)

In this chapter I propose, via 'tortured hair-splitting semantics' rather than 'common sense', to show how some of the issues raised so far can be seen in action. For this purpose I shall refer throughout to a BBC 'Nine O'Clock News' by way of an extended example. How in practice do good journalists avoid propaganda, provide us with genuine information, and throw up (into sharp relief) their gut feeling about objectivity?

The story I've chosen to analyse was screened on 1 February 1979. It was the main domestic story of that day, preceded in this bulletin by a long film report from Tehran about the return of the Ayatollah Khomeini to Iran after fifteen years' exile.

Elements of news narrative: visual structures

As the major domestic story, it typifies many of the formal properties of news presentation on television. It has three *presentation elements* (see table 2, pp. 120–1):

A The *newsreader* (in this case Angela Rippon) who 'frames' the topic at the beginning, provides links between the other elements, and rounds the topic off at the end;

B The *correspondent* or commentator (in this case the Political Correspondent, Rodney Foster), who sets the topic in context and explains its significance;

C The *film report* (there are two in this story) which presents images and 'actuality' from 'out there' at the street level of experience.

Visually the story is signified by four *modes of presentation*:

1. The '*talking head*' (see pic. 10.1) Not just the newsreader, but also the correspondent invariably gets this 'neutral' treatment, except that the correspondent is differentiated by the addition of both graphics and nomination.

2. *Graphics* (including animation, computer-displays, etc.). These can fill the screen with voice-over supplying the commentary (pic. 10.2), or they can be used 'behind' the talking head, as in our story, where the correspondent is placed slightly right of centre, with a graphic depicting a line-drawing of Big Ben over the word POLITICS 'behind' his shoulder left of screen (shot 10.3).

2a. A sub category is the *still photograph* held full-frame (shot 10.23).

3. *Nomination* The captions or verbal introductions which literally name participants in the news; usually reporters (shot 10.14). Individuals from 'outside' the news are also nominated, usually by a caption superimposed over an interview (shot 10.8). This kind of nominating, according to Brunsdon and Morley (whose term it is) is for

> clueing the audience in as to the identity of extra-programme participants or interviewees; establishing their 'status' (expert, eyewitness, etc.) and their right/competence to speak on the topic in question – thus establishing their proposed degree of 'credibility'/authority within the discourse. (Brunsdon and Morley 1978, p. 59)

4. *Actuality* The film (or ENG – Electronic News Gathering) report. The backbone of TV news, so it is hardly surprising there are three sub-categories of presentation modes:

4a. *Film with voice-over* where reporter does not appear in the film;

4b. *The stake-out* (shot 10.14) where the reporter addresses his commentary direct to camera;

4c. The *vox pop* (see p. 90 and shots 10.17 and 18) in which the interviewee is usually seen talking full frame, to an unseen reporter outside camera-shot. Vox pop interviewees are almost never nominated.

On the subject of modes of presentation, it is interesting to note that the news never (in my experience) uses one of the most familiar and characteristic television modes of presentation, the studio discussion. This is a pleasure news editors do without because of their commitment to a separation of 'fact' from 'opinion'. The ideological productivity of the separation is obvious – if the news defines its content as facts and 'hard information', carefully excluding set-ups that *look like* forums for opinion, then, logically, whatever you see on the news *is* information, it is not the arbitrary opinion of the reporter or anyone else. Similarly, the news keeps 'faction' – fictionalized fact – at bay. The 'dramatic reconstruction' is a staple of documentary usage, but the only reconstructions you see on the news are the ones staged by the constabulary, in which policewomen stumble through a rape-murder victim's last walk through the neighbourhood.

Institutional and accessed voices: verbal structures

Given these visual elements, it follows that the predominant *voices* of the news are those of the newsreader(s), the correspondents(s) and the various reporters on location. However, these are by no means the only voices we hear. The familiar cast of élite persons are often called upon to have their say, and there can be contributions from lesser-known people who are either representatives of particular parties or groups involved in a story, or selected for vox pops. However, none of these voices simply speaks. They are all subordinate to the overall structure of a story as presented by the professional broadcasters.

In other words, they function very similarly to the way spoken dialogue functions in a novel: it advances the narrative, but it seems to be 'privileged' by not being simply the voice or opinion of the author. In a novel, it is easier to see the paradox. Even though the dialogue 'belongs' to the characters who speak it, it is *produced* by the author. In television news the same principle holds. Whatever an individual character may say, its meaning will be determined not by his or her intentions or situation, but by the placing of the interview in the overall context of the story. The terms s/he uses may be taken up approvingly, or be contradicted and appear to be cynical, shortsighted or bloody-minded.

Further, the things some people say in interviews, or are quoted as saying, can perform the important task of making sense of a story in terms that are denied to the 'impartial' professionals. If the Prime Minister says a strike is the work of an 'irresponsible minority', then so be it, but the BBC cannot on its own behalf say any such thing. However, by using the quotation, the BBC can make sense of the strike in these terms.

All the individual voices, like individual notes in a musical score, are then orchestrated together within the overall news story. The effect of this on the narrative is to provide it with authenticity, the *reality effect*. This is not to say that outside voices are simply accepted into the narrative as 'right', or as definitive. Far from it. All quoted material or interviewed voices are treated as highly provisional in status. They are open to re-interpretation in the light of the other voices in the story, particularly those of the professionals themselves. We can distinguish the professional from the outsider by identifying two voices: the institutional voice and the accessed voice.

The institutional voice

The only voices which are fully 'naturalized' are those of the newsreaders, correspondents and (with certain exceptions) the reporters on location. These voices deny their constructed, provisional status – the things they say are said as if they were completely transparent. 'Reality' simply appears through them.

One of the tasks to be performed in any news programme, then, is to separate out the two kinds of voice, simultaneously 'marking' each type. When quotations are used, the marking of accessed voices is done by a conventionalized code of intonation-change. Hence, in our story, Angela Rippon (the newsreader) says, 'In the Commons the *Prime Minister urged* the strikers to "go back to work" while negotiations could continue on *what he called* a "proper basis".'

The phrases 'go back to work' and 'proper basis' are uttered, as it were, in quotation marks, and the quotation is further separated by stressing that the words 'belong' to the Prime Minister. The effect of this procedure, of course, is to naturalize all the parts of the discourse that are *not* in quotation marks. The viewer is offered the chance to interpret the quoted material in the light of what is known about the original speaker, but the institutional voice isn't quoting anything except reality.

The accessed voice

Similarly, accessed voices which take the form of interviews or on-the-spot comments are separated from the reporter's own account. There is a code of 'being interviewed': the individual is filmed in close-up, but never addresses his or her remarks directly to camera; instead, s/he appears to be talking to the unseen reporter, who is stationed discreetly off-camera. On the other hand, when reporters are seen on camera, it is always to address their remarks directly to 'us': they don't need to be accessed *through* an institutional mediator. This is the technique I've called the 'stake-out' (following American terminology).

There are some accessed voices, however, which don't appear in their own guise, but rather in that of the institutional voice itself. These are the voices who issue press releases. There is absolutely no way of telling in detail from the news broadcast itself how much of a newsreader's or reporter's script is written by the news organization and how much comes from press releases. By their very nature press releases cannot be impartial – they present the case of whatever organization issues them. There have been constant complaints in Northern Ireland, for example, that the coverage of events there is uncannily similar to versions emanating from the army, RUC or Northern Ireland Office. In a rare discussion by a working journalist of this issue, the *Guardian*'s Simon Hoggart reported in *New Society* that:

> Most journalists working in Northern Ireland are almost completely dependent on this [army] information service (and the smaller one run by the police), simply because there is no other source for news of day-to-day violence. This means that the army has the immense advantage of getting the first word, and it is left up to the integrity of the journalist to check that word one. Some do, some don't. Most only check when there is time or the incident looks like becoming controversial, and a few hardly bother at all. When the British press prints an account of an incident as if it were an established fact, and it is clear that the reporter himself (sic) is not on the spot, it is a 99 per cent cer-

tainty that it is the army's version that is being given. (*New Society*, 11 October 1973)

The advantage gained for such versions in being presented as the institutional voice is enormous. Their particular view is signified on screen in such a way that it looks like *the* view, the natural fact.

Meanwhile, back in the studio, there is another curious device for separating out the identifiably accessed voice, namely the 'noddy' (see pic. 8). This is where a reporter sits in a corner of the location

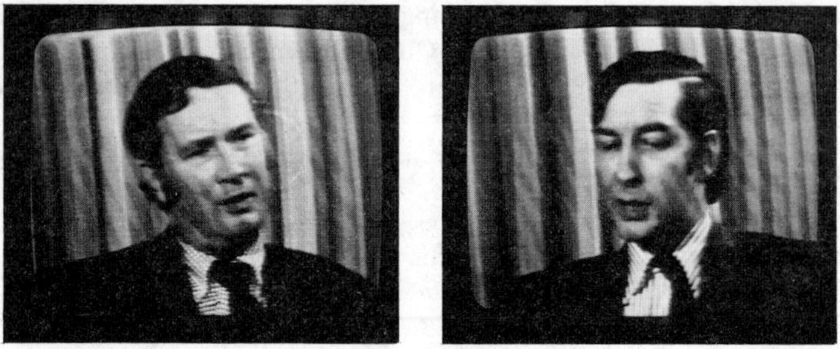

8 *The noddy: who is the interviewer, who is the accessed voice? (The home affairs correspondent and Dr David Wardle on 'News at Ten', 7 January 1976)*

where an interview is being held, and – with an expression of encouraging attentiveness – nods. These nods are later inserted into the film wherever there is an edited cut in the interview. The device is interesting because it performs contradictory functions. On the one hand it artificially 'naturalizes' the interview, making it look like a conversation between equals (and not like an edited selection); but on the other hand it reminds 'us' that the interviewer is there asking questions on our behalf, and that the status of the interviewee's comments is precisely that they are being listened to – they are not free-standing. In short, whilst accessing the voice, the institution simultaneously *appropriates* (steals) it.

Just as there is a code of being interviewed, so there is a code of interviewing. Interviews are visually of two kinds, either in a *studio* (or studio-like surroundings), or *on the spot*. The consequences of these two forms on the production of meaning can be decisive. As Walton and Davis argue, with reference to the coverage of industrial disputes,

> Although in the news as a whole there is the semblance of balance between the 'two sides', they appear in different contexts. Workers are more likely to be interviewed in groups, in the street, in noisy surroundings etc., while management are more likely to be filmed in surroundings which help to lend authority to their statements. . . . Workers tend to be stereotypically filmed by the factory gates or on a picket line. They are rarely accorded a studio and almost never shot talking directly face on to camera – as those of 'higher' status are. (1977, pp. 129–30)

In short, and as the Annan Report (1977) commented in response to the research on which these arguments are based (see Glasgow Media Group, 1976 and 1980), 'Management statements were treated as "facts", whereas the unions were depicted as being involved in "events" ' (Annan Report, p. 272).

Verbally, interviews usually take one of three forms. I have distinguished them on the basis of the type of question used to elicit a comment from the interviewee. But again it is noteworthy that some groups of interviewees get asked only one type of question, whereas others – perhaps involved in the same news event – get a different type. The three types are:

1. *How does it feel. . . ?* The standard 'Nationwide' vox pop question. What is the experience you're part of like for you as an individual? Tell us your emotions. An example of the absurd lengths to which this question can be taken occurred in the BBC's flagship science programme, 'Horizon', screened in November 1980. The programme set out to investigate whether there is a 'scientific' basis to astrology. It traced the astrologer who had predicted that a 'spy' would be unearthed within Buckingham Palace. In the light of the subsequent discovery of Anthony Blunt's activities, the obvious question to the astrologer concerned would be 'how did you do it?', 'What other successes do you claim?', etc. But the actual question asked was – 'How does it feel to be the man who. . .?' This question accords well with the news value of personalization, of course, and it is very common when 'ordinary people' are interviewed.

2. *Isn't it. . .?* This is the question designed to let the interviewee get on with the statement of his or her case, in their own terms. Used for 'experts' who have been wheeled in to explain a particular issue, it is also common when the 'expert' in question is the high-prestige management 'spokesman' in an industrial dispute.

3. *But surely. . .?* The classic 'tough' question, which is put 'on our behalf' to public figures who are trying to make their case in their own terms, but are reminded by the interviewer of other priorities, other ways of looking at the issue. Sir Robin Day is widely associated with this type of question, which he puts on our behalf to Prime Ministers, but it is also frequently found on a humbler level – that of the picket line. In our 'Nine O'Clock News', it is the only question we hear being put to a NUPE union shop steward. He is interviewed on-the-spot, as you would expect, and the question is not about the reasons for the dispute, or the nature of the claim, or even about the union's tactics. It is: 'But surely this sort of action isn't going to gain a lot of public sympathy?'

9 *How to be interviewed: On the left, a junior doctor spells out the government's inadequacies in the comfort of a studio interview. Responding to a series of 'isn't it' questions, he puts the government 'on probation' ('News at Ten', 7 January 1976). On the right, a NUPE shop-steward from the same health service is involved in the same activity – seeking a pay rise for his members. But he is placed, semiotically, out in the cold.*

Despite the care with which institutional and accessed voices are marked and separated from each other, there is a higher level of organization of the material in which they are re-integrated. This is at the level of the news-narrative as a whole. At this level, all the voices contribute to the production of the reality effect. The story as a whole is 'about' all that is included in it, no matter what the origin of particular statements. Indeed, the credibility of the news story depends on 'knitting together' the apparently transparent, neutral discourse of the institutional voices and the contending mêlée of accessed voices. What the story means, then, depends on the successful integration of a known and trusted institutional discourse and an 'authentic' representation of the 'factual' world of phenomena 'out there'.

News narrative: fact and fiction

One of the most interesting consequences of this narrative structure of the news is that it bears a very close resemblance to the structure of certain key types of television fiction, especially the police series. In these, it is normal for the 'heroes' like Regan and Carter in 'The Sweeney' or Starsky and Hutch, or their more recent successors in series like 'Minder', 'Hazell', or 'Tenspeed and Brownshoe', to survive as characters from week to week, series to series. Their antagonists – the villains – on the other hand, are not so fortunate. Not only are they refused a guarantee of survival beyond the individual episode, they are positively required to efface themselves (i.e. be defeated by the heroes) in each and every one. Only their *function* survives: our heroes cannot exist as such without their opposition, so villainy continues even though individual villains always get what's coming to them. In the news, similarly, the cast of 'newsworthy' characters is different from day to day, whilst on the contrary the institutional presenters are always there to guide us through their otherwise mysterious doings. *The news*, then, as a social institution (like *the law* in police series), is personalized, made human. The news *means* Richard Baker, Anna Ford, etc. Their continuing characteristics unify all the diverse voices they articulate together.

Conversely the accessed voices in the news, which do not survive the individual episode, only achieve continuity through their function. This means that in order to function at all, they must be very strongly 'marked' to identify them with other voices that perform the same function. In other words, accessed voices are routinely *stereotyped* to make them meaningful within the continuing saga of news-discourse. A routine shorthand for these stereotypes is easily obtained by personalizing events. Ministers, trade-unionists, etc. do achieve a personal continuity from news to news – their own characteristics provide the stereotypes, which are then exploited to render events 'meaningful'.

The marking of stereotypes is similar for villains in police series, as has been noted by Drummond. He gives the example of a 'Sweeney' episode screened in September 1975 called *Supersnout*. Here the role of informer, or 'snout', is signified by a character who literally 'constantly picks his "snout"' (1976, p. 24). There aren't many nose-pickers on the news, but even so the principle holds good that accessed voices, denied continuity, function to signify a limited number of stereotypes.

One of the ways in which stereotyping is achieved is by the production within the news of basic oppositions. Police series proceed on the basis of the opposition

police : criminal

within the terms of which all manner of values can be opposed, for instance good:bad, central:deviant, subject:object, order:chaos, etc. In just the same kind of way the news proceeds on the basic opposition

us : them

where 'us' is the culture/nation/public/viewer/family/newsreader/news institution, and 'them' is striker/foreign dictator/foreign power /the weather/fate/bureaucracy/accessed voice, etc. The implication of this is that once an individual or topic has been stereotyped it will always be presented in terms of the stereotype, and further, it will never be selected as newsworthy unless it does or says something that fits the stereotype. The classic examples of such stereotyping are, for example, spectacular youth subcultures on the domestic front, and foreign 'dictators' on the international scene (an example for all time being General Amin). Furthermore, once a topic has been assigned a place on the 'negative' (them) side of the basic opposition, its doings cannot be seen in positive (us) terms. Thus it seems to be with industrial disputes. Here the opposition is

us : them
management : strikers
government : unions

with the added spice of an opposition between those who suffer because of a dispute (in our bulletin, hospital patients) – 'us' – and those who act in it.

Within the resemblance between police series and the news, it is noteworthy that there is an opposition between those who initiate negative action and those who 'hold the fort'. Fiske and I found this opposition very pronounced in the ITN 'News at Ten' of January 1976 which we analysed in *Reading Television* (1978), and it is still strongly marked in the BBC 'Nine O'Clock News' of February 1979 where in an industrial dispute it is the workers (not employers) who initiate negative action 'against' the public.

In the 1976 ITN bulletin, there were reports on the British response to supposed IRA initiatives in Ireland, and to Icelandic gunboats in the so-called Cod War. In each case the way those events were signified in the news resembled closely the way our heroes act in response to criminal initiatives in police series:

> *The Sweeney*'s world is not one where 'white hat' restores the accepted moralities by the mere act of shooting 'black hat'. Their world is unpredictable, episodic, present-tense. They react to events rather than manipulating them – just as British frigates react to Icelandic gunboats and the British army to the IRA. (Fiske and Hartley 1978, p. 186)

Given what we have already said about the media-image of a 'non-political' consensus operating at the level of the family (p. 94), to which the news media address their remarks, it is not surprising that the basic opposition between 'us' and 'them' should also prove to have implications for that image. As Brunsdon and Morley have pointed out, there is an 'underlying preferred structure of absences and presences' in 'Nationwide' which follows the us:them model. At the level of *meaning*, this structure ascribes certain basic social and cultural activities firmly to 'them'. Brunsdon and Morley propose these oppositions:

Absent	: *Present*	
world	: home	
work	: leisure	
production / reproduction	: consumption	
workers (functions)	: individuals (bearers)	
structural causation	: effects	
THEM	: US	(1978, p. 25)

In other words, meaning in news-discourse is not only determined by what is there, but also by what is absent, not selected, discursively repressed. In addition, the 'absent' elements, whenever they can force an entry into the news, will be 'interrogated' through the perspective of the 'us'/'present' elements. The world will be meaningful to the extent that it impinges on (threatens) the 'home' culture. Work is significant to the extent that it affects consumption, disrupts family life, and so on.

It may seem odd to suggest that the news and television fiction are structured in the same way. After all (and quite apart from the difference between 'fact' and 'fiction'), the news is made up of separate and unconnected items, whilst police series, like plays in general, proceed by connected scenes towards a dramatic resolution. This argument, whilst obvious, is not true. We have seen that at the organizing level of narrative, and at the integrating 'character' level of the newsreaders, news is much more than an aggregate of distinct bits. On the other hand, one of the basic devices of TV fiction is *also* to proceed by means of apparently disconnected scenes. The viewer is presented with a job to do – the apparent irrelevances and contradictory directions of different scenes are *clues* – what is going to happen? How does this bit fit in? Whodunit? I'm not suggesting that news is a game of the same kind, but clearly the different stories often do cohere into a pattern – they break their individual boundaries and collectively signify particular themes, issues and meanings in the world. We select clues from *different* stories to construct a 'photofit' picture of our culture, of its state of play.

The 'Nine O'Clock News'

The various structural elements I've outlined are more or less common to all TV news programmes. But simply outlining these elements will not yield up the meaning of particular stories. For that we need to look more closely at the individual text, to see how the discourse is 'inflected' in particular ways.

Here then, in table 2, is the sequence of our 'Nine O'Clock News' story of 1 February 1979.

If we read 'vertically' down the grid we can see how the story develops. Again, this development is common to most major stories on TV news, and it has the following four narrative 'moments':

1. *Framing* At the outset, the topic – and its associated discourse – is established by the newsreader (section I). The newsreader's later contributions within the story serve to *link* other moments

in the development, but they also perform the critical task of 'fine-tuning' the framing. In other words, the links (III and V) progressively narrow the frame of the story.

2. *Focusing* The topic is focused here by section II, where the political correspondent explains what the events are 'about'.
3. *Realizing* The topic is 'made real' by accessing voices from the world out there, and especially by using actuality film to verify the 'reality' of the news's version of the story (IV and VI).
4. *Closing* Stories never just stop. The whole idea is to produce sense, which will be left behind in the viewer after the story is over. Hence closing does not refer to the 'end' of a story, but to the discursive 'end in mind', as it were – the closure of various possible interpretations of the event and the *preferring* of just one 'reading' of it. The story means *this*. Of course alternative readings are rarely closed explicitly; usually stories are closed by presenting only one (commonsense) interpretation. Thus closure begins right at the start of a story and gathers momentum as it develops; the role of section VII will therefore be merely to confirm the closure that has already been achieved.

One of the things to look out for in the analysis of any news story, then, is what is *not* there. In this story it is particularly important, since the translation of the event into a public commonsense idiom is achieved by *excluding altogether* the two main parties to the dispute in question. This is a remarkable feat that is in fact so smoothly achieved that you hardly notice it. Here's how it is done.

The story is framed to begin with as an industrial dispute. Here is the opening sequence, as read by Angela Rippon (10.1):

> Here at home the dispute by public service workers is still spreading.
>
> Half the hospitals in England and Wales and some in Scotland can now open their doors only to emergency cases.
>
> Apart from the hospitals the strike is affecting more ambulance services and schools, as well as water and sewerage workers.
>
> In the Commons the Prime Minister urged the hospital ancillary workers to 'go back to work' while negotiations could continue on what he called 'a proper basis'.
>
> The Prime Minister also said (10.2):

Table 2

Visual		*Verbal*	
Element	*Mode*	*Institutional*	*Accessed*
I Angela Rippon; newsreader (A)	(1) Talking head + (2) graphic – the PM's pic. & quote on red background.	Dispute 'by' public service workers; hospitals, etc. affected.	*Callaghan* (PM) urges 'go back to work'; involving the sick is 'not acceptable'.
II Rodney Foster; political correspondent (B)	(1) + (2) + (3) Talking head + back-graphic + nomination (2) Standard graphic for recorded speech from parliament.	Report on debate in Commons: Tories 'angry'; Labour 'disgruntled'.	*Thatcher*: demands volunteers go in to help hospitals. *Callaghan*: co-operation not 'free collective vandalism'.
III Angela Rippon (A)	(1) Talking head	The situation at two children's hospitals	
IV Film report by Christopher Morris at Great Ormond Street Hospital for Children (he is nominated by Rippon) (C)	(4a) Actuality with voice-over; outside hospital showing picket, NUPE banner, hospital sign, etc. On-the-spot interview. Inside hospital showing food, nurses sorting linen, rubbish piling up. Outside showing bemused child + adult approaching entrance.	Porters & kitchen staff give 5-min. warning of strike. Interview. Disruption: lunch late, 'senior nursing staff' sorting linen – 'it took up much of their valuable time', rubbish a health risk. Non-urgent cases being turned away.	*Conway Xavier*: nominated as 'NUPE Shop Steward'. Guarantees help if children at risk; in response to question expresses hope for 'public sympathy' for a 'traditionally very passive workforce'.

Visual		*Verbal*	
Element	*Mode*	*Institutional*	*Accessed*
V Angela Rippon (A)	(1) Talking head	Union's voluntary Code of Conduct not being observed. Dispute over what counts as an 'emergency'.	*Un-named* NUPE official: tactics will be 'to put the screws on tighter'.
VI Film report by Philip Hayden at hospital in Romford, Essex (he is nominated by Rippon and by caption) (C)	(4a) Actuality with voice-over showing pickets + banner. (4b) Stake-out in empty accident ward. (4a) Volunteer women cleaning. (4c) Vox-pop with two volunteer women. (4a) Makeshift arrangements and baby being taken away by car.	Strikers withdrew cleaners; hospital authorities close emergency ward. Describes emptiness of usually busy ward. Nominates and interviews volunteers. Morale is high despite 'irritations'; parents of 'tiny baby' did 'not complain'.	*Mrs Munns*: neighbour ill, asked her to help. Asked 'Has it been worth it, coming?' – 'Oh yes, they are so appreciative.' *Un-named* patient who has helped with washing-up until she had to go for an x-ray.
VII Angela Rippon (A)	(1) Talking head (2a) Black and white still photo showing wreckage? of vehicle.	Army called in to help at 'worst affected hospital' where ambulance and van found with slashed tyres across entrance.	*Un-named* 'Hospital spokesman' called the incident 'sabotage', claimed other breakdown services couldn't help; hence army.

10.1 *Section I: The dispute by . . .*

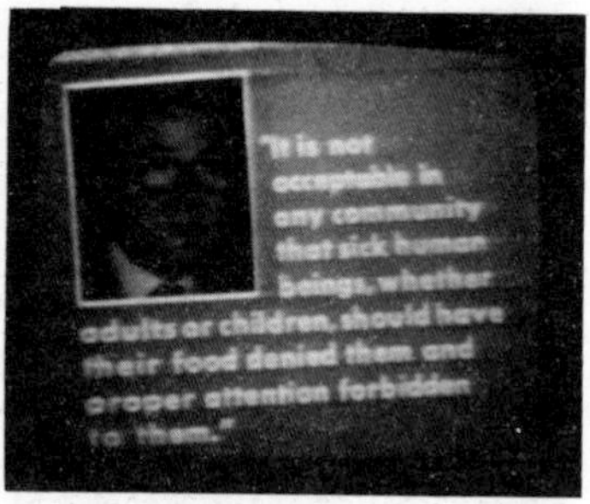

10.2 *The red graphic treatment*

10.3 *Section II: POLITICS*

10.4 *Balance: First the Tories said . . .*

10.5 *. . . and then Labour said . . .*

10.6 *Section III: Children's hospitals*

10.7 *Section IV: Them – not waving but being drowned*

10.8 *The accessed voice: On-the-spot interview*

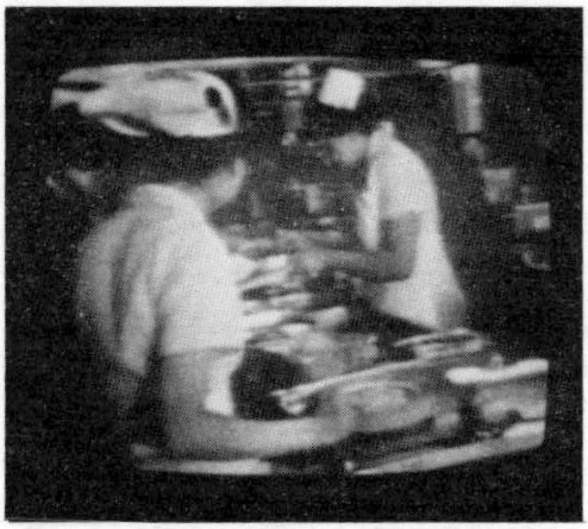

10.9 *Nurses serve food . . .*

10.10 *. . . and sort linen. It 'took up much of their valuable time'.*

10.11 *Rubbish piles up*

10.12 *Turning away 'non-urgent' cases*

10.13 *Section V: 'Put the screws on tighter.'*

10.14 *Section VI: The stake-out*

10.15 *The Strikers . . .*

10.16 *. . . and their message*

10.17 *Vox-pop with Mrs Munns*

10.18 *Vox-pop with patient 'volunteer',*

10.19 *The paper plates: 'no patient grumbled'*

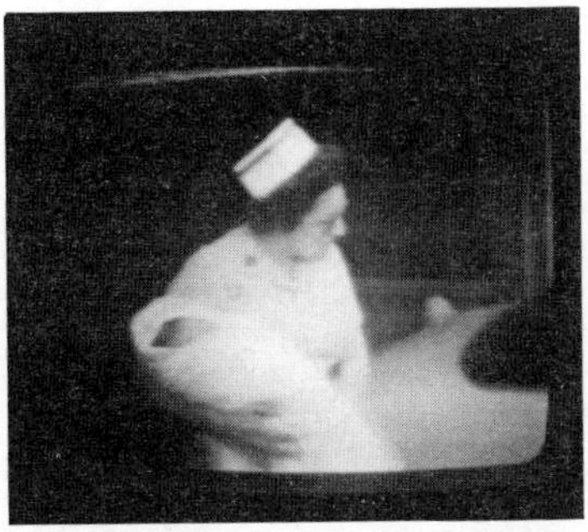

10.20 *'This tiny baby'*

10.21 *The baby's parents 'did not complain'*

10.22 *Section VII: 'Sabotage'*

10.23 *Trial by Semiotics ('Nine O'Clock News', 1 February 1979)*

> 'It is not acceptable in any community that sick human beings whether adults or children should have their food denied to them and proper attention forbidden to them.'

Initially, then, the story concerns a dispute between workers in hospitals, the ambulance service, schools, water and sewerage services, and their employers: the area health authorities, local education authorities, water authorities, etc. But already a *structured absence* is built into the news-framing of the story. At first sight it looks like a grammatical error, but '. . . the dispute by. . .' is ideologically very productive. Disputes are by definition *between* two people or parties: it takes two to tangle. The framing of the story as a dispute *by* just one group signifies the public service workers *alone* as the initiators of negative action. The employers simply disappear from the bulletin, apart from two references to 'hospital authorities' being 'able to keep essential services open', or 'being forced to refuse all but emergencies' (signified as passive reactions to negative initiative); and two references to the hospital authority which defined cleaners as part of the emergency service, and therefore closed the accident unit when they were not forthcoming.

However, it would be wrong to think that the invisibility of the employers means that the workers are signified as being in dispute with thin air. Far from it. The structural opposition common to all TV news, as we have seen, is the opposition us:them. The negative pole of this opposition is filled by the public service workers, and the positive side by the hospitals. However, the hospitals are not signified as employers, but as *places*, where there are 'sick human beings, whether adults or children' (10.2). It is the public service workers, according to the Prime Minister's doubly-accessed voice (quoted both verbally and visually) who are 'denying' and 'forbidding' these people their 'proper attention'. Hence:

us:them
(children) patients:public service workers.

The patients, of course, are not seen as the direct adversaries of the workers, so the basic opposition also includes:

government: strikers.

There is a nice distinction in the treatment given to James Callaghan as Prime Minister and as leader of the Labour Party in the House of Commons. As Prime Minister his statement is given the red graphic treatment (10.2), and his 'definition of the situation' is accepted as one of the key framing agents in this story – the strike is 'not acceptable'. But when we move on to section II of the story, things change. Here the main focusing work is done. Throughout this section there is a graphic reminder on the screen (10.3) that we are in the world of POLITICS (rather than industrial relations), and Rodney Foster, the Political Correspondent, takes up the framing reference from section I ('. . . in the Commons the Prime Minister urged. . .') thus: 'To be fair to the Prime Minister he's been among the first to condemn action by what he sees as an irresponsible minority. Action which he's already decried as totally unacceptable to any decent trade unionist.' So there we have it. This is not an industrial dispute at all. It is a political dispute between

children:public service workers
government:strikers
decent trade unionist:irresponsible minority
us:them

At this point the 'Prime Minister' has served his ideological purpose, and he becomes plain old 'Mr Callaghan', leader of the Labour Party. Foster spends most of his time scanning the inter-party arguments (10.4 and 5), but he introduces another element which will be taken up later (section VI). This is the demand by the Opposition for what its leader, Mrs Thatcher, calls 'volunteers' to be sent in to help the nursing staff. No-one could possibly see the well-meaning and agreeable 'volunteer' Mrs Munns (10.17) with her broom-of-office as a *blackleg*, could they? Thus the Opposition seems to get the discursive victory in this story, especially as Mr Callaghan is left sparring with his own side, after his reference to 'free collective vandalism': 'Well, a parting shot which did nothing to endear him to his left-wing MPs; and certainly these troubles won't go away for the government. . . .' Nor did they, of course. Three months later Labour lost a General Election which was fought largely in terms of the industrial 'winter of discontent' preceding it, of which this dispute was a major feature.

Back in our story, we find that the 'realizing' sequences simply illustrate the meaning that the story has by now been given. The frame is further narrowed – we are not offered film of just any old hospital, but of children's hospitals (what happened to the sewerage workers?). Even the second film from a general hospital (section VI) concludes with a shot of (10.20 and 21) 'This tiny baby, only thirty hours old, (who) was discharged from hospital a day early to help relieve the pressure. . . .' And though we see huddled groups of strikers sheltering under umbrellas (10.15) we never hear the voice of an ordinary worker in the dispute. Even the 'representative' shop steward, Conway Xavier, whose voice is accessed (10.8), has to answer a question about 'public sympathy' – he gets no chance to put his union's case, never mind the views of his 'own' workers. The only sign of their point of view is given when the camera pauses momentarily on a banner (10.16) which reads: 'Even "dragons" must eat.'

However, this silence of the workers follows discursively from the original framing, where the us:them opposition is established. The 'realizing' sections are free to get on with making the cap fit. Hence:

> The porters and kitchen staff didn't give much warning about their strike – just five minutes' notice. Then they walked out to join the picket line (10.7)
> Inside the hospital the disruption was more than just the minimum the union had promised: only two cooks were allowed to remain (10.9) (section IV)

> One NUPE official said tonight their tactics would be to 'put the screws on tighter'. More hospitals are being forced to refuse all but emergencies (10.13) (section V)

> This hospital's strikers refused to supply any cleaners because they say that's not part of their emergency service. The authorities think differently (10.14) (section VI)

Which all leads up to section VII, where Angela Rippon reports an un-named 'hospital spokesman' accusing the strikers of 'sabotage'. And sabotage it is; the army and a black-and-white still photograph are called in to provide the charge with semiotic credibility (10.23). The photo looks like the kind of photo we associate with war (army) coverage – it conforms to the *code* of military-style photography. The ideological closure is complete – once again, dissent is (subversively) criminal, and once again trial by semiotics wins a conviction.

But just to make sure we know our place on the us:them opposition, there has been a simultaneous narrative development of the signifiers for 'us'; namely the patients, staff and volunteers within the hospitals. From the initiative granted to the accessed voice of the Opposition leader (10.4): 'It is . . . precisely because many of the tasks could be done by volunteers that I ask him: where does his duty lie? Is it towards the patients and the doctors and nurses to help them . . . ?' we are conducted through the intricacies of lunch in *both* the 'realizing' sections (IV and VI):

> . . . so lunch was a little late today for nearly 300 young patients (10.9) (section IV)

> . . . morale on this ward was high. No patients grumbled about the paper plates or having to help with the washing up afterwards (10.19) (section VI)

And, as we've seen, the cheerful atmosphere of muddling through is personalized twice (10.17 and 18) in the form of the two interviewed 'volunteers'.

All this is set against the threat faced by these patients – the starkly empty accident and emergency ward in section VI which is shown through the device of the stake-out. The reporter stands amid the empty beds and says, in effect, look, see for yourselves. (I wonder who let him in though?)

Hence the opposing elements are orchestrated together throughout the story. This accords well with the structure of narrative in general – as Roland Barthes has shown, 'sequences move in counterpoint; functionally, the structure of narrative is fugued: thus it is that narrative at once "holds" and "pulls on"' (Barthes 1977, pp. 103–4). In other words, whilst you concentrate on one element, say the situation of the patients, or the contribution of the volunteers, you are simultaneously encouraged *by the narrative structure* to use that element to make sense of the opposing one. In this case, then, it is difficult to see the strikers as anything other than to blame for the patients' situation, and hence as an 'irresponsible minority', just as the framing section of the news had suggested.

8 PRODUCING THE NEWS: FOR OURSELVES

The first freedom of the press consists in its not being a trade.

Karl Marx (cited in Harrison 1974, p. 237)

Producing the audience

News is largely a product of history. And the history of news since the nineteenth century has been the history of a translation from popular defined as 'for the people', to popular as 'for the market'. Hence the way news is produced resembles in many respects the way commodities are produced. And one of the commodities newspapers like to produce is *readers*. Unable to survive at a price people can afford to pay without including advertising (see Dyer 1982), newspapers deliver readers to advertisers. And not just any readers. The *Daily Herald*, last of the radical popular dailies, closed down in 1964 despite having a circulation of over a million and a half and a total readership estimated at 4,744,000. This readership was almost double the *combined* readership of the quality papers (*The Times, Financial Times* and *Guardian*), but it was, as James Curran has pointed out, 'too small and too poor to sustain a paper in the mass market' (1978, p. 74. See also Harrison 1974, p. 223).

Similarly, television delivers viewers to advertisers. As Monaco suggests, this is particularly true of American television:

> The structure of network television is unlike the structures of the entertainment and information media that have preceded it. Networks don't sell entertainment, as the Hollywood studios did; they sell audiences, whose size and quality depend almost as much on the talent and luck of the programming executive in placing shows effectively as they do on the inherent value of the shows. (1977, p. 366)

In this context, argues Monaco,

> The networks produce their own news and public affairs programs mainly for the prestige it affords them (even though many news programs draw considerable revenue). CBS first established itself as a respectable challenger of NBC through its news coverage of World War II. (ibid., p. 365)

In other words news provides a credible excuse for 'up-scale' viewers to turn on and see the ads. The competition for readers with 'real disposable income' has been influential in shaping the map of currently available newspapers in Britain. Along with the *Daily Herald*, other major Fleet Street casualties have been the *News Chronicle* (1960), the *Sunday Citizen* (1967), the *Daily Sketch* (1971) and the *Evening News* (1980). The *Daily Express* was thought to be a candidate for closure until it was taken over by the multinational conglomerate Trafalgar House (owners of Cunard, the Ritz and other property, and Cementation Construction, etc.). The new owners decided not only that the *Express* was viable, but that the 'bottom' end of the market could bear a new title, so they launched the *Daily Star* to compete with the *Sun* and *Mirror*. With a circulation of around a million, it still has a long way to go: the market is dominated by the 'big two'. The current map of national dailies is shown in table 3, and of the national Sunday papers in table 4.

Table 3 (*Benn's Press Directory, 1982*)

Title	*Owner/Controller*	*Circulation (1979)*	*(Jan-June 1981)*
Sun	News International	3,851,719	3,622,720
Daily Mirror	Reed International	3,650,106	3,504,377
Daily Express	Trafalgar House	2,358,993	2,196,492
Daily Mail	Associated Newspapers	1,948,323	1,963,054
Daily Telegraph	Daily Telegraph	1,510,766	1,400,935
Daily Star	Trafalgar House	961,588	1,336,116
Guardian	Scott Trust	366,429	393,729
The Times	News International	360,257	282,186
Financial Times	S. Pearson	200,703	199,233
Morning Star	Communist Party (GB)	34,558	32,676*

*July-Dec 1980

Table 4 (*Benn's Press Directory, 1982*)

Title	*Owner/Controller*	*Circulation (1979)*	*(Jan-June 1981)*
News of the World	News International	4,666,811	4,003,067
Sunday People	Reed International	3,973,315	3,712,485
Sunday Mirror	Reed International	3,927,208	3,740,629
Sunday Express	Trafalgar House	3,205,739	2,996,447
Sunday Times	News International	1,470,438	1,431,707
Sunday Telegraph	Daily Telegraph	1,225,778	955,407
Observer	Lonhro	1,003,949	918,460

The picture is completed by the addition of provincial morning and evening dailies, a few surviving provincial Sundays, and a very large number of weekly newspapers. The numbers of these are given in a chart (table 5) compiled by Murdock and Golding (1978, p. 132).

What is striking about the 'map' as a whole is the difference in choice between the top and bottom ends of the market. Westergaard and Resler (1975) point out that the 'non-manual' socio-economic groups comprise only a third of the population, but there are four national dailies (*The Times, Financial Times, Guardian, .Telegraph*) which draw about 80 per cent of their readership from these groups. Further, the same four papers draw roughly half their readership from the top socio-economic group of businessmen, administrators and professionals. The other two-thirds of the population are served predominantly by only three papers (*Mirror, Sun, Daily Star*) which moreover are being driven to look more like each other every year. The 'middle-brow' papers (*Mail, Express*) command roughly equal proportions of readers among the four main socio-economic classifications, and the *Mail*, at least, is read by more women than other papers.

The conclusion drawn by Westergaard and Resler is that

> the hierarchical cultural structure of the Press is a product of economic inequality in a market system; and directly so, not obliquely. In this, as in other fields, the privileged escape the uniformity of mass production to which ordinary earners are confined. (1975, p. 267)

In short, commercial newspapers need a few readers with a lot of money, or a lot of readers with a little money. It's choice for the 'quality', and uniformity for the 'width'; both are markets for the advertisers.

Table 5 *Number of newspapers published, 1921–75*

	1921	*1937*	*1947*	*1975*
National and provincial Sundays	21	17	16	12
National morning	12	9	9	9
Provincial morning	41	28	25	17
Provincial evening	89	79	75	78
Weeklies	–	1,348	1,307	1,079

Note: 'Provincial' refers to England, Scotland and Wales, but the figure for weeklies also includes Northern Ireland.

The total combined circulation of these papers is also given by Murdock and Golding (1978):

Table 6 *Newspaper circulations in Great Britain, 1937–75 (figures in millions)*

	1937	*1947*	*1961*	*1975*
National and provincial Sundays	15.3	28.3	25.4	19.7
National morning	9.98	15.6	15.9	14.1
Provincial morning	1.6	2.7	1.8	1.96
Provincial evening	4.4	6.8	6.8	6.3
Weeklies	8.6	11.9	12.7	12.3

Losing the audience

But this is not the whole story. It is clear that market forces have a decisive influence on the 'established' national press – so alternatives must occupy other territory. The effects of market forces have been noted by Murdock and Golding. The first effect, they suggest, is that the range of material will 'tend to decline as market forces exclude all but the commercially successful' (1977, p. 37). Second, they argue that this 'evolutionary process' of exclusion is not random:

> On the contrary, the underlying logic of cost operates systematically, consolidating the position of groups already established in the main mass media markets and excluding those groups who lack the capital base required for successful entry. Thus the voices which survive will largely belong to those least likely to criticise the prevailing distribution of wealth and power. Conversely, those most likely to challenge these arrangements are un-

> able to publicise their dissent or opposition because they cannot command the resources needed for effective communication to a broad audience. (ibid.)

This situation is quite different from that in which the popular press first started in the early- to mid-nineteenth century. Then it was possible to keep a paper going on relatively small circulations, relying mostly on sales rather than on advertising. The popular press was largely the creation of political radicalism and was a crucial element in the development of working-class consciousness through the Labour and Chartist movements.

But, as Curran has shown, times changed. Escalating running costs and declining cover-prices for newspapers marked the later nineteenth century. Starting a newspaper became a little tricky for anyone without several million pounds. Curran makes the comparison:

> The change is illustrated by comparing the *Northern Star* in 1844 with the *Sunday Express* in the early 1920s. The *Northern Star* needed a sale of about 6,200 copies before it broke even, whereas the *Sunday Express* was running at a loss with a circulation of over 250,000. The *Northern Star* became profitable almost immediately, whereas nearly £2 million had to be spent *after the launch* of the *Sunday Express* in 1918 before it made any money. . . . A public subscription from northern towns was sufficient to launch and establish the radical *Northern Star*, but it needed the resources of an international financial empire to launch and establish the *Sunday Express*. (1978, p. 68)

More recently, the resources of another international financial empire proved inadequate. After losing or spending a total of around £70 million on *The Times* and the *Sunday Times* (part of which financed a bitter dispute and an eleven-month lock-out), the Thomson Organization put both titles up for sale in late 1980.

The 'other' news

Hence 'effective communication to a broad audience' is difficult without money. But having been dealt a bad economic hand, the 'disestablished' press is turning it into advantage by playing a different political game. They have found a practical flaw in the argument for an alternative press which nevertheless seeks a broad audience. Audiences of this kind tend to be addressed as undifferentiated 'masses'. In the absence as yet of an oppositional 'mass' class, aware of itself as such, and with a counter-hegemonic ideology, any oppositional appeal to broad audiences is liable either to fall on deaf ears, or drift into dominant ideological codes, or both. Newspapers on their own cannot create class-consciousness.

The alternative press as it now exists has therefore turned away from the 'mass', and is seeking to build counter-hegemonic consciousness in specific areas of cultural and political activity. Thus there are several different kinds of alternative news, addressing different but interlocking 'constituencies' of readers. Many of these are simply based on a particular locality, forming a 'community press'. One of the most successful of these is the *Rochdale's Alternative Paper* (*RAP*). Others include the *Islington Gutter Press* in London, recently joined by the *East End News*, which was partly financed by the Campaign for Press Freedom and the trade union movement. You can find a full list of community and neighbourhood papers in the Minority Press Group's pamphlet, *Here is the Other News* (1980b).

Other alternative papers are addressed to particular movements and struggles. *Camerawork* and *Radical Philosophy* are among the better-known, as is *Undercurrents* (alternative technology, ecology). Among the biggest sellers, with circulations of 20,000–25,000, *Spare Rib* is addressed to the women's movement, and *Gay News* speaks for itself. There are various politically-oriented papers, usually associated with sections of the political left, including *Socialist Worker, Socialist Challenge, Militant, Tribune* and *Labour Weekly*.

There are, however, a number of alternative news sources devoted to a less specialized 'constituency', and some of them have been highly successful. Chief among these is *Time Out*, which began in the 'underground' days of the late 1960s, but has moved with the times and become part of the established press. So much so, in fact, that it has now spawned its own 'alternative' competitor, *City Limits*. Between them they offer some of the best news sections of any papers (including the national press). *Time Out*'s success is derived from its events-listings and advertisements for London – it is unlikely that its formula could succeed in any other city, but prosperous Bristol's *Out West* is trying. Then there is the fortnightly *Leveller*, which aims at being a national alternative paper and therefore often ends up by serving no-one. It is, however, a source of the stories, treatments and politics that are so hard to find elsewhere. In South Wales, the investigative news magazine *Rebecca* built up a circulation of almost 10,000 in its seven-year history. This was enough to make it the biggest selling magazine of its type (including 'national' news magazines like the now defunct *Now!* and the *New Statesman*) in Wales, but not enough to pay the staff. In September 1981 it was relaunched as a monthly magazine. Finally we should mention *Private Eye*, which often provides a home for the more scurrilous stories Fleet Street journalists cannot get past their sub-editors, and includes a large amount of gossip, humour and cartoons.

Finding the audience

One of the least discussed determinants of what news is available to you (and whether it is) is the distribution system. This is dominated by two distributor/wholesaler groups, W.H. Smith and John Menzies. These wholesalers, together with the much smaller firm Surridge Dawson, distribute 57 per cent of newspapers in England and Wales, and 69 per cent of the magazines. In Scotland, Menzies alone distributes 79 per cent of newspapers and 93 per cent of magazines (1975 figures: see Minority Press Group 1980c, p. 33).

The trouble with this system is that it lends itself to under-the-counter censorship. A source of continuing frustration for alternative magazines and newspapers is that they are often refused by the wholesalers for being too small and ephemeral, with not enough advertising and promotion, or for being outside the range of 'family' interest. But of course without commercial distribution through the near-monopoly of firms like Smiths and Menzies, these are the very qualities a magazine will lack. Hence demand for alternative papers is said to be small, but they are denied the means to increase it. Furthermore, the wholesalers will certainly refuse to handle 'radical' material when they disapprove of its contents – even something as established as *Private Eye*. But there is rarely direct evidence of this; meanwhile the radical press is alive and well, but invisible among the consumer commodities in the High Street.

11.1 *Alternatives: Community*

11.2 *Alternatives: Movements*

11.3 *Alternatives: Struggles*

(11.2 shows cover pages from: *Undercurrents* no. 39; *Spare Rib* no. 89; *Camerawork* no. 6; *The Leveller* no. 16)

9 CONSUMING INTEREST

Linda: No, I never watch the news, never!
Lorna: I can't ask him to turn it over 'cos he likes it, so I go in the kitchen till it's finished.
(Cited in Hobson 1980, pp. 109, 111).

I have devoted most of my argument to the news 'text' as it appears on the TV screen or in the newspaper. There are several good reasons for this. First, texts are the way most of us normally encounter the news. There is a lot you can do to understand the role of news in society by taking some of the systematic concepts I have described and prizing open news texts with their aid. Second, most of the work from which I have drawn my analysis is concerned with the text. The growing areas of semiotics and communication studies developed largely out of textual analysis of various kinds. Finally, and as a result, there is currently a gap in research into social discourses like the news. Most of what happens when the text is 'realized' as a 'live' discourse, when it is read by the consumer, is a mystery. As Patrick Moore says about other mysteries of the cosmos, 'we just don't know'.

But certain things about the way news is read can be said. Primary among these is that news, like television as a whole, does not have direct ideological effects which necessarily coincide with the 'intentions' of the producer of the text. As Connell puts it, 'there is *no* evidence to suggest that all the social groups that comprise the audience for the media's accounts of a given situation will accept, without qualification, the orientations and positions those accounts offer' (1978, p. 78). In other words, news-discourse has its 'effect' in the same way as language has its effect: not directly on behaviour, but as a structuring agent of mediation between the discursive self and the social/physical world.

But this does not mean that you are free simply to make of the news what you like. In fact the same relations and social forces operating to 'close' news-discourses in particular ways act on your discourses too. So we need to look into the consumption as well as the production of news-discourse.

Experience and mediation

First it is useful to make a distinction between two domains of 'lived culture'. These are the domains of *experienced* and *mediated* meanings.

Experienced meanings are those which result from *personal interaction* at the subjective level. They are generated primarily in conversation. They are 'institutionalized' primarily in the areas of family, school, work, friendship. This domain is the realm of what Berger and Luckmann (1966) call reality-maintenance, where *primary socialization* takes place. It promotes a *subjective reality* which organizes and confirms our consciousness of ourselves, and our (more or less successful) habit of assuming a central place for our consciousness, with the world outside receding in circles of ever-decreasing relevance.

Mediated meanings reach through experienced meanings and bring that outside world to bear on them. We get them from television and the other media, as well as from teachers, parents, etc. In other words, we produce mediated meanings in the same context as experienced meanings, and in fact our interaction with *objective reality* in the process of *secondary socialization* is achieved by translating mediated into experienced meanings. News clearly belongs to the domain of mediated meanings, and it is one of the most important means by which the 'outside' world reaches into our personal space.

An example of what can happen to people whose experience of a particular topic is confined largely to its news-mediated meaning is given by Hartmann and Husband in their discussion of the media and racial conflict. On the basis of an analysis of media coverage of racial issues and of surveys carried out in schools located in areas of high and low immigration, they found that

> Children who live in areas of low immigration rely perforce more heavily on the media for their information about coloured people

than do others. Media-supplied information carries the inference of conflict more often than that from other sources. As a result these children are more prone to think about race relations in terms of conflict than are those in 'high' contact areas, even though they (the 'lows') live in places where the objective conditions for inter-group competition or conflict are absent.
(1973, p. 282)

Hartmann and Husband conclude from their study that the children from 'high' contact areas are able to modify their attitudes on the basis of local experience; but for them, and even more for those without that local experience, the 'interpretive frameworks, ways of thinking, are heavily structured by the mass media'.

Two implications follow from this. First, where experienced meanings are at odds with mediated meanings, a 'negotiation' takes place in which both can be modified. But, of course, they can stay at odds too, remaining 'in contradiction'. Second, mediated meanings are important in structuring the ways in which we see the world – even the world of experience.

Subjectivity

Mediated meanings, then, only become actively meaningful *as* experienced meanings in the sometimes uncongenial company of contradictory ones. But nevertheless they are actively captured by us in our subjective reality (interactive relations) and used to classify and make sense of the world. However, our subjective reality is not a 'given' object which is unaffected by the meanings it encounters. On the contrary, it is itself a product of its relationship with them. The experienced meanings we construct in conversation are constructed out of the potential offered by language. And language, as we have seen, is social. That is to say, our subjectivity is itself a social phenomenon, determined by the discourses (language-potential realized in use) that we encounter from birth.

Our individuality is not pre-given. All that is pre-given is our biological existence. Individuality is constructed on that site, as it were, and it is constructed by the way in which the various discourses (both experienced and mediated) we encounter are 'negotiated'. That is, some discourses will appear to work in parallel, producing mutually confirming meanings, whilst others will intersect and contradict them, making our individuality a 'site of struggle'.

Halliday has drawn a map, reproduced in figure 4, of the way in which the 'nature of the individual' is not biological but social.

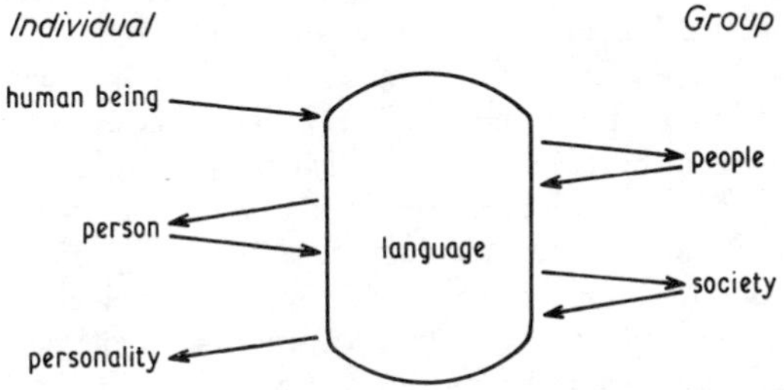

Fig. 4 (Halliday 1978, p. 15)

It shows how a (biological) human joins a group of people through language; through language s/he is differentiated from the group as a person; the person has social relations within a structured society (not a 'mass' of undifferentiated people), in which many roles are played through many discourses; out of these discourses and roles the personality of the person is constructed.

In short, as Volosinov puts it, 'The individual, as possessor of the contents of his (sic) own consciousness, as author of his own thoughts, as the personality responsible for his thoughts and feelings – such an individual is a purely socio-ideological phenomenon' (1973, p. 34). And you can see that the logic of the map suggests that the construction of the subject/consciousness/personality is a continuous interactive process, whereby, as Buckminster Fuller once said, 'I seem to be a verb.' All the arrows also 'point the other way'. Our socially constructed personality is where social relations are reproduced through language – language of which our personalities seem to be 'the author'.

How is ideology 'consumed'?

The way we make sense of both our own personal environment and the world at large is through discourses which themselves have made us what we are. In fact there is a definition of individuality which suggests that it is no more than the 'site of intersection' of many different and differing discourses. A discourse is a continuous, generative, interactive process. So our individuality produces and re-produces these discourses whilst being produced by them.

Implicit in this notion is the idea of a relationship between the two poles of 'objective' (mediated) reality and 'subjective' (experienced) reality. This relationship determines what meanings will finally be produced out of the interaction between the two poles. It follows that both poles have a say in the 'dialogic' production of meanings, and this goes for ideological meanings as much as for any others. Hence we cannot construe ideology as a finished product flowing into our consciousness from outside (from the 'objective' to the 'subjective' pole). News *texts* do not result in ideological *meanings* without being 'realized' by our active subjective consciousness. Thus we need to consider how ideology is re-produced at the moment of its 'consumption' as we read news texts.

In seeking to assess the effectiveness of the 'subjective' pole, however, we are faced with a difficulty, since it is not easy to analyse. Indirect evidence, like the continuing social dominance of dominant ideology, points to readers as relatively helpless creatures, subjected rather than subjective. And many analysts have taken this notion further by suggesting that ideology's main purpose is to 'construct people as subjects', the better to work its dominating will on them (see Althusser 1971, p. 160 and Belsey 1980, chapter 3). But the indirect evidence also points the other way. Given the prestige of dominant ideology, and its reproduction in so many influential spheres (family, school, media, politics), the continuing existence of so many forms of resistance to it suggests that its 'readers' are not so easily duped. The structural fissures in class-divided societies keep throwing obstacles in the way of the smooth sway of dominant ideology. It has an uphill struggle on its hands, and it has to engage in this struggle every day, on all channels, at full volume. And still, when their 'real interests' are at stake, people refuse to listen.

How can we begin to account for this? First, it is by no means clear that news is 'read' as information by many people. I have referred elsewhere to the fictional structure of news narrative (chapter 7, pp. 115 ff.) and to the quality of entertainment encoded into television news (chapter 3, pp. 46 ff.). It is quite possible that the

12.1 *'Dramatic end to the six-day siege.'*

12.2 *The explosion: headline*

12.3 *The explosion again: story*

12.4 *The explanation: dropped*

12 *SAS bomb Iranian embassy (BBC news, 5 May 1980)*

'preferred readings' so carefully structured into news accounts of events are simply not noticed – the 'readers' have their minds on other levels within the discourse. The newsmakers are of course aware of the quality of 'news-as-entertainment'. For instance, Reuven Frank, an executive of NBC (one of the three main American networks) instructed his staff that 'Every news story should, without sacrifice of probity or responsibility, display the attributes of fiction, of drama' (Tunstall 1977, p. 36).

In British news, the same 'news value' of dramatic entertainment can be seen. For example, the day the SAS stormed the Iranian Embassy in London (5 May 1980), both the BBC and ITV channels interrupted their normal programmes to bring live pictures of the

13.1

13.2

13.3

13.4

13.5

13.6

13.7

13.8

13 *SAS bomb Iranian Embassy (ITN news, 5 May 1980)*

event. By the end of the same evening, their construction of it was clear. Headlining the bulletins with film of the bomb blast (by means of which the SAS got into the building), both channels played up the drama. Jan Leeming, newsreader for the BBC, opened their bulletin with 'Dramatic end to the six-day siege' (pics. 12 and 13). And the voice-over commentary by Michael Sullivan on the ITN bulletin was presented entirely in the present tense: talking us through the screams, shooting, attack, dogs barking, sirens, fire, firemen, and hostages (13.2–7).

Whilst both channels also 'made sense' of the event through the accessed voices of police and government spokesmen, this was clearly a low priority. For example, the BBC did show Home Secretary William Whitelaw in their 'Nine O'Clock News' (12.4), where he said, among other things, that the event 'showed that we in Britain are not prepared to tolerate terrorism in our capital city'. But in the special bulletin later in the evening (which was shorter), it was Whitelaw's 'ideological inflection' of the event which was left out. Neither channel used the word chosen by both Whitelaw and the Metropolitan Police Commissioner to describe the hostage-takers in the Embassy – instead of 'terrorists' they were referred to throughout as 'gunmen'.

However, ideology and entertainment are not incompatible. If you're not looking for it, that doesn't make it go away. In fact it can be argued strongly that the more entertainingly an ideological message is encoded, the more we are likely to be 'subjected' to its ideology. The SAS example is relevant here. For once defined as entertainment, politics and cause have disappeared. Few people can have known very much about the situation in Arabstan, and after the siege we knew very little more. The event became an isolated 'dramatic' act, into which all sorts of patriotic pro-SAS 'meanings' were then inserted. It may well have been a dramatic triumph for the British military, but that is by no means *all* that it meant.

Man-made news

It would be unwise to suggest that lack of interest in the ideology of the news necessarily disables that ideology. But the notion that news appeals to people differently may be useful. For some may escape its ideological inflections by not being appealed to at all. One such group is women. News is not simply mostly about men, but it is largely by men. As Bruce Page, editor of the *New Statesman*, has put it:

> The difference between the men and the women on the editorial staff is that the men, collectively, have a much wider and more active experience of journalism. Therefore, operationally, they have more to say. This, of course, isn't due to greater inborn ability: it's due to the disgraceful fact that the existing structure of journalism offers *routinely* to men a breadth of experience which it offers only exceptionally to women. (*New Statesman*, 9 January 1981, p. 14)

News is not only about and by men, it is overwhelmingly seen through men. For example, Walton and Davis report that there is a bias against women interviewees: 'The BBC seems to have slightly more interviews with women than ITN. Of the 843 named interviewees in the first three months of 1975, only 7.7 per cent were women. They were more likely to be interviewed in connection with disaster or sports stories than in industrial or economic stories' (1977, p. 128). And, as the *Sunday Mirror* referred to elsewhere (p. 28) makes all too clear, women newsreaders are noteworthy not for being newsreaders but for being women: they are themselves 'made meaningful' as objects of the gaze of men.

Some evidence that news and current affairs programmes can fail to appeal to women because such programmes simply fail to notice women has been offered by Morley: 'Ideologies do have to function as "descriptions" or "explanations" of the "reader's life", and it is in so far as they succeed or fail to do this that the "ideological viewpoint of the text" is accepted or rejected' (1980, p. 122). Morley conducted interviews with numerous groups of 'Nationwide' viewers, and found that certain groups of women saw nothing in it to identify with. Others were explicit that its 'irrelevance' was located in its abandonment of women. One critic said of an item about family finances: 'When they were talking about it . . . they said to her, "How does Ken's money go?" They didn't ask her about her money, what she did with her money. As far as they were concerned that's pin money' (p. 122). Others criticized 'Nationwide' not so much for abandoning women as for showing families in an artificial light: 'Don't they think of the average family', and 'They show it . . . like all the husbands and wives pitching in to cope with it, cope with looking at problems. I mean, they don't show conflict, fighting, things that we know happen. I mean it's just not, to me it's just not a true picture – it's too harmonious, artificial' (p. 122). Of course, one of the interesting things about this criticism is that it is aimed at 'Nationwide'. If the current affairs programme which most clearly and explicitly appeals to families (and therefore, in its terms, to women), fails to find the mark, then it seems probable that the news is even wider of it.

Negotiating with ideology

Nevertheless, despite its 'man-made language' and reference to a man's world, the news is still watched by men and women alike. Indeed, my emphasis in this book on television news derives largely from the fact that it is watched by so many people. The Annan Report (1977) estimates that three in five people in the UK watch or listen to a full news bulletin (excluding summaries) every day, and 'News at Ten', with an audience of 12 to 15 million people, regularly appears in the 'top twenty'. In America too, television overtook newspapers as the prime source of information for most people in 1974 (Roper poll, quoted in Monaco 1977, p. 479). The Annan Report further noted that 'the public watches the news, likes the news and considers both BBC News and ITN to be more trustworthy than the newspapers' (p. 266).

But large numbers don't make a mass. Simply because the 'same' message goes out to twenty million people, it does not follow that twenty million people interact with it in the same way to get the same 'meaning' and the same understanding.

Hence there is a need for a 'model' of the communication of news which does not simply assume that what is said is what is heard. Little work has been done so far. Many analysts tend to accept the broadcasters' Olympian view of the 'audience' as a large mass of undifferentiated individuals. But there are two approaches which begin to map out the territory. The first is derived from the work of Frank Parkin (1972), and has been taken up by Hall (1973b), Fiske and Hartley (1978, pp. 103–5), and particularly by Morley (1980). The second comes from the work of Basil Bernstein (1973 and 1975), as taken up by Fiske and Hartley (1978, pp. 116 ff.) (see also Halliday 1978, *passim*).

Parkin suggests that the class structure forms the basis from which differently situated social groups develop different 'meaning systems' within the terms of which any message from dominant ideology is 'decoded'. He identifies three meaning systems, from which three distinct 'codes' develop:

1. *The dominant code* Within this code, messages encoded in the dominant ideology are likely to be accepted.

2. *The negotiated code* Here, the decoding is partial or partially resisted. For example in a news item on unemployment, it is possible to accept the assumptions on which employment policy is based (the 'need' to 'master inflation', perhaps) whilst at the same time resisting its particular application here and now ('I need a job'). However, given the multiple discourses within which all individuals interact, and given that certain of these discourses will contradict each other, whilst others confirm and reinforce each other, there is a sense in which *all* decoding is 'negotiated'. This notion could lead us back into consideration of the audience as a 'mass' of negotiators, all very much alike. It is necessary, then, to maintain the force of Parkin's argument by showing that negotiated codes (however many of them there turn out to be) are *socially structured* and not idiosyncratic codes.

3. *The oppositional code* Here the dominant ideology is refused, being decoded in the discursive context of an oppositional ideology which may be radical, feminist, and so on.

Morley uses Parkin's framework among others to analyse responses to 'Nationwide'. One of his conclusions is that it is no longer adequate to speak of generalized 'effects' on an audience.

> We must not assume that the dominant ideological meanings presented through television programmes have immediate and necessary effects on the audience. For some sections of the audience the codes and meanings of the programme will correspond more or less closely to those which they already inhabit in their various institutional, political, cultural and educational engagements, and for these sections of the audience the dominant readings encoded in the programme may well 'fit' and be accepted. For other sections of the audience the meanings and definitions encoded in a programme like *Nationwide* will jar to a greater or lesser extent with those produced by other institutions and discourses in which they are involved – trade unions or 'deviant' subcultures for example – and as a result the dominant meanings will be 'negotiated' or resisted.
>
> (1980, p. 159)

But, as Morley notes, 'more work needs to be done' (p. 163).

The second approach I mentioned comes from the work of Bernstein. His work on sociolinguistic coding orientations has in fact been applied very little to media analysis, but it has valuable possibilities. It concentrates on the role of language (discourse) in transmitting social–structural relations and suggests that there are systematically different ways of 'decoding' the 'orders of meaning and relevance' offered as implicit assumptions in any discourse. In other words, any message expressed in 'elaborated' code offers systematic possibilities of resistance to anyone decoding it in 'restricted' code. The two codes are:

1. *Elaborated code* Abstract language, not dependent on immediate context for its meaning, which is verbally explicit and directed towards individualized response. 'Literate' communication. Also verbosity.

2. *Restricted code* Based on communal relations, realizing its meaning as much in intonation, word-stress, expressive features, as in verbal planning. Reinforces the solidarity of relationship rather than the niceties of the 'authorial' statement.

Bernstein's interest is largely in the sphere of education, where elaborated code is accepted and promoted as 'correct' (and is associated with the discourses of dominant ideology), and where restricted code is stigmatized as 'wrong' (and is associated with working-class children). However, it is clear that the two codes are in principle available to all, and orientation towards one or the other implies no difference in linguistic ability.

Bernstein's work focuses attention on exactly how social–structural divisions are realized in discourse. Despite the fact that any language (like the English language) is spoken by all the members of a speech community whatever class position they occupy, it does not follow from this that all the members of a speech community utilize the potential of that language in the same way. In Balibar's phrase, language is 'indifferent' to classes – all classes use the 'same' English language system. But, of course, not all classes speak the same English. Once the language system is realized in discourses, it enters the contentious world of historical and economic determination, with the result that different classes are far from 'indifferent' to language – it becomes a 'site of struggle'. Bernstein's notion of differential 'coding orientations' which are socially structured offers us a way of understanding how television messages in general, and news-discourse in particular, are differentially decoded by different groups in the overall audience. The message is indifferent to different classes in the audience, but it does not follow that they feel the same way.

Fiske and I, for example, have suggested (1978, pp. 116–26) that a fundamental contradiction is structured into television discourse. It occurs between the literate (elaborated) codes of clarity, balance, impartiality, the consistent tone of voice and the tendency towards abstraction which are the preferred codes of news, and, on the other hand, the oral (restricted) codes of episodic, dramatic, concrete television presentation. In short, the television *mode* constantly subverts the television *message*. What remains to be seen is whether some sections of the audience 'prefer' the mode and others the message.

One of the sources of differential coding orientations for Bernstein is the organization of the family. He suggests that the organization of family role-relationships is socially structured. Thus there are, according to Bernstein, *positional* and *person-oriented* family role-relationships. In the positional family, control and decision-making are invested in the family member's formal position as father, mother, grandparent, boy or girl. In person-oriented families, on the other hand, roles are less clearly distinct, and control and decision-making takes more account of the individual's unique attributes (1973, p. 176). Bernstein relates the positional family with the restricted code and the personal family with the elaborated code.

What is significant in this hypothesis for our purpose is of course the influence that the family situation may have on news-decoding. Television is a consumer product located largely in the family environment. Its meanings, then, are likely to be realized differently in different kinds of family structures. Hence it is not possible to assess the effect of a given ideological message without taking some account of the immediate (family) viewing structure.

Decoding is not, therefore, a simple individual act, but one in which socially-structured contexts will be manifested. In other words, I suggest that taken together, the contradiction between the oral modes and literate message of television, and the contradiction between elaborated encoding (oriented towards personal individuals) and restricted decoding (oriented towards the solidarity of structured roles) supply certain social groups with *structural resistance* to the 'flow' of ideology; that is, resistance not based on individual will but on the structure of the relationship between socially-located 'reader' and 'text'.

DAILY Mirror

Wednesday, May 7, 1980 10p

PICTURE EXCLUSIVE!

Hostage who lived six days in fear

BEAUTY OF THE SIEGE

Cheery heroine was a lifesaver

THIS beautiful girl helped the terrified siege hostages to live through their ugly ordeal.

She is 21-year-old Nooshin Hashemian, one of the people who were held by gunmen at the Iranian embassy in London.

By ANTON ANTONOWICZ

Nooshin, an embassy secretary, was yesterday helping police to build up a detailed picture of the six-day siege, which ended when SAS troops stormed the building.

The courageous brunette was among the first survivors to be seen by TV viewers as police escorted the freed hostages to waiting ambulances.

Calm

Her arms were still tied behind her back. She was shoeless. Her tights were torn at the knee. But she called out cheery words to the friends following her.

Relatives who managed to snatch a few words with the survivors in hospital were later full of praise for Nooshin.

If Police Constable Trevor Lock was the siege hero, they reckoned she was the heroine.

One man leaving the hospital said: "She kept the others calm. She built up a special relationship with the gunmen. She helped to save many of the others.

"She is so young, but she showed special bravery."

Someone already knew that Nooshin was special—her 30-year-old husband

He is waiting to welcome her back to their London home with a huge bouquet of flowers, a bottle of champagne . . . and a kiss.

NOOSHIN: She kept the others calm and helped to save many lives.

SALUTE TO THE HERO —PAGE 3

OPERATION THUNDERFLASH PAGES 4 and 5

PORTRAIT OF AN SAS SQUAD —CENTRE PAGES

I QUIT says the DOC

SEE BACK PAGE

14.1

Daily Mail

WEDNESDAY, MAY 7, 1980

10p

48 PAGES WITH MONEY MAIL

Police question lone survivor of the Embassy hit squad

ENVOYS ARMED TERROR GUNMEN

By PETER BURDEN and JOHN DICKIE

POLICE believe the terrorists in the Iranian Embassy siege were supplied with arms after they arrived in Britain–by Arab diplomats who had the weapons smuggled into the country in diplomatic bags.

Two Embassies have come under strong suspicion—that of the Iraqis, who have become desperate enemies of the Iranian regime in recent months, and that of the Libyans, who are known to be arms suppliers for terrorist movements worldwide.

Detectives of Scotland Yard's Anti-Terrorist Branch under Commander Peter Duffy last night were questioning the lone survivor of the terrorist team, which, it is now believed, totalled six.

Charges

They hope to learn from him exactly where the group set up a base in London before it took over the Embassy — and exactly from whom it picked up its carbines, pistols and hand grenades.

The arrested gunman faces charges of murder and kidnapping. And it became clear that he will be tried here, probably at the Old Bailey ,rather than be sent back to Iran.

Without waiting for any extradition demands from Tehran, Whitehall stood its ground for a British trial on the basis of a United Nations convention on the prevention and punishment of crimes against internationally protected persons.

While diplomatic premises enjoy inviolability under international law, embassy buildings are not regarded as being 'foreign soil.'

Police have accounted for more than 30 people involved in the siege: 19 hostages brought out alive, five released ealier and two executed; one gunman in custody, one who died on the way to hospital, two whose bodies were found in the debris, and at least one more and possibly two whose bodies have yet to be found.

Detectives sifting the tons of rubble by hand were also hoping to find all the terrorists' weapons. Each will be checked by ballistic experts against each bullet in each victim. So will all the SAS men's guns.

The hope is eventually to identify the source of each part of the terrorist armoury.

A full-scale inquiry has already been mounted, with the help of Foreign Office

Turn to Page 2, Col. 1

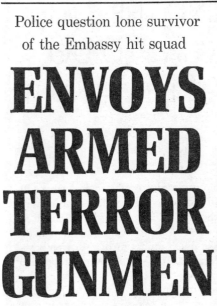

The two faces of courage

ON HIS face the smile of a brave man with the knowledge of a job well done.

On hers, courage of a different sort, of a wife who waited for six days while her husband faced a frightening ordeal as a hostage in the Iranian Embassy.

Police Constable Trevor Lock and his wife Doreen held hands and exchanged glances frequently as they met the world's Press yesterday.

PC Lock, 41, his face still bearing the cuts sustained when he was overpowered at the Iranian Embassy, heard Sir David McNee, the Metropolitan Police Commissioner, say this of him to reporters:

'You have all written about bravery — now look at it.'

Deputy Assistant Commissioner Peter Neivens said: 'If you notice, he wears the letter K on his epaulette — which denotes that he is an officer stationed on a local

Turn to Page 2, Col. 1

INSIDE: Lynda Lee-Potter 7, Femail 12-13, Diary 17, Prize Crossword 31, TV 32-33, Classified 36, 40-42, Motor Cycling 37, Letters, Stars & Strips 38, Sport 43-48

14.2

10 CRITICIZING THE NEWS: WHAT TO DO AND WHERE TO FIND IT

Simply following the news from day to day can be an enjoyable and interesting occupation in itself. But you can do more than merely get what you're given. Whilst there is little choice in the texts you're offered to read, you can choose several different ways of reading them. In this way you can make much more out of the given news texts and transform consumer enjoyment into a more productive activity.

For example, you can concentrate in turn on the way the news text is made to 'make sense'; on the ideological meanings it promotes; and on its appeal to your desire and pleasure, by which means it seeks to establish an identification between your 'discursive formation', or sense of self, and its own. And whether your reaction to the news is one of pleasurable involvement or critical opposition (or, more typically, both), you don't have to abandon these reactions when you learn to 'read' the news critically.

As always, in any situation where your resources don't match those of the other side, the first thing to do is – get organized. What follows is a series of three different ways in which you might get organized to develop a critical understanding of the news. First (pp. 155–86), illustrated projects for analysing news output. Second (pp. 186–7), some alternative images and sources of news to set against the mainstream. In this context, I suggest, one of the best alternatives is for you (individually and collectively) to produce a news text yourself. Third (pp. 187–90), a programme of suggested further reading and study which will develop more fully some of the perspectives I've used in this book.

Projects

Newspapers
The best place to start is with the national wide-circulation papers. I've presented samples from a number of these throughout this chapter. Using them as examples, you can begin to ask questions.

* In any one instance, what is the relationship between copy, headlines and pictures?
* How does the overall layout help to promote a particular 'meaning' for the event reported?
* What role do the photos play in 'closing' the meaning of the stories? What codes are at work in producing this effect?
* What is the relationship between different stories on the same page? For example, the popular dailies often juxtapose political stories and images with showbiz or glamour stories and images (see 15.1 and 15.2). Does this type of juxtaposition itself produce any meaning which is not 'contained' in either of the stories on their own?
* How are the events in politics and the other spheres of social life translated into a popular idiom?
* Consider the headlines of 16.1 and 16.2. What is their ideological productivity? That is, what benefit for a particular ideological position is to be gained by selecting and signifying the events in this way? What alternative possibilities can you suggest to 'make sense' of the event (i.e., what paradigmatic choices have been made)?
* How are 'accessed voices' used to make the story's 'preferred meaning' seem to emerge 'naturally'?
* Can you find any evidence of a consensual model of political relations, or of a commonsense mode of address to the reader?
* Is there any evidence to suggest that some interests in a dispute are presented as natural and general interests, whilst with others (for example in 16.1, the unions, or in 16.2 the 'left' or demonstrators) a convergence is proposed between their interests and deviant/criminal behaviour?
* How far is political conflict signified in the rhetoric of violence?

DAILY STAR

TUESDAY, MARCH 4th, 1980 8p (10p C.I.s, Eire) Printed in London ★

VOTE! VOTE! VOTE! FOR YOUR Colour STAR BIRD
CENTRE PAGES

ROBBIE VINCENT'S DANCE GUIDE
PAGE 13

WIN £10,000 TO GIVE YOUR HOME A FACE-LIFT—PAGE 18

Major Disaster

'Heart op' joy for a doggie!

BRITAIN'S first heart "op" on a dog looked to be a tail-wagging success last night.

Major Disaster, an 18-month-old Labrador, has had a heart pace-maker fitted by a team of surgeons.

The operation was carried out at Musgrove Park Hospital, Taunton, Devon.

The dog is recovering at the Langford Veterinary Institute near Bristol.

Hoping

Major Disaster belongs to Mrs. Vivienne Harcombe and her family. They are hoping to have him home today.

Mrs. Harcombe said: "It's wonderful. Without the pacemaker he would have died."

Her pet's heart trouble was diagnosed three months ago.

The £1,500 operation was carried out free of charge by Mr. Richard Palmer and his team.

And last night he defended the decision. "There is no waiting list for human patients," he said. "If a human needs a pacemaker the operation is carried out almost immediately."

SIX COPS ARRESTED

by JAMES NICHOLSON

Drama of swoop after break-in at top men's store

SIX policemen were in the cells last night after a break-in at a fashionable men's shop.

They were arrested after a burglary at Austin Reed's Fenchurch Street branch, in London.

The officers—an inspector, two sergeants, two detectives and a constable — were being questioned last night at Bishopsgate police station. They are expected to appear in court today.

City police had been keeping a special watch on the shop after burglars had made three attempts to break in.

The vigil ended when a car was seen parked near the premises. As torches were switched on in the darkened shop the intruders fled. Goods were found loaded in the parked vehicle and the homes of officers were later searched.

A senior police spokesman said: "Six City officers are in custody. The matter is being investigated and I expect a result very soon."

Mr. Geoffrey Tubb, company secretary of Austin Reed, said at his office in Thirsk, Yorks, last night: "Money was taken from a safe—maybe a couple of hundred pounds—and a quantity of goods have been stolen.

"Whether the intruders were policemen or not, to us it's just an insurance matter."

He said staff at the premises in Fenchurch Street had been told to make no comment.

The arrests shook the City force, whose Cheapside headquarters are less than a mile from the raided shop.

A spokesman denied that goods were found in a police vehicle.

Laughin' Judy a stunner!

LAUGH-IN girl Judy Carne bounced back to happiness last night after the car crash which nearly killed her. Judy got a rapturous welcome from the audience at a top London nightspot with her song-and-dance routine.

Picture: DAVID WILLIS

15.1

THE Sun

Tuesday, March 4, 1980 9p TODAY'S TV: PAGES 14 and 15

TODAY IN YOUR No 1 SUN

GEORGE AND MILDRED MAKING WHOOPEE

See Centre Pages

PICTURE EXCLUSIVE

THE MAN IN THE LIFE OF ATOMIC BLONDIE Page 9

WIN £100 FOR NOTHING! Page 11

THE SUN'S GREAT TEAM SLIMMING RACE IS UNDER WEIGH—Page 21

25% Rail union leader slaps in his claim

SUN EXCLUSIVE
by TREVOR KAVANAGH

RAILMEN'S leader Sid Weighell will slap down a massive 25 per cent pay claim for his men tomorrow.

It will lead to a bitter head-on clash with the Government.

And Mr Weighell issued the warning yesterday that there will be industrial strife unless Ministers release enough money for cash-starved British Rail to pay up.

He said rail chiefs will be forced to increase fares in the summer — possibly by ten per cent.

Cheap

Mr Weighell said he felt sorry for commuters who have already coughed up for 20 per cent fare rises in January.

He said: "I commute every day and I agree the service is getting worse."

But he added: "I've said the day of the cheap railwayman is over and I mean it."

Mr Weighell's National Union of Railwaymen will make its formal demand for a "substantial" pay rise tomorrow.

It will be backed by the other rail union ASLEF.

KIDNAPPERS CAGED

Boss's wife taken naked from bed

Angela Rippon in London yesterday Picture: ROGER BAMBER

NO, I'm NOT a naughty girl! See Page 3

By JOHN ASKILL

EVIL blackmailer John Easthope was jailed for seven years yesterday for a heartless kidnapping that went badly wrong.

Easthope hired two henchmen—they got five years each—to snatch his former boss's wife for a £36,000 ransom.

The pair dragged terrified Emily Dewhurst, 57, naked from her bed and bundled her blindfolded into a van at gunpoint.

They left her husband Bill tied to a bedpost with the ransom note.

Then Easthope's master-plan started going wrong.

THE HUSBAND struggled free within minutes and dialled 999.

THE VILLAINS — "so nervous, they were shaking" — took a wrong turning and drove into a police roadblock.

Sobbing Emily collapsed into a policeman's arms crying: "Oh, thank God, I was so frightened.

EVIL

"I thought they were going to kill me."

Yesterday Easthope, a 32-year-old father of three, was branded an "evil, contemptible man" by Judge Kenneth Taylor at Stafford Crown Court.

The judge told him:

Continued on Page Two

15.2

THE SUN, Tuesday, March 4, 1980 3

PAGE 3 WINNERS

THEIR KNICKERS ARE IN A TWIST!

You're a sizzler, Sharon

★ IT'S Day Two in The Sun's super Sizzling Six Week, and here's another No. One newcomer

Today's fresh face belongs to smiling Sharon Clayton, a 17-year-old stunner from Rushden.

She is hoping for a stage career that will have everyone's eyes popping. Meanwhile, she collects £200 for reaching the last six in our Be A Page Three Girl Contest.

I'm not a naughty girl, says Angela

AN ANGRY Angela Rippon yesterday flew off to sign autographs on a Japanese car and said: "I don't know why everyone is getting their knickers in a twist."

By TONY SNOW

The newsreader, who will be on a stand at the Dublin Motor Show, added: "I haven't been a naughty girl. I am not in trouble with the BBC."

Angela said she could not understand the storm over her involvement in the launch of the Datsun Cherry hatchback in Ireland. She explained:

"I am only doing what other newsreaders and everybody else who appears on television does.

Contract

We are allowed to do trade launches. Peter Woods, Richard Baker and the others all do it.

They are called public appearances. We have been doing them for yonks — opening supermarkets, car showrooms or garden fetes. It's not advertising, it's a personal appearance.

I have not overstepped the terms of my contract in any way."

Angela, 35, said she was not promoting Datsun cars. A car was being auctioned for charity on the stand and "they have asked me along to drum up more interest for charity."

She is being paid for her appearance today, but would not say how much.

The figure is believed to be more than £1,000.

A BBC spokesman said: "Angela has not been on the carpet."

But he added: "At some stage she and the editor of TV news, Alan Protheroe, will have a conversation about this.

"Television news are concerned if any newsreader appears to be endorsing a commercial product.

"He will decide wether this has happened in this case."

Involved

The spokesman said Angela's contract did not specify what she could not do. "But there is an unwritten convention about what newsreaders do," he said.

"We leave people to be sensible themselves about it."

A spokesman for Datsun in Dublin said: "We are obviously employing Angela because she is well known. But she is not being paid to endorse our product."

Curse of The Exorcist—Page 24

PLAICE OF FAME FOR A CHIPPY

A FISH and chip shop has sizzled its way into a good food guide.

The Seashell Fish Bar in North London battered posher restaurants out of sight.

It was especially praised for its "huge servings."

The shop is commended in The Good Food Guide published by the Consumers' Association.

The guide also praises an Indian takeaway restaurant and a **JAVANESE** snack bar—both in London.

Three restaurants got triple top honours for wine, food and cooking skill.

They are the Connaught in London, Miller Howe at Windermere, Cumbria, and Arbutus Lodge in Cork, Ireland.

● In the association's Good Hotel Guide, also published yesterday, notable absences include London's Hilton and Dorchester.

15.3

THE SUN, Tuesday, March 4, 1980 13

MY NO-SEX PACT, BY A JP

A MAGISTRATE who left his wife and seven children to live with his best friend's widow said yesterday: "There is no sex between us."

Burly 49-year-old Mr George Cunningham added: "When your marriage breaks up and your life is shattered at my age, the question of sex doesn't enter your head."

Mr Cunningham, a local councillor, admits he has been living at the home of attractive Mrs Jean Taylor since leaving his family last August.

Last year, he was the centre of a row over the allocation of a new council house, in Bramford, Suffolk, to Mrs Taylor.

He was reported to the Director of Public Prosecutions for allegedly failing to declare an interest at a meeting of Mid-Suffolk District Council's housing committee.

But the Director decided to take no action.

Mr Cunningham said yesterday:

"We have both agreed that there should be no question of a sexual relationship.

I know what people are saying but when I go to bed at night I know I have absolutely no recriminations."

Mr Cunningham's wife, Janet, said at her home in Suffolk: "I intend to divorce George."

Eagles fall to the sly poisoners

FARMERS and gamekeepers using illegal poisoned baits could be killing off Britain's dwindling flock of golden eagles, it was claimed yesterday.

The Royal Society for the Protection of Birds said the eagles and other birds of prey are being slaughtered to protect lambs and grouse.

They are also picking up laced baits left for pests like foxes, crows and gulls.

Pop goes £500 for an Elvis napkin!

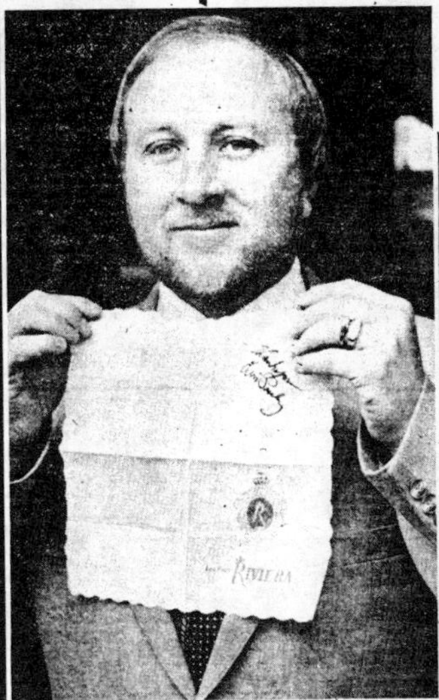

By JANET MIDWINTER

PUBLICAN Brian Brodie shows off an Elvis Presley souvenir that set an auction rocking yesterday.

Mr Brodie paid £500 for a paper serviette autographed by the rock superstar.

And that was just for starters.

POP went another £480 for a collection of 14 early Beatles photographs.

And POP went £220 for four American dollar bills—each signed by a Beatle.

Brian's big spree

After his groovy £1,200 spending spree at London's Sotheby's, Mr Brodie said: "I was prepared to pay whatever was necessary."

Detour

He will give the rock mementoes to his daughter Samantha for her 13th birthday next Monday.

And they will be on show in the upstairs bar of his pub — the Cross Keys in Endell Street, Covent Garden.

Mr Brodie, 34, was driving Samantha to school when he heard the sale advertised on radio . . . and made an expensive detour.

Sotheby's were amazed by the bidding. They thought the Elvis napkin would fetch £120 at the most.

But the price may have soared because the napkin was from the Las Vegas Riviera Hotel, where Elvis gave his last public performance.

DIA'S DAD GOES ON SAFARI

RODDY'S dad, Sir Harry "Foxhunter" Llewellyn, has taken on a job as a tourist guide in Africa.

He will guide holidaymakers on a "never to be forgotten" journey through Zambia and northern Kenya.

Sir Harry, an Olympic show-jumping winner on Foxhunter in 1952, has been angry at the antics of his other son, Dai.

He wrote of Roddy's relationship with Princess Magaret in the News of World.

SUN SPOT

ELEVEN 18th-century oak doors were removed by mistake from Nottingham's Shire Hall court yesterday and put in an auction sale. Embarrassed court officials managed to recover them all and return them to the Hall's dungeons.

15.4

OUR NO-SEX PACT, BY JP AND A WIDOW

A MAGISTRATE told yesterday of his "no-sex" pact with the widow of his best friend.

George Cunningham, a local councillor and father of seven, left home last year.

Since then he admits he has stayed at the home of attractive Mrs. Jean Taylor.

But he said they had both agreed there was no question of a sexual relationship.

Mr. Cunningham, 49, said: "I have an office at Mrs. Taylor's home and when I stay there I have my own room.

"I know there has been gossip and it has been very upsetting for both of us.

"But when your marriage breaks up and your life is shattered at my age the question of sex doesn't enter your head.

George Cunningham

"Mrs. Taylor has been a family friend for many years."

Mrs. Taylor said: "It is rubbish to say we are having an affair."

At Mr. Cunningham's former home in Bramford, Ipswich, his wife Janet said: "I can only say I intend to divorce George and the grounds will be adultery.

"He walked out last June and he has been living at Mrs. Taylor's house since August."

Inquiry

Mr. Cunningham, who works as a British Rail signalman, is an independent member of Mid Suffolk Council and has been a magistrate for eight years.

Last year he was at the centre of a row over the allocation of a new council house to Mrs. Taylor.

But after an inquiry the Director of Public Prosecutions decided to take no action.

TERROR OF DISCO MONSTER

A RAPIST who preyed on disco girls was back in prison last night.

Former Coldstream Guardsman Barry Jarvis, 22, was jailed for two years at Exeter — his third sex-crime conviction in three years.

His latest victim was his best friend's girl.

Jarvis is already serving two years, imposed last November, for rape. Yesterday's sentence will be added on.

Juries at both trials were told how he prowled discos in search of girls. But if his chatting-up failed he was prepared to rape.

I've not been naughty — Angela

by JAMES WHITAKER and ROBERT BRADY

AN UNREPENTANT Angela Rippon is to tell her bosses at the Beeb: "I've not been a naughty girl."

Top newscaster Angela is at the centre of a row over promoting Japanese cars.

She is to be called in by the editor of TV News Alan Protheroe to explain why she is appearing on the Datsun stand at Dublin Motor Show.

For BBC news readers are banned from promoting commercial products.

Sign

But Angela will plead she is not doing anything that other newscasters haven't been doing for years.

She said yesterday: "I am not endorsing a commercial product. I am just making a personal appearance on the Datsun stand to sign a few autographs."

She said she had already appeared on the French Renault stand at the Ulster Motor Show in January

And Angela, who drives a Mini and a Saab, added: "I have no particular allegiance to Datsun. In fact, from a personal point of view, I would much rather be promoting a British car.

"We are allowed to do these trade launches. It is not advertising. I am merely following a tradition. And I have in no way overstepped my contract."

Datsun announced yesterday that Angela will go ahead with her £1,000-a-day appearance.

Asked whether her appearance would boost Datsun sales, a spokesman for the firm said: "What do you think?"

Angela — still smiling yesterday

'SOCCER-STYLE THROW KILLED BABY'

by DAVID NEWMAN

BABY Michelle Buck died after her mother's lover hurled her "like a footballer taking a throw-in," a court was told yesterday.

Martin Cook threw 11-month-old Michelle across the room because she wouldn't stop crying as he watched football on TV, it was alleged.

Michelle landed on a bed, struck her head on a wardrobe, and hit the floor, Bristol Crown Court was told.

She died four days later from concusion of the brain with a fractured skull, said Mr. Thomas Field-Fisher, prosecuting.

On other occasions Cook—said by Michelle's mother Christine Bulk, to be in a "furious temper" — is alleged to have given the baby a heavy slap to the head because she cried.

Mrs. Buck, 22, claimed Cook had also hit Michelle with a paint tin and punched her in the eye.

Cook, 19, of Arlington Villas, Clifton, Bristol, denies murdering Michelle and two charges of cruelty to her.

The case continues.

Tomorrow in your top-class STAR College girl fashions

15.5

DAILY STAR, Tuesday, March 4, 1980 7

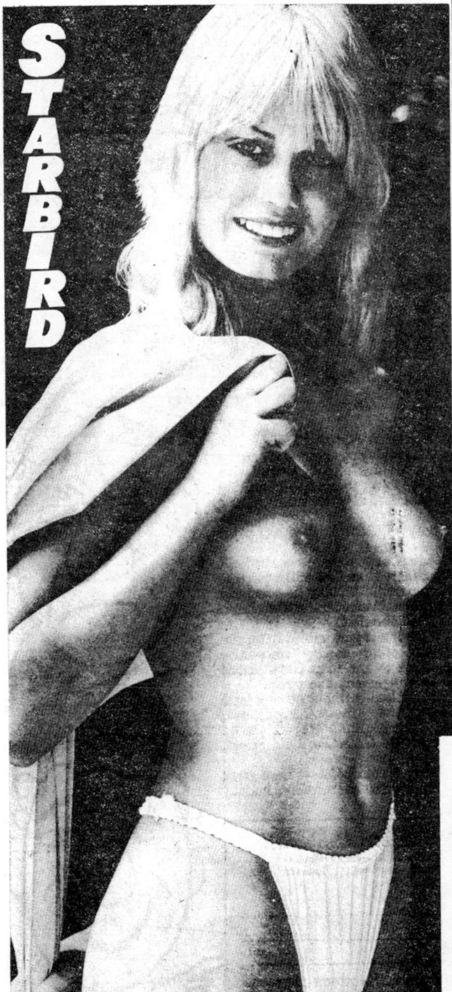

BRIAN PAYS £500 FOR A SCRAP OF NOSTALGIA!

by DON MACKAY

PUB landlord Brian Brodie paid £500 yesterday — for a paper napkin.

And he reckons he got a real bargain.

For Brian's scrap of nostalgia was autographed by Elvis Presley just before he died.

And it was used by the King at his last public performance.

Brian, who runs the Cross Keys pub in London's Covent Garden, also picked up a vintage collection of Beatles souvenirs.

Rock on! Brian and his Elvis souvenir

Early hits

He shelled out £220 at a Sotheby's auction for 14 autographed photos, a postcard written by Ringo, signed discs of the group's early hits "Love Me Do" and "Please Please Me" . . . and four dollar bills autographed by the fab four.

Now Brian plans to put the souvenirs on the walls of his pub. And he's keeping his fingers crossed that wife Jackie shares his enthusiasm for the Swinging Sixties.

He said: "I hope she still loves me after she finds out how much I spent.

"I only popped into the auction on the spur of the moment after hearing about it on the radio.

"But this stuff was too good to miss. I would have paid twice as much to get it."

The day's highest price £550, was paid for an album of photographs signed by such Hollywood greats as Gary Cooper, George Raft the Marx Brothers and Mary Pickford.

Kim's a tasty dish!

CURVY Kim Mills worked as a waitress in a posh restaurant before helping herself to a slice of fame as a model.

Now she is dishing up the goodies on the international glamour circuit. And wherever she goes, the boys are always asking for more.

Off duty Kim likes surfing, collecting unusual wine bottles and listening to Bryan Ferry records.

Picture: JOHN PAUL

'Curse of death' on sailor Jack

by GEORGE DEARSLEY

EX-SEAMAN Jack Jones went pale with fear when he opened a parcel. For it contained a dead crow—an ancient curse on mariners.

Now Jack is dead. He collapsed after weeks of brooding over the "gift," sent to his local by drinking pal Malcolm Thompson as a prank over an unpaid debt.

Mr. Thompson, of Dunoon Road, Hartlepool, was recently bound over by a court because of the incident.

Yesterday he denied he was linked with the tragedy. "I didn't know the crow was a symbol of death," he claimed.

Omen

But a black magic expert said: "It was a stupid thing to do. A black bird has been an omen of death since the 16th century."

Regulars at the Park Hotel, where father of three, Jack, 45, collected the parcel, said: "He was very superstitious."

His wife Lorna was too upset to talk at her home in Park Road, Hartlepool.

CLIMBERS KILLED

The bodies of two English climbers were found yesterday at the base of Lochnagan mountain, Aberdeenshire. Their names will not be revealed until relatives have been told.

£18m for slur on Guccione

WORLD record libel damages of more than £18 million have been awarded to Bob Guccione, boss of the Penthouse publishing empire.

After a two-week trial a jury in Columbus, Ohio, made the award against Larry Flint, and his magazine Hustler, over a long campaign against Guccione.

The record may not last for long, though. Guccione will soon be the defendant in a £45 million libel action.

● The greatest damages for defamation ever awarded in the United Kingdom were £117,000 against Associated Newspapers.

But the 1961 action was settled out of court for a much smaller amount.

15.6

* How do the papers use the signs, codes and conventions at their disposal to present not just the stories and images, but also their appeal to 'us'? In other words, what signs are there in the texts themselves of 'our' pleasure, demand or desire, and what strategies are used in the selection and combination of these signs to promote our identification with the discourse?
* How are myth, connotation and multi-accentuality (see pp. 21–30) exploited to limit the meaning-potential of the texts?
* How far does our successful recognition of the preferred reading require our simultaneous consent/submission to a hegemonic 'definition of the situation'? How far do we have to be implicated in the ideology of the news to make any sense of it at all, and how far does its attempt to entertain as well as inform depend on our unwitting connivance in its ideology?
* What alternative discourses can be set against those used in the news to show how they are oriented towards a particular (but unstated) 'map' of social/cultural relations? Here, you might 'read' each newspaper by means of the alternatives offered by the discourses of, say, feminism, radicalism and multi-culturalism in turn, and then begin to ask why these are only presented *as* alternatives (at most) in the national, 'popular' press.

One of the most valuable methods you can use to tease out the answers to some of these questions is *comparison*. Comparison brings out the distinctive features of the object or study, by showing which of its characteristics are *unique to itself*, which are *common with others*, and what possibilities are *absent altogether*. Here is a number of ways in which you can isolate the distinctive features of newspaper discourse by making comparisons.

1. *Compare topics, treatment and rhetoric* Collect all the daily, Sunday or local papers for a particular day or week. Compare their choice of topic for front page coverage, and compare the way different papers treat the same topic. A good example of the latter is 14.1 and 14.2, where the aftermath of the SAS storming of the Iranian Embassy in London is treated quite differently in the *Daily Mirror* and the *Daily Mail*, both of 7 May 1980 (see also p. 143). This kind of comparison can help to expose the news values that are at work, not only in single newspapers, but in the press as a

whole. The shared codes common to all newspapers are important as well as the differences; look in particular at the priority given to stories, and the possible elements selected for treatment or emphasis. Often the tabloids will show quite different front pages, as do the *Daily Star* and the *Sun* of 4 March 1980 (15.1 and 15.2). However, on closer inspection the inside pages reveal remarkable similarities in the choice and treatment of stories. In this example, the two papers share an interest in Angela Rippon's attendance at the Dublin Motor Show; in a JP's 'No-Sex Pact'; in pin-up glamour pictures; and in a pub landlord's purchase of pop memorabilia (15.3 and 15.4; 15.5 and 15.6). Further, these four items are presented in a similar way in the two papers – there is little within each one to tell you which is the *Daily Star* and which the *Sun*.

Have a look at the language of rhetoric; the classic definition of rhetoric is as the art of using language to persuade or influence others. Newspapers use it all the time. Examples can be taken from any of the papers I've illustrated (and from many others), but see in particular 16.1, where even the headline seeks to persuade us to make sense of a strike in a particular way. Note that this story concerns Conway Xavier, the same NUPE shop steward who featured in the BBC 'Nine O'Clock News' of 1 February 1979 (see also pp. 114 and 128). His appearance here is in connection with a different story, and at a different time – 5 December 1980 – but once more his voice, though accessed, is largely stifled, this time in the iron grip of the headline juxtaposed alongside his mugshot.

Similarly, 16.2 shows the *Daily Express* of 24 April 1979. Its rhetoric, or use of language to persuade or influence its readers, is the dominant feature of the story. Clearly it concerns conflict between police and demonstrators. But the *Express*'s textual strategy is to translate police tactics into the rhetoric of individual heroism:

> There were policemen with faces covered in blood and white paint, policemen with stab wounds – one apparently in serious condition.
> One young constable, blood streaming from a gash on the head, told colleagues: 'I'm O.K. Let me go back'.
> Others were helped by policewomen to the sanctuary of the local police station.

The demonstrators' tactics, however, are another matter. They are

THE
NEW STANDARD

Friday, December 5, 1980. Price 12p

Incorporating the **Evening News**

LATE PRICES
STOP PRESS

Great Ormond St. walkout over sack for NUPE man

STRIKE AGAINST THE CHILDREN

ANCILLARY WORKERS picket the Hospital for Sick Children, Great Ormond Street, today.

by Peter Dobbie

PORTERS, cooks and cleaners at the troubled Great Ormond Street Children's Hospital walked out on strike today.

Union officials were claiming that all services would be withdrawn and that the management had provoked them.

At least 170 workers walked out in protest at the dismissal of militant deputy head porter Mr Conway Xavier, branch chairman of the National Union of Public Employees.

He was sacked after a stoppage at the hospital last week. Now nurses, doctors and senior staff will be left to clear up the laundry, move patients and clean hospital wards.

But the hospital will keep going, according to administrator Mr Austin Lythe. "We have had strikes at the hospital before and the patients always come first. Senior staff and nurses usually rally round in times like this."

The dispute which has led to this latest stoppage at Great Ormond Street, which looks after 250 children, began at the Queen Elizabeth Children's Hospital in Hackney.

It was there that a porter was asked to carry laundry during his lunch hour, refused, and was disciplined. Other porters, all with NUPE, stopped work and Mr Xavier called out ancillary staff at Great Ormond Street in support.

That stoppage, which occurred last month, lasted two days and yesterday Mr Xavier was dismissed after the hospital accused him of disloyalty to management, neglecting his duty and taking unauthorised leave.

But today, Mr Xavier was back at the hospital to say: "If the management didn't like my work, they should have demoted me.

"I am a union official and I take what action my members ask. I have worked in the hospital for five years and proved my commitment, more of a commitment than officials at the hospital."

Mr Xavier was non-committal about how the strike might affect the children but said that vital supplies would be allowed to reach the premises when picket lines were set up.

NUPE area officer Mr Ian Barber said the workers considered Mr Xavier's dismissal was a direct attack on their right to appoint union officials.

In an attempt to spread the strike, NUPE's London area hospital committee will be meeting next week to discuss support with NUPE members at other hospitals.

Mr Barber said: "We hope the stoppage will have a minimal effect on the care of patients

SACKED — deputy head porter Conway Xavier: "Talk first, strike last."

Benn and Heffer: We'll stay on back benches

by Robert Carvel

LEFT - Wingers Tony Benn and Eric Heffer told Labour leader Michael Foot today that they will fight for real Socialism and not join his Parliamentary Front Bench team.

Both were defeated in the elections for 12 places in the Opposition Shadow Cabinet. But Mr Foot has discretion to make a few extra senior appointments.

Messrs Benn and Heffer made it clear they would not be interested in receiving such patronage.

After a telephone conversation with Mr Benn, who is in Washington, Mr Heffer had a 20 minute talk with Mr Foot.

Later he said: "Michael was very friendly and understanding."

Mr Benn's office said that he will not comment until Monday.

However, Mr Heffer understood that he had Mr Benn's support for a statement he issued complaining that Labour needs a "truly balanced" Shadow Cabinet and has not got that.

Mr Heffer promised to continue as a Back Bencher in supporting Mr Foot and added: "The truth is that although Michael Foot has been elected leader, the majority of the Shadow Cabinet does not really reflect the new spirit and views of the party in the country.

Messrs Benn and Heffer intend to campaign for the return of a Labour government "to carry out fully Labour's Socialist policies."

These policies—as approved

Continued Page 2, Col. 1

NEW CHALLENGE FOR BOMB P-c
PAGE THREE

REES-MOGG TO LEAVE TIMES
PAGE SIX

MATRON MAGGIE — BY HEALEY
PAGE SEVEN

IS THERE LIFE AT 40?
PAGE 19

TV 26 • Entertainment Guide 30 • Ad Lib 20 • Compton Miller 23 • Patric Walker 28 • City 42

16.1

Win a £25,000 home!
SEE PAGE 24

DAILY EXPRESS

THE VOICE OF BRITAIN

No. 24,510 Tuesday April 24 1979 *Weather: Heavy showers* 9p ★

Election riot: Police injured as 300 are arrested in Left protest

BATTLE OF HATE

The tough arm of the law

By Colin Bell and John McCormick

POLICE and demonstrators in thousands fought pitched battles last night in the streets of Southall in West London.

Sixteen policemen were taken to hospital along with 24 rioters, and dozens more were hurt. Some 300 were arrested.

Flashpoint of the violence was Southall Town Hall where the National Front was staging an election meeting.

Trouble first broke out four hours before the meeting. Police squads arriving to take up positions were stoned by a mob of youths, Asian and white.

As the time for the meeting drew near huge crowds of demonstrators became involved.

As has happened at National Front meetings before. It was the police who caught all the aggro.

At the start 1,000 chanting people confronted police near the railway station and then attacked "without the least provocation," said an officer.

Then the gang seized a double-deck bus. Police went in and, as all the bus windows were smashed, arrested 30 people.

SIEGE

In Park View Road West Indian squatters locked themselves in a house and refused orders to come out—so, said police, "we went in and got them." A number of officers were injured.

Nearer the town hall mounted officers were knocked off their horses by flying bricks and fireworks. At one point a cavalry round-up was staged in the ground of Holy Trinity Church.

Smoke bombs were thrown at a line of officers behind riot shields and then a mob of boys and girls—little more than school children—dashed in.

Innumerable minor scuffles erupted, with demonstrators being dragged to police wagons while the casualties reeled back for help.

Picture Extra: Centre Pages

There were policemen with faces covered in blood and white paint, policemen with stab wounds—one apparently in serious condition.

One young constable, blood streaming from a gash on the head, told colleagues: "I'm O.K. Let me go back."

Others were helped by policewomen to the sanctuary of the local police station.

Among those arrested was Asian militant Tariq Ali.

Sir David McNee, the Police Commissioner, spoke of "unprovoked attacks against the police and property by groups of people determined to create an atmosphere of tension and hatred."

And that election meeting? It was attended by just 40 members of the Front and 20 others.

While outside 2,000 police faced 5,000 demonstrators.

PICTURES BY JOHN ROGERS

Law and disorder: One of the hundreds of arrests in Southall

Secret pact shock for Jim

By JOHN CHRISTOPHER

THE Prime Minister was last night faced with a real fight on his hands to keep his Commons seat.

The Liberal candidate in Cardiff South-East pulled out after a secret pact with the Tories and advised his supporters to vote against Mr Callaghan.

Liberal Chris Bailey, who deliberately arrived too late to hand in his nomination papers, said: "Mr Callaghan deserves to lose his seat. I hope Liberals will vote Tory."

In the October, 1974 General Election Mr Bailey—who fought a successful battle to save his Bristol Channel Ship Repair Company from nationalisation—polled over 8,000 votes.

Mr Callaghan's majority was 10,718 and if the Liberals follow Mr Bailey's appeal a swing of five per cent would be enough to put the Prime Minister out.

Liberals in the constituency will actively campaign to get Tory Mr Alun Jones elected.

Last night a Tory official said: "We have every hope of winning the seat now."

TV GUIDE Pages 22 & 23 • Weather Page 2 • Hickey Page 13 • Letters Page 24 • Property Page 26 • Finance Pages 30 & 31 • Startime & Crosswords Page 32 • Sport from Page 33

16.2

signified as the initiators of negative action (see pp. 116 f and 126). They 'stoned', 'confronted', 'attacked "without the least provocation"', 'seized', 'locked themselves into a house and refused orders to come out'.

Whilst it is clear who the police are – the terms 'police', 'policemen', 'officers', 'constable' or 'policewomen' are used seventeen times in a story of nineteen paragraphs – it is by no means so certain who is opposing them. They are, variously, 'demonstrators', 'rioters', 'a mob of youths, Asian and white', '1,000 chanting people', 'the gang', 'West Indian squatters', 'a mob of boys and girls – little more than school children' and, finally, 'Asian militant, Tariq Ali'. This rhetorical strategy has a double effect: it denies a coherent identity to the demonstrators (the organizers, the Anti-Nazi League, are not mentioned). But it also enables the *Express* to signify *all* the participants as 'left' and as 'rioters', as in '300 are arrested in Left protest' and 'sixteen policemen were taken to hospital along with 24 rioters'. It could not have been known at the time that all those civilians taken to hospital had been active in rioting, as the subsequent inquest on one of them who died, Blair Peach, made clear.

What, then, of the 'meaning' of the story? It is twofold in the *Express*. First, it is a story of violence: 'Battle of Hate', 'pitched battles', 'Flashpoint of the violence', etc. Second, it is a story of police firmness and bravery in the face of violence. The pictures accompanying the story are captioned 'the tough arm of the law', and 'law and disorder: one of the hundreds of arrests in Southall', whilst the text 'reminds' us that 'as has happened at National Front meetings before, it was the police who caught all the aggro'.

If you want to test out the way the *Express*'s rhetoric works, you can take the terms we have been considering, and apply them to the opposing faction. But, of course, such an exercise will not 'balance' the story. Part of the reason for that is the need for a rhetorical (persuasive) discourse to suppress certain information altogether. In other words, one of the most important aspects of the *Express*'s rhetoric is what is *not* there on the page.

2. *Compare 'genres'* Most newspapers carry only a little news. The single largest amount of space is occupied normally by advertisements, with the rest of the space devoted to letters, cartoons, features, editorials, pin-ups and the like. Such cultural spheres as sport, fashion, showbiz, gardening, cooking and motoring are often

given their own sections, forming a grey area between news and features. It can be quite revealing to take a 'hard' political story and compare it with others from, for instance, fashion/glamour features or 'human interest' stories. The *Daily Mirror* (14.1) is a good example. Perhaps this 'angle' on the SAS story is deemed newsworthy because the picture of Nooshin Hashemian (one of the hostages in the Embassy siege) *looks like* an image from the fashion/showbiz star system, and the accompanying story *reads like* an episode of popular fiction. The story of this 'courageous brunette' concludes: '"She is so young, but she showed special bravery". Someone already knew that Nooshin was special – her 30-year-old husband. He is waiting to welcome her back to their London home with a huge bouquet of flowers, a bottle of champagne . . . and a kiss.'

You can extend this kind of comparison to show how news discourse compares with genres other than news; for example popular fiction itself, both on TV and in magazines. Look at the language, the topics, the stereotyped characters and the social setting of stories in fiction and in the news. How are the potentialities of myth, connotation and multi-accentuality exploited in both genres? How does the narrative sequence of stories in TV news compare with the sequence of scenes in TV fiction, and the layout of magazines with that of popular newspapers? By what distinctive features does news-discourse announce that it is *not* fictional?

3. *Compare across time and cultures* How does the presentation and signification of news differ over time and across different cultures? Clearly the eighteenth-century newspapers shown (17.1 and 17.2) differ considerably from modern conventions in layout, stories and language. Even so, the diet of public affairs, advertisements, gossip and letters has recognizable affinities with contemporary news output.

Within the twentieth century still more telling comparisons can be made. There is a fifty-year gap between the *Daily Chronicles* illustrated (17.3 and 17.4) and the *Daily Mirror* and *Daily Mail* (14.1 and 14.2) – May 1930 to May 1980. Similarly, fifty years separate the *Daily Expresses* shown in 17.5 and 16.2 – 1929 to 1979. Using these examples, compare the coverage of particular topics. For example, the use of images of women in the headline stories of the *Mirror* (14.1) and the *Daily Chronicle* (17.3); or the coverage

The St. James's CHRONICLE; OR, BRITISH EVENING-POST.

Price Two-pence Half-penny.] From TUESDAY, December 11, to THURSDAY, December 13, 1770. No. 1530.

WEDNESDAY, Dec. 12.

COUNTRY NEWS.

Portsmouth, Dec. 9.

YESTERDAY several Drafts of Shipwrights, to the Amount of 120, came here from the different Yards to assist in compleating the Superbe and Chatham, now undergoing a thorough Repair in the Dock, in order for the Royal William and Sandwich, two 2d Rates, to go in, which Ships are to be fitted for Sea with the greatest Expedition; and in order to forward them, an additional Number of Shipwrights are ordered to be entered. The Northumberland, Lenox, and Warwick, are ready to receive Men. Rear-Admiral Buckle is come down this Evening to command under Vice-Admiral Geary at this Port.

SHIP NEWS.

Deal, Dec. 10. Wind N.W. Came down and sailed with his Majesty's Ship Tartar, the Nelly Frigate, Gregg, for Virginia; Britannia, Wade, for St. Vincent's; Emperor of Germany, Lewis; and New Parham, Brown, for Antigua; and Henry Dawkins, Henderson, for Jamaica; the Cerberus Man of War is preparing to sail. Arrived and sailed for the River, the Lady Irvin, Padgett; and Katharine, Knowles, from Jamaica; Nancy, Ogilvie, from Salo; and Friends Adventure, Roberts, from Gatcombe. Came down and remain with the Romney Man of War, and Speedwell Sloop, the Eclipse, Trueman, for Venice.

Arrived,

At Philadelphia, Hetty, Leach, from Lisbon; Elizabeth and Mary, Sparks; and Philadelphia Packet, Osborn, from London.
At Piscataqua, Irish Oak, Greenough, from the West Indies.
At Boston, Hannah, Jarvis, from London.
At Leverpoole, John, Belton, from New York.

LONDON.

It is a known Fact that a certain great Man in the Law, who presides in one of the Courts at Westminster made a constant Practice, during the last Term, as soon as he left the Bench, and was disrobed, to alter his Dress from that of a grave Law-giver, to a snug bob-wigged Stock-Jobber, and repaired every Day to Change Alley to take every Advantage of his Intelligence, and by that upright Method to increase the Profits of the empowered the Lord Mayor to raise the City Militia, on any Emergency, on calling a Court of the Commissioners to meet within 24 Hours afterwards. This is a Power delegated every Year to the Lord-Mayor for the Time being.

Yesterday Col. St. John set out to join his Regiment at Minorca.

The Mary Harriot, Austin, from Jamaica for London, was lost last Thursday at Padstow; there is some Hope of saving Part of the Cargo: The Crew consisted of 18 Men, nine of whom are lost; the Captain and the rest are saved.

Extract of a Letter from a Gentleman at Calcutta to his Friend at Glasgow, May 16, 1770.

"It is certain that Cossim Aly Kawn is in Motion for Bengal, and that as soon as he crosses the Jumna there will be two Brigades sent to meet him. The French are said to have joined with Sowjah Dowla, which I really believe to be the Case, by the Pains taken in enticing away our European Soldiers.—The Country is in a deplorable Situation; you will no Doubt be surprised and astonished, when I inform you that Provisions are so scarce here, that Parents come in to us offering their Children for a Handful of Rice, and if they cannot get that, they are glad to get rid of them on any Account."

Extract of a Letter from Plymouth, Dec. 8.

"By Ship Intelligence from a Western Port, there seems to be a Certainty, that the Brest Fleet, which consists of near twenty Ships of the Line, is sailed, and that the Spaniards have twelve Sail in Cadiz Bay. It is not unnatural to suppose that those Ships are ready for Action."

Extract of a Letter from Dublin, Dec. 4.

"The Bank of Sir George Colebrooke and Co. having advertised their being under a Necessity of deferring the Payment of their Notes for a short Time, which may cause a Diffidence in the other Banks in this City, that may prove extremely injurious to the Trade and Manufactures of this Kingdom: His Excellency the Lord Lieutenant, the Nobility, Gentry, principal Merchants, and Traders of this City, being sensible of the secure Foundations of the Houses of Messrs. David Latouche and Sons, Mess. William Gladowe and Co. Mess. Thomas Finlay and Co. and Mess. John Dawson Coates and Patrick Lawless, have advertised that they will continue to take the Notes of the said Houses as Cash, in all Payments would have well served (for what you modestly inform us it was originally intended) "as a Supplement to a larger and more *solemn* Dictionary." I am sorry however to say, that it is not in my Power to bestow the same Applause with equal Justice on the Execution, as Impartiality obliges me not to deny to the Plan. But, that I may not seem to pass so severe a Censure without sufficient Cause, let me be permitted to quote a few Examples, in order to show how well you have succeeded in the glorious Task of *Elucidation*. I very much fear, Sir, that the Goodness of your Intentions has made you think too highly of your Abilities; and that, while with the true Spirit of the Times you have been endeavouring to correct one *Barbarism*, you have unwittingly fallen into a greater. Language certainly was intended to be the *Vehicle* of our Thoughts; that Language therefore is most to be preferred which effects the End proposed with most Facility. Now it may perhaps be doubted whether those *familiar Phrases*, which you have undertaken to *elucidate*, are not in themselves more intelligible and expressive than the very Explications you have annexed to them; and some Readers may possibly think the simple Terms *see saw* and *ding-dong* better calculated to convey the Ideas intended, than the more sublime ones *alternate Preponderation*, or *tintinnabulory Chimes*. Perhaps, Sir, it might have been as well if you had condescended to have used a Mode of Expression, more suited to the Intellects of those Readers who may be supposed to receive their Knowledge from a *fugacious* Paper.

These, Sir, are a few Examples how well you have succeeded in the Business of *Elucidation*. I leave the Rest to the Reader's Sagacity to *investigate*, and will only beg Leave to offer you one Piece of Advice, which seems to arise from the Occasion, which is, that whenever you again attempt a similar Undertaking, you would be pleased to descend a little nearer the Language of common Conversation, lest the Reproach, so often bestowed upon Interpreters, should be found applicable even to you, that your Endeavours to *elucidate* have served only to confuse, and that (to use your own Simile) you have sifted the Cinders till your Readers are blinded by the Dust.

Oxford, Dec. 6. I am, Sir, &c.
ACADEMICUS.

To The Printer of the St. J. CHRONICLE.

I know, Mr. Baldwin, your Predilection to Politicks, but when you shall be disposed to descend from political to real Life, you will perhaps find Room in your Paper for this Letter.

I am, Sir, your's, &c.
CELEBS.

Custom-House, Dec. 7, 1770.

THE Commissioners of his Majesty's Customs being informed, that the Dealers in Foreign Thread Lace have large Quantities of those Commodities sent them by the Post, by which Means the Payment of the Duties is evaded; they think proper to give this Publick Notice, that notwithstanding any Sums paid for the Conveyance of such Goods, they are still liable to Forfeiture for Non-Payment of the Customs, and the Receivers thereof to the Penalties inflicted by Law.

EDWARD STANLEY, Sec.

CROSBY, Mayor.

A Common Council, holden in the Chamber of the Guildhall of the City of London on Thursday the 15th Day of November, 1770,

Resolved and ordered, That the Sum of Forty Shillings for every able Seaman, and Twenty Shillings for every ordinary Seaman, over and above the Bounty granted by his Majesty, be given by and during the Pleasure of this Court, and not exceeding one Month from this Day, to every such Seaman that shall enter, at the Guildhall of this City, into the Service of his Majesty's Navy. HODGES.

THURSDAY the 22d of November, 1770, at a Committee for carrying into Execution the Resolution of the Common-Council for giving a Bounty to Seamen entering into his Majesty's Navy,

Resolved, That this Committee will meet in the Council-Chamber, at Guildhall, every Monday, Wednesday, and Friday, until the 15th of December next, from Eleven in the Forenoon until Two in the Afternoon, to carry the above Resolution into Execution.

HODGES.

SILK WEAVERS WAREHOUSE,

Pall-Mall, Dec. 5, 1770.

VAN SOMMER and Company, at first opening this Warehouse were, for many Reasons, obliged to sell for ready Money only. The great Encouragement they have met with upon those Terms, has induced them to enlarge considerably their Manufacture: And in order to render their Plan for reducing the Prices of Silks more extensive, they now propose the following Regulations with respect to Payment, having fixed their Prices, as usual, at the very lowest Rates they can afford as Manufacturers.

To allow Five per Cent. for ready Money.

Four per Cent. on Silks paid for within Three Months. And

17.1

It is said, that no Persons, except Peers eldest Sons, an Heir apparent of a Peer, all the Judges, the Attorney and Sollicitor General, his Honour the Master of the Rolls, the four Kings Serjeants, and the Masters in Chancery, are to be admitted for the future into the House of Lords.

We are told, that the Passing of the Defaulter's Accounts is to be postponed till the Thane's Son is an Auditor of the Imprest, as the Perquisites on so vast a Sum are an Object of the Favourite's Attention.

We are informed that 259,074l. will be wanted for defraying the Charge of the Office of Ordnance for the Land Service, for the Service of the Year ensuing.

We are also informed that 35,433l. will be wanted for defraying the Charge of the Office of Ordnance for Land Service, not provided for by Parliament in 1770.

By the Danish Ship lately arrived from Bengal, which on her Way touched at Mauritius, Advices have been received, that 16 Sail of Transports, with a Regiment on board, were then lately arrived at that Island from France; which confirms the Suspicion that the French have been long meditating a Blow in India.

The Land-Tax is settled at 4s. in the Pound for one Year only.

An Appeal is made against the Verdict given at the last Assizes at York, relating to the Beldy-Hill Lead Mines.

His Majesty having received Information, that Hemp, Flax, Human Hair, and Feathers, are frequently brought on board Ships coming from Hamburgh and Bremen, which Goods are more especially liable to retain Infection; his Majesty's Order in Council, dated Dec. 9, is published in last Night's Gazette, that all Ships coming from Hamburgh or Bremen, and having Rags, Cotton-Wool, Hemp, Flax, or Human Hair, or Feathers on board, that are already arrived, or shall hereafter arrive, in any of the Ports of this Kingdom, or of the Isles of Jersey, Guernsey, Alderney, Sark, or Man, do make their Quarantine for forty Days.

It having been represented to the King, that a Number of desperate Men, armed with Fire-Arms, on the 13th Day of October, and on the 20th Day of November last, broke open the Guard-House erected at the Entrance of the Black-Lead Mine near Seathwait in Cumberland, and forcibly entered into a Part of the said Mine, with Intent to carry away Black-Lead from thence; and did also threaten the Lives of the Persons who had the Care of the Mines: His Majesty's Pardon, and a Reward of 50l. are promised to any Accomplice, on Discovery of the rest of the Offenders.

At the Court of Aldermen held Yesterday at Guildhall, an Order was made for the lowering the Price of Bread Half an Assize, or a Penny in a Peck Loaf, which takes Place To-morrow.

Yesterday was held a Court of the Commissioners of the Lieutenancy at Guildhall, when the Court made to them.

On Saturday one Robinson was taken up at a House near Whitechapel Church, for exercising his Function as a Romish Priest, and was bound over for his Appearance the next Sessions at Hicks's-Hall, himself in 400l. and two Sureties in 200l. each.

Married.] Thursday, at Blackmore, in Essex, Benjamin Barnett, Esq; of Lombard-Street, Banker, to Miss Avice Wheate, Daughter of the late Sir George Wheate, Bart. and Sister to Sir Jacob Wheate, of Lechlade, in Gloucestershire.—Thursday last, the Rev. William Slade, of Warminster, Wilts, was married to Miss Frances Abbott, at Winterborne Dancey.

Died.] Saturday, at his House at Maidstone in Kent, Samuel Fullagar, Esq.—Monday, at her House at Fulham, Mrs. Thory, a Widow Lady.—Yesterday, Mrs. Reessen, Wife of Jacob Reessen, Esq; Merchant, in New Broad-Street.—A few Days since, at Hampstead, Mrs. Goddard, Sister to Sir Henry Parker, Bart. of Talton in Warwickshire, and half Sister to the present Earl of Clanricarde.—Saturday, at his Seat at Lingdell, near Dunmow, in Essex, Thomas Purkiss, Esq.—A few Days since, at his House near Wigan in Lancashire, Peter Swan, Esq.

BILIOUS Complaints, visceral Obstructions, the Tortures of Indigestion, and all Disorders incident to the Stomach and Bowels, are speedily and effectually cured by a Physician from the University of Padua, professedly addicted to that Branch. He is to be heard of at the St. James's Coffee-House, St. James's-Street; and whoever chuses to consult him, by leaving proper Directions at the Bar, will be waited upon.

For The St. James's Chronicle.

To Dr. S——l J—hn—n.

SIR,

I Shall make no Apology for addressing myself to you, as the Writer of a Paper signed Lexiphanes, which was published in the St. James's Chronicle of the 4th Instant. The *heterogeneous* Words, the *anomalous* Expressions, and above all the *aerial Inanity*, so happily diffused through the whole, betray to us the Author of the Prince of Abyssinia as clearly as if it had been signed with your Name.

You undertake, Sir, to *elucidate* those *colloquial Barbarisms*, which have crept into the Language of our Country from the "*Ebullitions* of convivial or epistolary Humour, the Sallies of *dramatic Hilarity*, and the sportive and dry Intelligence of *diurnal, nocturnal*, and *hebdomadal* Historians." The Design, I confess, is an Undertaking worthy of that Genius, who is already distinguished by his *Capability* "to trace every *radical* Word thro' a *collateral* Series of *Ramifications*." And if the Execution had been but moderately *adequate*, it

SIR,

MARRIAGE proving daily a Source of the most severe and lasting Calamity in Life, though little new perhaps is left to be said upon the Subject, any Thing which serves to discountenance the meretricious Arts and Duplicity of Coquetry, and to expose the senseless Vanity of giddy unfeeling Flirts, may be attended with some publick Utility.

I mean not to animadvert upon the cruel Industry of that Herd of impertinent, unfeeling, treacherous Wretches, called Match Makers, who haunt publick Places, and intrude themselves into Families, to betray and gradually to warp the Affections of innocent young Creatures. I have ever considered this numerous conscientious Tribe of designing Beings, as more pernicious to Society and to the Peace and real Happiness of Families, even than Bawds themselves. The Attacks of the latter are more easily guarded against than the artful Insinuations of Match Makers, who make their first Approaches under the Disguise of Friendship, and watch every Avenue and rising Passion of the unguarded Breast, till, by their baneful Industry and treacherous Insinuations, they find Means to sap the Foundation of every virtuous Principle. The deluded Victim is, contrary to her first and best Resolves, sacrificed at last to the loathsome Arms of a worn-out impotent Dotard, or ignorant Sot; from which unnatural Junction, nothing can be expected but a barren Bed, cold Indifference, and secret pining Discontent. But the original Purpose of the sottish Husband is fully answered by the Fortune of the poor betrayed young Creature, which goes either to satisfy the impatient Demand of a gaping Mortgage, or in Liquor for his sporting drunken Companions.

Vanity and female Friendships have in all Times been the Ruin of more than half the Sex. But the vicious Modes of the World tend to corrupt and debauch the infant Mind from every Principle of Virtue, and to give it a wrong Direction. What are the Effects of Raffles and Lottery Tables, which are going on from Morning to Night at Bath and Tunbridge, and at which it is common to see Children of eight Years old engaged with the utmost Impatience and Anxiety! It is here that wrong Impressions are received, virtuous Principles effaced, and the Mind early tinctured with a Love of Vanity, false Shew, and a mean Attention to Interest. Daily but woeful Experience evinces, how many deluded young Creatures have, in various Shapes, met their Ruin in the Schools of Vanity, and fashionable Folly.

It is surely little to be wondered at, that Minds thus early infected with the Contagion of vicious Habits, and dazzled with the superficial Glare of false Appearances, should be betrayed into unhappy Marriages, and be sometimes dead to the Calls and Feelings of Generosity, Gratitude, and Honour.

COVENTRY AND THE MERCURY:

Warwickſhire, Northamptonſhire, Leiceſterſhire, and Oxfordſhire

GENERAL ADVERTISER.

PRINTED BY N. ROLLASON, IN HIGH-STREET.

Price Three-pence Halfpenny.] MONDAY, FEBRUARY 7, 1791. [No. 2666.

THRUSDAY's POST.

From the LONDON GAZETTE.

Vienna (Germany), Jan. 12.

NEWS has been received here of the Fortreſs of Iſmail having been ſtorm'd and taken by the Ruſſian forces, under Gen. Suwarow, on the 22d of laſt month The aſſault is ſaid to have laſted upwards of 7 hours; but no authentic particulars are yet received here of the loſſes on each ſide, which are reported to have been very conſiderable.

War Office, Jan. 27, 1791.

OFFICERS appointed (from the under mentioned regiments, &c.) to INDEPENDENT COMPANIES.

To be CAPTAINS.

Capt. Thos. Steel, late 85th—Capt. Lt. J. Macpherſon, late 82d.—*Lieutenants*—John Bonamy, from 76th reg —Lord Sinclair, 17th—Hon. Francis Stuart, 16th—John Armſtrong, 73d—Thos. Ger. Elrington, 14th—Thos. Hardyman, 36th—Iſaac Brock, 8th—The Mar. of Huntley, 67th—Henry Miller, 50th—Rob. Macdonald, 42d—Geo. Taggart, 19th—John Robertſon, 55th—H. D. Fraſer, 42d—W. Anne John Crawley, 40th—H. Bromley, 2d Batt. Royals—Donald Robertſon, 69th—Walter Ovenden, 2d—Thos. Stewart Briſbane, 54th—Rob. Campbell, from the Royals—David Dewarr, 22d Foot—Henry Johnſon, 66th—Wm. Grant 55th—Ja. O'Connor, 19th—Cha. Rawdon, 18th—Claus Pell, 11th—Wm. Armſtrong, 8th—Geo. Anderſon, 55th—Wm. Troughton, 50th—Rich. Neate, 18th—Duncan Drummond, 35th—John Stewart, 25th—Perkins Lindſay, 22d—Donald Macdonald, 22d—Nath. Levett Peacocke, 50th—John Sandieman, 44th—Edw. Baker Littlehales, 58th—Barnard Bowes Foord, 26th—Thos. Probyn, 38th—Francis Cuninghame, 34th—Edw. Hutchinſon, 65th—J. C. Cowell, 1ſt Batt. Royals—Geo. Pigot, 2d Batt. Royals—Wm. Earle, 50th—John Hext, 22d—John Alexander, 31ſt—Lord Dungarvan, 34th—Rob. Balfour, 30th—Wm Purvis, 39th—Patrick Macdowell, 7th—Rob. Alex. Dalziel, 20th—Rob. Biſſett, 37th—Hon. Cha. Colville, 28th—Sylveſter Muirſon, 52d—Richard Quarrell, 43d—Hon. Wm. Stewart, 67th—Wm. Harneſs, 29th—Thos. Urquhart, 37th—J. Delves Broughton, 76th—Geo. Garnier, 53d—T. Vincent Reynolds, 34th—Mundiford Allen, 56th—Dugald Campbell, 57th—Wm. Beecher, 31ſt—Archibald Kennedy, 16th—Wm. Byng, 33d—John Timms, 22d—Alex. Maclean, 6th—John Oſwald, 7th—John Majoribanks, 19th—Geo. Strickland, 8th—John Biſſett, 36th—Tho. Bowyer Bower, 59th—Carr Bereſford, 16th—Hon. Alex. Hope, 64th—Geo. Hobart, 7th—Lewis Will. Brounker, 62d—W. Palmer Auckland, 17th—Hon. James E. Stuart, 7th—John Macdonald, 21ſt.—*Enſigns*—J. Spencer, from Coldſtream foot guards—Rob. Lawley, 1ſt foot guards—Hon. Edw. Bligh, 1ſt Foot Guards—Hon. J. T. Capel, from Coldſtream Guards.—*Cornet*—E. of Dalhouſie, from 3d D.

of Cheſter, from the 2d chapter of the firſt book of St. Peter, verſe 17th: "*Fear God, honour the King.*" His Lordſhip from this text enforced the neceſſity of ſubordination in all ſociety—he ſhewed that Kings had prerogatives, and that the people had rights, neither of which ought to be deſtroyed or infringed upon—he exhibited the conſtitution of Great Britain as the greateſt conceſſion of the Almighty to the wiſdom of ages, and as a happy medium between the towering hierarchy of Rome, and the republican and levelling principles of ſeveral ſects of *Proteſtants*—he exhorted his hearers to a maintenance of the Church and State, and ſhewed the dager of admitting the profeſſed enemies of the former into power, as they would (if admitted), to a moral certainty, diſturb the peace of both, if not annihilate them. He ſaid the church and State were admirably interwoven, and that one could not ſtand without the other. Forcibly impreſſing the bleſſings enjoyed under the preſent conſtitution, he conjured his hearers to maintain it upon the principles on which it was founded, of religion and of reaſon, prudence, virtue, and a love of the country.

In the courſe of his ſermon he touched upon the ſtate of Europe, and particularly upon the revolution in France, where all government was deſtroyed, and twenty millions of people melted down to a ſhapeleſs maſs. He ſhewed the abſurdity of recurring to natural rights, which could be permitted alone in an unaſſociated ſtate; and gave it as his opinion, that the people of that country were to wait for a government to be produced by the virtues or vices of one man.

To-morrow the Houſe of Commons will meet, purſuant to their laſt adjournment.

Mr. Pitt, it is imagined, will bring out his Budget in the courſe of next week, or the week after; many new ſchemes of finance are in report; but which of them will be adopted, we cannot as yet ſay with any degree of certainty.

Mr. Dundas follows with the India Budget, which perhaps will be delayed until the next arrivals from Madras, which are expected to be about the latter end of February, or the begining of March.

Yeſterday arrived a mail from New-York, brought to Falmouth by the Sandwich packet in twenty days.

The GOUT: a moſt extraordinary CURE of it.—A Gentleman of Fortune and Character, at *Chipping Norton*, having been for a long time confined to his bed, ſo violently with the Gout in his Head, Stomach, and Limbs, as to induce his Phyſician and Apothecary to pronounce it ſcarcely poſſible for him to live *Twenty*

And, as an additional Encouragement, ſhould the Number of the Quarter be the firſt drawn Ticket on Wedneſday the Ninth Day of February, the above ONE HUNDRED TICKETS (Value 1650l.) ſhall immediately be delivered to the fortunate Holder of the Quarter, over and above the 250l. it is entitled to—as FIRST-DRAWN.

A Receipt for an Eighth, at 1l. 1l. will produce Half the above Benefits, with FIFTY TICKETS on the firſt drawn.

A Receipt for a Sixteenth, at 10s. 6d. will acquire, on the

L.		L.	s.	L.		L.	s.	d.
20,000	— —	1250	0	500	— — —	31	5	0
10,000	— —	625	0	100	— — —	6	5	0
5,000	— —	312	10	50	— — —	3	2	6
2,000	— —	125		25	— — —	0	10	6
1,000	— — —	62	10	1ſt 10,000 Blanks,		0	5	0

With TWENTY-FIVE TICKETS on the firſt drawn.

And the Shares at Five Shillings and Sixpence, will produce Half of the Sixteenths, with THIRTEEN TICKETS on the firſt-drawn.

Thus, the Shares in this Plan (though Cent. per Cent. cheaper than the uſual Prices) will receive, and are entitled to their full Proportion in all the Prizes, without any Deduction; to the Purchaſe-money in the Prizes of 25l. and to the Return of 1l. each Quarter; 10s. each Eighth; 5s. each Sixteenth; and 2s. 6d. each Five and Six-penny Share,—on the 10,000 Blanks. They are only excluded the Benefit of the 20l. Prizes. So that by relinquiſhing the trifling Benefits of the 20l. there is, in the firſt Inſtance, a Saving of Two Guineas on the Purchaſe of each Quarter, One Guinea on each Eighth, Half-a-Guinea on each Sixteenth, &c. beſides the

EXTRAORDINARY ADVANTAGE

of becoming poſſeſſed of the above numbered WHOLE STATE LOTTERY TICKETS on the firſt Morning of Drawing, and which will be inſtantly delivered to the fortunate Holder thereof, over and above the Prizes they are entitled to as firſt-drawn. With theſe Tickets, the fortunate Purchaſer comes into the immediate Poſſeſſion of upwards of SIXTEEN HUNDRED AND FIFTY POUNDS, and has the faireſt and beſt founded Hopes of acquiring the Capital Prizes of 20,000l. 10,000l. 5,000l. &c.

OBSERVATION.—*If in all former Lotteries, although there have not been any Prizes between 50l. and 20l. and yet thoſe Shares excluding the 20l. Prizes, had the Preference, and were bought with great Avidity,—what then muſt be the caſe in the preſent Lottery? where there are 5000 Prizes of 25l. entitled to the Purchaſe Money; nay more, 10,000 Blanks, being entitled to 1l. on each Quarter, 10s. on each Eighth, 5s. on each Sixteenth, and 2s. 6d. on each ſmaller Share—which favourable circumſtances, properly conſidered, muſt place this Mode of Adventure above any objection, even of the moſt cautious and ſcrupulous, the Depoſit being only* Two Guineas *a* Quarter; *which, if drawn any of the 5000 Prizes of 25l. the Money to be returned,—If any of the 10,000 Blanks, 1l. to be returned:—Conſequently, for the Riſque of 1l. 2s. only, the*

A Saving of near *Thirty per Cent!*

And the Whole Purchaſe-Money returned on both the 25l. and 20l. Prizes!

JENKINS and Co.

At their Old Eſtabliſhed Houſe,

No. 125, *FLEET-STREET, LONDON,*

Reſpectfully ſubmit the following œconomical and truly-advantageous Mode of adventuring in the enſuing Lottery, to the Attention of their numerous Cuſtomers and the Public.

LEGAL RECEIPT SHARES,

At THREE GUINEAS, ONE GUINEA and a HALF, SIXTEEN SHILLINGS and EIGHT SHILLINGS,

For the Whole *Time of Drawing; and are as follows;*

For 3l 3s. inſtead of 4l. 10s.

You have ONE QUARTER, which produces on

L.20,000	—	L.5,000
10,000	—	2,500
5,000	—	1,250
2,000	—	500
1,000	—	250
500	—	125
100	—	25
50	—	12 10s.

And the Whole Purchaſe returned if either 25l. or 20l.

For 1l. 11s. 6d. inſtead of 2l. 5s.

You have ONE EIGHTH, which produces on

L.20,000	—	L.2,500
10,000	—	1,250
5,000	—	625
2,000	—	250
1,000	—	125
500	—	62 10s.
100	—	12 10s.
50	—	6 5s.

And the Whole Purchaſe returned if either 25l. or 20l.

For 16s. inſtead of 1l. 3s.

You have ONE SIXTEENTH, which produces on

L.20,000	—	L.1,250
10,000	—	625
5,000	—	312 10s.
2,000	—	125
1,000	—	62 10s.
500	—	31 5s.
100	—	6 5s.
50	—	3 2s.

And the Whole Purchaſe returned if either 25l. or 20l.

For 8s. you have as follow

17.2

To be LIEUTENANTS.

Ensigns John Crew, from 29th regt.—Alex. Houston, 97th Fames Smith Bailie, 33d—Ed. Whitehead, 54th—Arthur Miller, 53d—Tho. Mullins, 24th—Ph. Brampton Gurdon, 24th—Hugh Macpherson, from half-pay of the late 89th—— Raitt, from half-pay of 46th—J. F. Castello, from half-pay of the late 94th—Donald Macdonald, 2d bat. Royals—And. Pilkington, from half-pay of Major Elford's corps—Wm. Patterson, 57th—Ed. Robinson, 43d—Ed. Hull, 3d Tho. Norton Poulett, 31st—David Hunter, 14th—Hugh Rob. Duff, 35th—Wm. Belford, 18th—Cavendish Sturt, 34th—Rob. Donald, 68th—Geo. Fox Bruce, 32d—David Erskine, 31st—Arch. Butter, 17th—Lord Blaney, 32d—Rich. Lytter, 12th—Second Lieut. Wm. Law Dundas, 23d—Ensigns Ronald Ferguson, 53d—Robert Young, 66th—Geo. Carnagie, 14th—Wm. Halton, 17th—Rowland Hill, 38th—David Oswald, 29th.

To be ENSIGNS.

Irving Brock—Steuart Trotter—G. Lauder—J. Christie R, G. Elrington—D. D. Quereville—Andrew Foster—Alex. M'Dowell—John Geffrard, jun.—Walter Largent.

BANKRUPTS.

Richard Jackson, now or late of Oxford-street, Middlesex, haberdasher, Feb. 8, 15, March 15, at Guildhall.—Attorney, Mr. Smith, Thavies Inn.

John Simson Spencer, of Gracechurch-street, London, hatter, Feb. 5, 15, March 15, at Guildhall.—Attornies, Mess. Hunt and Swain, Old Jewry.

Robert Wellum, late of Old Ford, Middlesex, victualler, Feb 5, 19, March 15, at Guildhall.—Attorney, Mr. Macquillin, Lion's Inn.

DIVIDENDS.

Feb. 26. James Smith, of Coventry-street, Middlesex, man's mercer, at Guildhall.—22. Andrew Veziam, late of Gould Square, London, merchant, at Guildhall.—March 1. John Ellis, late of Friday street, London, gauze-weaver, at Guildhall.—1. Thomas Welch, of Ross, Herefordshire, mercer, at Guildhall.—1. John Wilkinson, late of Bernard-street, Middlesex, money scrivener, at Guildhall.—1. Robert Harvey, of Dover, Kent, shopkeeper, at Guildhall.—Feb. 24. John Brooke and Paul Randall, both of Melksham, Wilts, clothiers, at the Bush, Bristol.—March 1. John Williams, late of Narbeth, Pembrokeshire, dealer, at the Angel, Haverfordwest.—Feb. 24. John Tengatt, of Pannal, Yorkshire, innholder, at Mr. Forrest's, Sulphur Wells.—March 15. William Emes, of Bath, Somersetshire, shopkeeper, at Guildhall.—8. David Fraser, of Brewer-street, Middlesex, saddler, at Guildhall.—Feb. 22. Thomas Thorley, of Lombard-street, London, wax chandler, at Guildhall.—22. John Pearsall and Benjamin Pearsall, of London, hardwaremen, at Guildhall.—March 1. Richard Garratt, now or late of Fish-street Hill, London, linen-draper, at Guildhall.—Feb. 26. John Quilter, of St. Osyth, Essex, grocer, at Guildhall.—29. William Cordy, of Cornhill, London, carver, at Guildhall.—18. Richard Weale, the younger, of Maidenhead Bridge, Bucks, innholder, at Guildhall.—26. Philip Baker, Tothill-street, Middlesex, linen-draper, at Guildhall.—28. John Duke, of Bolton upon Dearne, Yorkshire, linen-draper, Great Black Bull, in Wakefield.—Feb. 3. Thomas Needham Rees, of Watlington, Oxfordshire, Surgeon, at Guildhall.

CERTIFICATE.

Feb. 23. Philip Constable, (Partner with Redmond Barry,) of Birmingham, Warwickshire, factor.

LONDON, *Feb.* 1.

Yesterday, soon after eleven o'clock, the Lord Chancellor went to the House of Lords, where his Lordship ordered that no petitions for private bills be received in that House after the 15th of April. At half past twelve o'clock the House was adjourned till this day; after which his Lordship, attended by the Archbishop of Canterbury, the Bishops of London, Rochester, Sailsbury, and St. Asaph, proceeded to the Chapel in Westminster Abbey, where they heard a sermon preached by Dr. William Cleaver, Lord Bishop

as a *Forlorn Hope*, to send to *Mr. Wagstaffe*, of that Place, for a Bottle of *Oriental Vegetable Cordial*, one Dose of which giving him such Relief as to encourage him to persevere in repeating it every third Hour, until he had taken half a dozen Doses, when he was enabled to walk about his Room, and the next Day to make his Appearance in the Town, to the great Surprise and Astonishment of his Friends. This inestimable Cordial is to be had in Bottles, of 5s. each, of the Patentee, B. CORNWELL, at his House, No. 13, *Conduit-street, Hanover-square.*

*** There are also Quart Bottles at 1l. 3s 6d. each, containing the Quantity of Six 5s. Bottles, for private Families and Exportation.

This celebrated Cordial is also sold by N. Rollason, Coventry, and one reputable Person in every City and Town in Great Britain, &c.

[*For the remainder of this Post see the last Page.*]

1791.

[No. 137, *FLEET-STREET*, LONDON.]

MARGRAY and Co. having had the Honour and Satisfaction to have their Schemes approved of and patronized by the Public during a Succession of upwards of THIRTY Lotteries; again most humbly submit the following Proposals to the Consideration of their old Friends, Patrons, and the Public in general:—

PLAN I.

A SAVING of CENT. PER CENT. in the PURCHASE of SHARES, with a Douceur of ONE HUNDRED TICKETS, Value about ONE THOUSAND, SIX HUNDRED and FIFTY POUNDS.

THE TICKETS,

No.	No.	No.	No.	No.	No.
3741	3763	5575	5592	5609	33015
3742	3764	5576	5593	5610	33016
3743	3765	5577	5594	32916	33017
3744	5561	5578	5595	32917	33018
3745	5562	5579	5596	32918	33019
3751	5563	5580	5597	32910	33020
3752	5564	5581	5598	32920	33021
3753	5565	5582	5599	32926	33022
3754	5566	5583	5600	32927	33023
3755	5567	5584	5601	32928	33024
3756	5568	5585	5602	32929	33025
3757	5569	5586	5603	32930	33026
3758	5570	5587	5604	33011	33027
3759	5571	5588	5605	33012	33028
3760	5572	5589	5606	33013	33029
3761	5573	5590	5607	33014	33030
3762	5574	5591	5608		

This Plan may justly be stiled, the Lottery's 'ne plus ultra;' it is out of the Power of Invention to suggest a more advantageous Mode of Adventure, at so small a Risque.

Price of Shares in this Plan:

A Receipt for a QUARTER,	£.2	2	0
Ditto for an EIGHTH,	1	1	0
Ditto for a SIXTEENTH,	0	10	6

Also, a SHARE at FIVE SHILLINGS and SIX-PENCE, entitled to Half a Sixteenth.

A QUARTER at 2l. 2s. will produce

On the £.20,000	£.5000	
10,000	2500	
5,000	1250	
2,000	500	
1,000	250	
500	125	
100	25	
50	12	10
25	2	2
First 10,000 Blanks,	1	

the Prizes—3 of 20,000*l.* 2 of 10,000*l.* 3 of 5000*l.* the 2000*l.* the 1000*l.* the 500*l.* &c.

*** *Besides the unparallelled Advantages of the above* ONE HUNDRED TICKETS, *and by which* all, *or the* major Part *of the Capital Prizes may be obtained,—and, at what Expence?—at 1l. 2s.*

PLAN II.

In order to afford a pleasing Variety, and to gratify those who are not inclined to be precluded the Benefits of the Twenty Pound Prizes,—this Plan is adopted; the Shares in this Plan, are entitled to the full Quota in all and every one of the Prizes, whether 20,000l. or 25l. they are also entitled to the Purchase-money in the 20l. Prizes, to the Benefit of the 10,000 Blanks; and to the additional Advantage of the Douceur of ONE HUNDRED TICKETS, on the first-drawn Ticket.

Price of Shares in this Plan:

A Receipt for a QUARTER,	£.3	3	0
Ditto for an EIGHTH,	1	11	6
Ditto for a SIXTEENTH,	0	16	0

Also, a Share at Eight Shillings and Six pence.

A Receipt for a Quarter, at 3l. 3s. in this Plan, will produce on the

£.	£.	£.	£.	s.
20,000	5,000	100	25	0
10,000	2 500	50	12	10
5,000	1,250	25	6	5
2 000	500	20	3	3
1,000	250	10,000 Blanks	1	9
500	125			

Should the Number of the Quarter be the first drawn Ticket on the Ninth of February, the above ONE HUNDRED TICKETS (Value 1650l.) shall immediately be delivered to the fortunate Holder thereof, over and above the 250l. it will be entitled to as first-drawn.

A Receipt for an Eighth, at 1l. 11s. 6d. will produce Half the above Benefits, with FIFTY TICKETS on the first-drawn.

A Sixteen Shilling Receipt, producing a Sixteenth Share, will acquire on the

£.	£.	s.	£.	£.	s.	d.
20,000	1,250	0	100	6	5	0
10,000	625	0	50	3	2	6
5,000	312	10	25	1	11	3
2,000	125		20	0	16	0
1,000	62	10	1st 10000 Blanks	0	5	0
500	31	5				

With TWENTY-FIVE TICKETS on the first-drawn.

And the Shares at Eight Shillings and Six pence will produce Half of the Sixteenth, with THIRTEEN TICKETS on the first-drawn.

TO THE PUBLIC.

MARGRAY and Co. would have been silent concerning themselves, were the Public not daily loaded with the fulsome Encomiums that other Houses heap on their own Conduct; whilst MARGRAY and Co. have scorned publishing an Account of the large Sums of Money they have paid, or exposed those they have paid it to. Whether they have punctually and strictly fulfilled their Engagements in upwards of Thirty Lotteries, they are proud to appeal to the Public at large;—they challenge every Individual in the whole Country, whether, in the Course of all their Concerns of the first Magnitude, there ever happened a Demur, a Dispute, or a Disapointment: but, in having scrupulously discharged every Engagement with the Public, they have but done their Duty, and have no more Right to claim a Merit on that Score than a Banker has, in paying his Customers' Drafts when presented; or a Merchant, in honouring his Bills of Exchange when they become due. And it is fair to ask,—What Opinion would the Public entertain of the Banker, who advertised that he paid his Customers' Drafts or of the Merchant, who publicly boasts that he is regular in paying his Bills?—After this Observations MARGRAY and Co. have only to add, that they will pursue the same Line of Conduct, which has secured to them Reputation and Confidence for a long Series of Years.

Begins Drawing on Wednesday February 9, 1791.

Being HALF a SIXTEENTH: upon

L.20,000	L.625
10,000	312 10s.
5,000	156 5s.
2,000	62 10s.
1,000	31 5s.
500	15 12s. 6d.
100	3 2s. 6d.
50	1 11s. 3d.

And the Whole-Purchase returned if either 25l. or 20l.

It is presumed that this Plan is so *plainly* advantageous, that no one can be at a Loss to decide upon it. Every Person must perceive that in the benefits of a Fourth Share they *save* no less than *One Pound Seven Shillings* in an Eighth *Thirteen Shillings* and *Six-pence*, in a Sixteenth *Seven Shillings*, &c. &c. being upon an Average, near THIRTY per Cent.

In point of Security, and Certain of just Payment, JENKINS and Co. presume they need not enlarge, during the Course of *Eleven* Lotteries, they have divided and paid, to their fortunate Customers, the following capital Prizes:

One of 20,000l.—Two of 10,000l.—Four of 5,000l.—Thirteen of 2,000l.—Twenty-five of 1,000l.—and Thirty-four of 500l.

The Receipts for all which, with Reference to the Parties who receive the same, may be seen at the Office.

JENKINS and Co. have Permission to publish the Three following Receipts:

Being 781l. 5s. gained for ONLY 1l. 19s. 6d.

"Received March 22, 1788, of Messrs. *Jenkins* and Co.
"Three Hundred and Twelve Pounds Ten Shillings, for a
"Guinea Share, No. 13,371, drawn a Prize of 5,000l. in
"the present Lottery.
"312l. 10s. "JAMES WHITE, *Wyre*, near *Pershore, Worcestershire.*"

"Received March 6, 1789, of Messrs. *Jenkins* and Co.
"Three Hundred and Twelve Pounds Ten Shillings, for a
"Half Guinea Share, No. 29,685 drawn a Prize of 10,000l.
"in the present Lottery."
"312l. 10s. "*Received for* H. CRITCHLEY, *Derby.*"
"JOHN BOWMAN, *Distiller*, No. 16, *Coppice-Row, Clerkenwell.*"

"Received March 11, 1790, of Messrs. *Jenkins* and Co.
"One Hundred and Fifty-six Pounds Five Shillings, for an
"Eight-Shilling Share, No. 29,321, drawn a prize of
"5,000l. in the present Lottery."
"156l. 10s. "T. JAMES, Tea-Dealer, *St. Thomas's, Southwark.*"

And in the last Irish Lottery the following capital Prizes were sold by them.

33,116, a Prize of 1000l, to Mrs. Duncan, near the Royal-Oak, Woolwich.

14,638, a Prize of 500l. to Mr. Parfitt, Dockhead, Southwark,

34.507, a Prize of 500l. to Mr. Joseph Bee, No. 31. Ironmonger Lane, Cheapside,

24.339, a Prize of 500l. to Mr. James Rough, Waterman, No. 11, Broad Street, Ratcliff, Cross,

32,928, a Prize of 500l. to a Gentleman at Wakefield, Yorkshire.

Besides several others to Persons unknown.

Jenkins and *Co.* conscious of the liberal Advantage that must, in all Probability, advert to those who may honour them with a Preference, presume they may, with much Propriety, claim the Encouragement and Patronage of a generous Public.

Begins Drawing the 9th of February, 1791.

Country Correspondents punctually attended to.

Good Bills, at a short Date, or Cash sent in a Parcel, (by Coach or otherwise) will have whatever is ordered, executed with the Punctuality as though personally present, and sent by Return of any Conveyance that may be pointed out.

Plans, at large, may be had (gratis) at No. 125 Fleet-street, London; and will be sent wherever desired.

Daily Chronicle

NO. 21,272. LONDON. FRIDAY, MAY 23, 1930. LEEDS. ONE PENNY.

MISS AMY JOHNSON MISSING ON LONE FLIGHT.

NOT SEEN SINCE EARLY YESTERDAY.

WIRELESS STATION CLOSES WITHOUT NEWS.

FORCED LANDING IN LONELY SPOT?

Miss Amy Johnson, the 26-year-old Hull girl, whose lone flight to Australia has roused the admiration of the world, is missing.

She set out early yesterday from Sourabaya, Java, for the island of Timor, from which she planned to make the last stage of the great adventure — the 500 miles flight over sea to Australia.

Six and a half hours later she passed over Bima (on the island of Sumbawa), but since then all is silence.

She had petrol for a ten-hours' flight—about 1,000 miles.

"NO NEED FOR UNDUE ANXIETY."

—*Sir Alan Cobham.*

Man of First Australian Flight on Lack of News.

SIR ALAN COBHAM, who made the first flight to Australia and back, in 1926, told a "Daily Chronicle" representative last night that he did not think there need be undue anxiety about Miss Johnson's safety.

"Her route," he said, "is over a great number of little islands, on most of which it is quite possible to make a forced landing in more or less safety.

"They are isolated and scattered, and without any means of rapid communication, and

it would not surprise me at all if nothing was heard of her for 24, or even 36, hours.

"It may take some time for the news to get across to Timor, where she should have stopped for petrol, before tackling the most difficult part of the route across the water to Australia.

"She should not have encountered adverse weather at this time of the year. It is early autumn in that part of the world, the rainy season is over, and I think this is the best time for flying that could have been chosen.

"Until there is definite news that she has crashed, I should not feel very much anxiety about her."

RAINBOW OMEN.

Auspicious Start, but Last Seen 400 Miles Away.

The latest news is given in the following Reuter cables:—

SOURABAYA (Java), Thursday.

Miss Amy Johnson left here for Atamboea (on the island of Timor) at 6.5 this morning.

After a trial run, yesterday afternoon, Miss Johnson was not satisfied as to the condition of the machine.

In consequence further repairs were carried out during the night.

This morning, at 5 o'clock, she was satisfied, and made a good start with the engine running smoothly.

She circled above the field and waved her hand to the many spectators, who cheered her enthusiastically.

Miss Johnson appeared to be in excellent spirits.

Before her departure there was a splendid rainbow in the sky, which Miss Johnson declared was a lucky omen.

She intended to fly straight to Atamboea.

Before she left Sourabaya, Miss Johnson said that she would alight at Bima if her motor was not running smoothly when she arrived over Sumbawa island.

SOURABAYA (Later).

Miss Amy Johnson passed over Bima, on the island of Sumbawa, at 11.30 this morning on her way to Atamboea.

[At this point she had flown 400 miles and had still 350 more to fly to reach Atamboea.]

BATAVIA, Thursday.

Some uneasiness is now being felt about Miss Amy Johnson, as nothing has been heard of her since she passed Bima.

The wireless station of Koepang, on the island of Timor, which is in telephone communication with Atamboea, was specially kept open until 11 p.m. Java time, but reported at the closing hour that there was still no news of Miss Johnson.

MISS JOHNSON'S FATHER.

Though naturally anxious about their daughter's progress, Mr. and Mrs. Johnson told a "Daily Chronicle" representative last night, at Hull, that they were not alarmed at the fact that no news had been received of her landing at Atamboea.

Atamboea, Mr. Johnson said, has no direct cable service. He had been informed by London that he need not be unduly concerned if news of her reaching there was delayed. The strain of waiting, however, was beginning to tell on Mrs. Johnson.

LONELY TROPIC SEA.

The Timor Sea (between the Sunda Islands, over which Miss Johnson was flying, and Australia) is one of the loneliest seas of the tropics.

In all the 900 miles of sea between

(Continued in next column.)

(Continued from previous column.)

Bima, where she was last reported, or Atamboea, for which she was making, and Port Darwin, in North Australia, there is, according to Lloyd's, only one small ship.

This is the Marella, a steamer of 4,340 tons net, belonging to a Sydney firm of shippers. She left Darwin on May 20. The maximum distance she could cover in a day would be about 250 miles. This, however, might now bring her within 100 miles of Miss Johnson's route between Bima and the island of Timor.

The Marella is equipped with wireless.

There is a possibility that other small coasting vessels are in the vicinity, but the route is little frequented, and the Marella is the only ship known to Lloyd's to be there.

ROYAL FUN AT A MUSIC HALL.

KING AND QUEEN'S HEARTY LAUGHS.

THAT NEW CAR.

FINDING THE SEA AT SOUTHEND.

By Our Theatre Correspondent.

One thing can be said very definitely about last night's Royal performance at the Palladium—the King and Queen thoroughly enjoyed their evening at a music-hall, their first for more than two years.

It was a great night for Variety. It had all the glamour and the excitement of a gala performance of pre-war days.

For hours before the Royal party arrived, a great crowd thronged the street. Inside, the auditorium was packed.

More than three-quarters of the audience in the stalls and the circle were in evening dress, and when the King and Queen, accompanied by the Duke of Gloucester, appeared in the flower-decked Royal box, they were given a rousing reception.

A PLEASANT BLEND.

All through the programme proved an excellent one, a pleasant blend of real music-hall acts of the best type.

Of the first half I should say that George Clarke and his Company in "His First Car" and Gillie Potter scored the biggest hits.

How the King and Queen laughed when the maid came out of the house into the yard where the Clarke family were gathered round admiring their new car and began lustily to beat a very dusty mat on its glistening bodywork! George Clarke's proud admonition to his wife, "You can forget your tramway habits now" was a joke which made all the Royal party chuckle.

Gillie Potter's absurd descriptions of a visit to Southend and a meal in a restaurant made the Queen rock in her chair with laughter.

HOMELY HUMOUR.

It was homely humour with the real music-hall tang, but every point got home.

"There was some talk about going down to the sea, but the man who knew the way was ill," was one of Gillie Potter's jokes about Southend that amused the Royal party.

The combined dancing ensemble which brought the first half of the bill to a close was as fine an act of the kind as the music-halls have ever seen.

As at previous Royal performances, the ballad singer was a very popular turn. This time it was Odali Careno, the operatic star. Her last number, "For You Alone," brought down the house, and at the end she had to take half-a-dozen curtain calls.

Will Hay and his company, who have previous experience of Royal performances, repeated their former success. Will Hay's sketch, "Entomology," is very funny indeed, especially the bit where he and his elderly white-haired pupil try to catch a red beetle which continually dodges across a grassy bank.

It was interesting to note that the turns which seemed to appeal most to the King and Queen were the broad comedy acts. That has always been so at these shows.

Of last night's performers, I should say that the outstanding successes were George Clarke, Gillie Potter and Will Hay—all British artists.

On being told that the amount taken was about £3,300, the King said that he was very glad that the occasion had been so successful.

THE KING'S PRAISE.

"It has been the best variety programme we have ever seen. Every act was splendid from beginning to end," the King told the organisers of the performance when leaving the Palladium.

"And I think so, too," said the Queen.

The King and Queen at the London Palladium last night.

RACING DOGS SENSATION.

TWO FOUND DEAD IN THEIR KENNELS.

POISON THEORY.

Two well-known London greyhounds, Munster House and Apelle, were found dead yesterday at the Burhill Kennels, Hersham, Walton-on-Thames, in circumstances suggesting foul play.

The Wimbledon Stadium veterinary surgeon, Mr. Alfred Sams, was summoned, and as the external symptoms pointed to strychnine poisoning, Mr. Stevens, manager of the track at Wimbledon, where the dogs have raced, ordered both cases to be sent to the Royal College of Veterinary Surgeons for a post mortem.

Apelle, a favourite for the Wimbledon Gold Cup, was owned by Messrs. Russell & Redfern, and was one of the best hurdlers in London. He won his last race, an intermediate round of the Cup, on Wednesday.

Munster House, a younger dog, had also shown great promise.

ONE RUN TO WIN —STUMPS DRAWN.

ANOTHER DAY'S "PLAY" NECESSARY.

An unusual incident marked the finish of the county cricket championship match between Hampshire and Notts at Southampton last evening.

Hampshire finished wanting only a single run to beat the champions, when stumps were drawn for the day.

Crowding round the pavilion, the spectators called long and loudly for the players to come out and finish the match, but their appeals met with no response.

EXTRA TIME PLAYED.

An extra half-hour had already been played, and cricket after that is not provided for by the rules.

Two years ago there was a similar occurrence. Lancashire, in a match against Essex at Colchester, having to wait until next morning to get the two runs they required to win.

Full story of the play is told on Page 13.

CITY (FOSTER) FATHERS

British Mayors to Visit French "Adopted" Towns.

From Our Own Correspondent.

PARIS, Thursday.

Arrangements are now complete for the visit to France of the municipal delegation from the cities and towns of Great Britain which have "adopted" a town or village in the regions of France which were devastated by the war.

Seventy Lord Mayors and Mayors will arrive in Paris on Wednesday next.

After being entertained in Paris, they will leave, on the following Saturday, for the respective places which their cities and towns have adopted.

OUTSTRIPPING GRANDMA.

"I once asked my typist to weigh her clothes," said Mr. Slater Willis, a Sheffield business man, at a conference yesterday. "Not in my presence," he added hastily, amid laughter.

"Her clothes weighed about 12 ounces. Probably those of her grandmother weighed twelve pounds."

THE GINGER GROUP'S CENSURE MOTION.

SIR OSWALD MOSLEY BACKED BY 29 LABOUR M.P.s.

By Our Political Correspondent.

THE latest development in the political crisis is the special meeting of the Labour party, held last night, to discuss Sir Oswald Mosley's motion of censure on the Government for its handling of unemployment.

It gave little reliable guidance as to the issue of events next week.

The meeting lasted for nearly three hours, and ended in the defeat of Sir Oswald's motion by 210 votes to 29.

Sir Oswald's motion expressed dissatisfaction with the Government's unemployment policy, and called for one more in harmony with the Labour party's pledges at the last election.

PREMIER'S REPLY.

The Prime Minister replied. He declared that Sir Oswald's proposals had been examined by experts and found impracticable.

Mr. Thomas also made a short speech.

Mr. Thurtle endeavoured to reconcile the opposing factions by an amendment which amounted to a compromise. It recognised the difficulties of the situation and promised intensive endeavours to deal with it on the lines of Labour policy.

Mr. Henderson made a valiant endeavour to patch matters up. He paid compliments all round and invited Sir Oswald to withdraw his motion.

CHANGED HIS MIND.

Sir Oswald appeared to be about to respond to the invitation, and then to change his mind. Many Labour members afterwards thought he had missed a great opportunity for showing magnanimity, which would have stood him in good stead later.

The chances in next Wednesday's division obviously depend very largely upon what the dissentients do. Generally the impression last night was that the 29 will be reduced to ten or even fewer on the vote in the House.

LIBERAL ATTITUDE.

The Liberals are to consider their attitude at a party meeting on Tuesday. The present feeling in the party is in favour of doing as they did on Monday and not voting, though a few take the view that, bearing in mind the problems ahead, and particularly the position in India, it would be better to make sure that the Government is not defeated.

Mr. Lloyd George will meet other Liberal ex-Ministers before the full party meeting.

As for the Conservatives, it is difficult to discover what exactly is in their minds. They profess the intention to do their utmost to defeat the Government, but I have reason to believe that they would be better pleased if the Government majority were to fall to half a dozen or so.

Their attitude is very much as it was on the second reading of the Coal Bill, when, after apparently strenuous efforts to muster all their forces against the Bill, they showed every sign of relief that the Government had won by a majority of eight.

SIR HERBERT SAMUEL'S COMMENT.

"The resignation of Sir Oswald Mosley has brought matters to a crisis," said Sir Herbert Samuel at Nottingham last night.

"I hope it may have the effect of stirring up the Government to a more complete realisation of the gravity of the unemployment situation."

Mr. Thomas's plans for road and bridge development were, Sir Herbert said, absurdly inadequate. There was need for a programme five or six times as great, for which special emergency powers should be put into operation.

CABINET'S FEELER ON UNEMPLOYMENT.

Mr. Tom Johnston, the Under-Secretary for Scotland and one of Mr. Thomas's collaborators on unemployment policy, made a statement last night which may have an important bearing on next Wednesday's debate.

Approving the suggestion of an inter-party conference on agriculture, Mr. Johnston said:—

"he would also welcome the extension of the plan to cover unemployment generally, an issue which, in his judgment, is too serious for any one party to administer or control."

It is unlikely that Mr. Johnston would make such a statement merely on his own authority.

If it represents the views of his colleagues in the Government, it might substantially affect the division in the Government's favour.

It is worth noting that the "pooling of the best brains" in all parties on unemployment is a main plank in the programme of Captain Berkeley, the Liberal candidate in the Nottingham by-election.

It would certainly have Liberal support in the House of Commons.

ITALIAN SCARE.

From Our Own Correspondent.

GENEVA, Thursday.

More than 2,800 arrests, including 200 Fascists, have been made in Milan since the arrival of Mussolini in that city, according to a statement published by the Socialist newspaper "Le Travail."

The report states that the post office, railway stations, and all public buildings are being occupied by the police.

Troops, it is added, have been notified for any emergency, and panic prevails among the inhabitants, whilst many foreigners are leaving the city.

According to the newspaper, the news had to be smuggled across the frontier.

[A speech by Mussolini is reported on Page 2.]

WOMAN'S NAME IN COMMONS.

AN APOLOGY BY MR. SNOWDEN.

BACCARAT STORY.

SIR ROBERT HORNE AND LE TOUQUET.

By HUGH MARTIN,
Our Parliamentary Correspondent.

WESTMINSTER, Thursday.

Comments on a new "baccarat case" were the cocktail provided to-day before the House of Commons settled down to a stodgy meal of Scottish estimates.

Shortly before midnight on Tuesday Mr. Snowden, in replying to second reading criticisms of the Budget by Sir Robert Horne, read an extract from the society gossip in a London daily paper with the object of showing that rich people in this country, who are bitterly complaining of over-taxation, have been wasting their money abroad.

The paragraph purported to describe incidents at Continental gaming tables when baccarat is played, and the words which the Chancellor read (after the Conservative Chief Whip had interjected the name of a member of the Government) were:—

Each player becomes banker in turn, and some of those who did so last night at Le Touquet were Sir Robert Horne and Mrs. —— (giving the name of a woman well-known in society). Sir —— ——, I am told, looked sardonically on.

Resentment at the reading of the paragraph was registered at the time by an uproar on the Conservative benches.

Mr. Churchill, who has a standing feud with the Chancellor, now further expressed this feeling by rising at the close of questions to ask the Speaker whether Mr. Snowden had been in order. Mr. Snowden was present, but Sir Robert Horne absent.

TRADITION OF THE HOUSE.

Mr. Churchill's point was: How far is a member, or a Minister, justified in referring in the course of debate to private persons outside this House, and in coupling the name of a woman with the name of a member of the House?

He argued that a point of order must arise, because, if such allusions became common, they "would lead on occasion to exceedingly disorderly episodes, which would be regretted by all."

Quite apart from the question of order, there was, Mr. Churchill submitted, the tradition and unwritten rule of the House, which forbade, for instance, all reference to conversations in the lobbies and smoking-room. (A Labour member: "And to telegrams.")

If such references were judged to be unsuitable for inclusion in debate a

Continued on Page 2.

Daily Chronicle

NO. 21,275. LONDON. TUESDAY, MAY 27, 1930. LEEDS. • ONE PENNY

TWENTY-SIX KILLED IN RIOTS IN RANGOON.

A ROUND TABLE ON UNEMPLOYMENT?

SIGNIFICANT HINT BY PRIME MINISTER LAST NIGHT.

NATIONAL PROBLEM.

MR. LLOYD GEORGE'S APPEAL.

Significant references to the unemployment crisis were made last night by Mr. Ramsay MacDonal dand Mr. Lloyd George.

Addressing his constituents, the Prime Minister said:—

"People were always saying, 'Why don't the Government ask the other parties to co-operate on unemployment?' I will give my answer.

"While the unemployment problem was the same problem as we faced at the last election, it would not be fair to ask the other parties to co-operate.

"The Labour party had its policy and the Tory party had its policy, and they could not be united together.

"Circumstances are now changing. The problems have changed, and if other parties care to co-operate with us we will let them know on Wednesday.

"On its national aspect of the problem of unemployment we shall welcome any amount of that sort of co-operation."

Mr. Lloyd George, speaking at Nottingham, said:—

"The figures are now approaching 1,800,000, and I should be very surprised if they stopped before they are two million.

"It is vital for this country that steps should be taken, and taken promptly, to deal with it.

"You cannot have an evil like this eating into the vitals of the nation without some permanent damage being effected on its constitution.

"Therefore it isessential that all men of good will should devote themselves to bring this matter right without loss of time.

"It is idle to say that this great nation cannot do it. It has faced greater things and triumphed. It can solve it if it only applies itself rationally, wisely and unitedly."

The Labour party had said that the programme which the Liberals put forward for dealing with unemployment was their policy.

"I say to them, here and now," said Mr. Lloyd George, "we renounce all rights in it. Act upon it; take it on, but do not lock it up."

It will be recalled that Mr. Tom Johnston, Under Secretary for Scotland, speaking last Thursday, said he would welcome an inter-party conference on plans to deal with unemployment, an issue which, in his judgment, was too serious for any one party to administer or control.

TO-MORROW'S CRITICAL DEBATE.

By Our Political Correspondent.

The Government are sparing no effort to ensure a full muster of Labour M.P.s for to-morrow's division on unemployment. A special appeal has been issued to Ministerialists individually, and it is confidently believed that there will be a full attendance bar casualties.

The Prime Minister's speech is awaited with keen interest. It is anticipated that, in addition to announcing his intention to give personal supervision to unemployment policy, he will ask Parliament to "think nationally" of the problem, and announce his intention of applying for emergency powers so as to speed up the Parliamentary procedure, which is blamed largely for the slow progress in municipal and other schemes of work-providing.

Such a plea by Mr. MacDonald would probably appease much of the unrest in the Labour party, reduce the number of Labour abstentions to the very minimum (Labour spokesmen declare there will be none), and make the Government safe in the division.

As already stated, the Liberal M.P.s will decide their line of action to-night. There is, however, a very definite disinclination among them at the moment directly to share responsibility for a policy they could not control.

It would be wrong, I think, to put any other interpretation on a decision, which they may reach to-day, not to embarrass the Government to-morrow.

I hear, by the way, that in addition to his new preoccupation on the unemployment question, the Prime Minister is also to take in hand personally the preparation of the Government's agricultural policy, which has caused difficulty up to now.

SIX OF FAMILY DEAD.

Killed as Car Hits Train at Level Crossing.

OTTAWA, Monday.

Six persons, members of one family, were killed when a motor-car was struck by a train at a level-crossing near Coburg, Ontario, to-day.

A baby, aged 18 months, was found by rescuers clasped in the arms of its mother, who was dead.

The infant was still alive, but died later.—Reuter.

A scene of the recent riots in Peshawar, showing the motor-cycle of the Royal Tank Corps dispatch rider who was killed and afterwards burned with kerosene by the mob, and the armoured car which went to his rescue and itself caught fire from the flames.

BIG FIRE IN BERLIN.

£75,000 DAMAGE ESTIMATED.

FLASKS OF GAS.

SHEDS AND CARS DESTROYED.

FROM OUR OWN CORRESPONDENT.
BERLIN, Monday.

One of the most spectacular fires which have occurred in Berlin for many years broke out in the east side of the city at noon to-day on ground belonging to the railway company.

Sheds, two-storeyed warehouses, motor-cars and railway carriages were soon in a blaze on a frontage of a mile.

The fire spread rapidly, and five immense sheds, covering an area of 11,000 yards, have been burned to the ground.

An army of firemen was quickly on the spot, fighting the flames.

While they were at their work there were a number of violent explosions as the fire reached a score of great flasks of oxygen.

The inhabitants of houses near the scene of the disaster were obliged to evacuate them because there was a fear that the fire might spread.

THREE FIREMEN INJURED.

Three firemen were injured by falling material.

By 4 o'clock the flames were extinguished.

It is estimated that the damage will amount to about £75,000.

Telegraphed picture of the great fire in Berlin yesterday afternoon.

£400 NECKLACE FOR 2/-.

Strange Wanderings of a String of Diamonds.

Reuter's correspondent at Toronto tells of a diamond necklace, worth £400, stolen by a domestic servant from her mistress.

It has been recovered by the police after changing hands several times, without its value being realised.

The last purchaser told the police he had bought it for 50 cents (2s.), not believing it was genuine, and had presented it to his wife.

LORD BYNG RETURNS.

To Be at His Desk in Scotland Yard This Morning.

Viscount Byng, the Chief Commissioner of the Metropolitan Police, and Lady Byng, returned to London yesterday after a six months' holiday in South Africa.

Both looked remarkably well. Lady Byng carried her right arm in a sling, and explained that she was suffering from a broken wrist caused by slipping in the forecourt of a house in which she was staying in South Africa.

"I have had a splendid holiday, and I shall start work at the Yard to-morrow," said Lord Byng. "As long as I retain good health I shall not think of retiring."

FLYING GIRL NOW IN 'NEVER-NEVER' LAND.

CUT OFF FROM COMMUNICATION WITH THE WORLD.

ESCORT OUTSTRIPPED.

FROM OUR OWN CORRESPONDENT.
SYDNEY, Monday.

Miss Amy Johnson has flown now into a never-never land, where she is cut off from all communication with the world.

Flying as strongly as ever, she left Port Darwin this morning for Daly Waters, 320 miles away.

She arrived there safely, and after refuelling set out again for Alexandra Station, 200 miles further south, on her flight to Brisbane.

At 5.30 p.m. (local time) she was reported over Brunette Downs, only 40 miles from her destination, and it may safely be presumed that she arrived at Alexandra Station not very many minutes later.

THE PRINCE'S TRIBUTE.

The Prince of Wales, in opening the Congress of the Federation of the Chambers of Commerce of the British Empire, at the Guildhall, yesterday, said:—

"We have all been watching a plucky single-handed attempt to shorten the distance between England and Australia. I am sure that you will join with me in congratulating Miss Johnson on her remarkable achievement."

The Prince's reference was loudly cheered, the delegates' womenfolk in the galleries waving their handkerchiefs.

But there is no communication, either by telephone or telegraph, between that place and the rest of Australia, and it is unlikely that anything more will be heard of this intrepid English girl until she arrives at Long Reach (Queensland) after her next hop to-morrow.

Telegrams and cablegrams of congratulation continue to pour in for Miss Johnson at Port Darwin.

No fewer than 800 telegrams alone were received to-day, and extra telegraph clerks had to be employed at the Darwin Post Office.

CHINESE WOMAN'S GIFTS.

A Chinese resident in Darwin has sent the airwoman a valuable green jade token and green silk pyjamas. In a message thanking the woman for the gift, Miss Johnson says:—

"It is so nice of you. They match my colour scheme perfectly."

To-day it was decided that Miss Johnson will be the guest of the Governor of Queensland during her stay in Brisbane. She will be taken to Government House in a motor-car, following her arrival at the Brisbane air field.

MORE PRESENTS.

Australian newspapers are publishing photographs of the presents which leading Sydney firms are giving to Miss Johnson. These range from silk underwear, gramophones, and hats to wristlet watches.

During the flight from Port Darwin to Daly Waters Station, the difference between the speed of the Jason, Miss Johnson's plane, and the escorting machines at times forced Miss Johnson to fly alone over monotonous and very dangerous stretches of country.

Despite the deadly flat nature of the country, with the vista unbroken even by trees, and a strong 50-mile-an-hour head wind, the English girl landed at Daly Waters as perfectly fit as though she had never left England.

After reaching Long Reach on Tuesday night, Miss Johnson's next lap—to Brisbane—a distance of 650 miles, will be commenced on Wednesday morning.

In a brief talk with the "Daily Chronicle" correspondent before she left Port Darwin, Miss Johnson revealed that, whereas other pilots who had flown from England to Australia and vice versa tried to belittle her attempt before she left England, Captain Kingsford Smith, the famous Australian airman, told her he thought she had a good chance of succeeding.

"'Don't worry. You can do it if you have got the guts to stick it out,' Capt. Smith told me," said Miss Johnson.

PARENTS IN LONDON.

Mrs. Johnson's Pride in Her Daughter's Feat.

Mr. and Mrs. Johnson, Amy's parents, arrived in London last night from Hull.

They were surrounded at the station by reporters and photographers. Mr. Johnson said it was a business visit, but Mrs. Johnson—dark and petite, and with a smile in her eyes—said, "We have come up from Hull for a good time, but, alas, we go back to-morrow."

Trying to answer half a dozen questions at once, Mrs. Johnson said: "I do hope Amy will not try and fly back again. She has done so well, and there is no need for her to run any further risks.

"When I heard of her arrival at Port Darwin I was so thankful I could hardly speak. I am so proud of my daughter, but really I have great confidence in her. You see, I have flown with her myself, and I just loved it."

"We do want to see our little girl as soon as we can," Mr. Johnson said, "and there is plenty of time for her to attempt any more spectacular flights."

AMY'S SPEECH.

"Overwhelmed" by Her Welcome.

PORT DARWIN, Monday.

Before leaving here for Daly Waters, Miss Johnson said the welcome she had been given here was absolutely beyond comprehension.

While it did not upset her, it overwhelmed her, and she could not find words to express what she felt.

When she failed to beat Mr. Hinkler's record, she said, she looked upon the flight more or less as a failure.

She thought public interest had been stimulated by her record flight to India, but that when she dropped back interest would wane.

"When it became impossible for me to keep level with Mr. Hinkler," she said, "I was most disappointed, and decided to finish the flight as quickly as possible. I wanted to reach Australia by air, for my ambitions are set on aviation.

"At no time did I have the slightest doubt about reaching Australia."—Reuter.

AMY JOHNSON, D.B.E.?

Suggestion That a New Honour Should be Created.

One of the questions to receive Mr. MacDonald's early attention on his return to London to-day will be that of a suitable recognition of Miss Johnson's historic flight. It will be for the Prime Minister to advise the King to the most appropriate form of recognition.

Commander Kenworthy, M.P. for Central Hull, who is taking an active interest in the question, said last night that he would like to see Miss Johnson made a Dame of the British Empire.

This would correspond with the honour conferred on Sir J. Alcock and Sir W. Whitten Brown, who made the first Transatlantic flight in 1919, and were created Knights of the British Empire.

In some quarters it is felt that a new honour for women should be established especially to meet the cases of such achievements as that of Miss Johnson.

EARL'S PLUCKY DAUGHTER.

LADY DAVINA LYTTON JUMPS INTO LAKE.

WOMAN'S DEATH.

How she jumped into a lake in a vain effort to save a life was told at an inquest yesterday by Lady Davina Lytton, younger daughter of the Earl of Lytton.

The body, that of Mrs. Elsie Ivory, 42, wife of a Stevenage councillor, was found in the lake at Knebworth Park, near the Hertfordshire seat of Lord Lytton, on Saturday night.

Lady Davina Lytton said at the inquest at Stevenage that she was walking with her cousin, Miss Lafone, when she saw the body floating in the water.

EARL'S EVIDENCE.

"I told my cousin to run for help," said Lady Davina, "and I called to my father, whom I saw standing on the footbridge.

"My father went to fetch the boat as the body was out of my depth.

"Another man came and I jumped in and got the body to the steps."

The Earl of Lytton said that when he arrived at the boathouse his daughter and the young man had got the body out of the water. They did all they could to restore life.

Lady Davina Lytton.

Mrs. Ivory, he said, must have been in the water for only 15 or 20 minutes.

It was said that Mrs. Ivory was missed from a Hitchin nursing home on Saturday evening.

A verdict of suicide during temporary insanity was recorded.

DUKE OF CONNAUGHT.

Suffering From a Cold: Engagement Cancelled.

The Duke of Connaught, who this month celebrated his 80th birthday, is suffering from a slight cold.

Acting under medical advice the Duke was not present at the annual dinner of the Royal Empire Society at the Connaught Rooms, W.C., last night.

MOB LED BY ARMED PRIESTS.

COOLIES BESIEGED IN HOMES.

600 INJURED.

POLICE FIRE IN BAZAAR BATTLE.

RANGOON,
Monday Midnight.

It is now estimated that 26 persons were killed during the Communal rioting here to-day between Burmese and Andhra collies.

Figures given by the General Hospital about 9 p.m. were 276 indoor patients and 300 outdoor patients, casualties being mostly Andhras.

It is further estimated that roughly 100 persons received treatment elsewhere than at the hospital.

A few Anglo-Indians and two European police officers were also injured, but not seriously.

["Andhra" is the name given to a race of Coromandel Coast Indians, many of whom have migrated to the eastward of the Bay of Bengal. As there have been dock strikes at the port of Rangoon, the battle of Andhras and Burmans would seem to be the outcome of labour as well as racial rivalry.]

PRIESTS WITH DAGGERS.

In the afternoon the quarrel took a communal turn.

Over 50 Burmans, armed with lethal weapons, led by phongys (priests) armed with dahs (daggers), paraded the streets, hunting the Andhras and belabouring them severely. Burmans also tried to make forcible entry into the Andhras' quarters.

The Andhras took shelter indoors, but the Burmans were in a recalcitrant mood, and stray assaults continued.

According to one version, the trouble arose owing to some of the Andhras abusing some Burmese coolies, who thereupon assaulted them.

Bazaars and shops were early closed and many offices shut up.

Andhras attacked three Burmese

Continued on Page 2.

LATE NEWS.

MINISTER HIT BY CAR.

As Mr. Arthur Greenwood, Minister of Health, was leaving the House of Commons at midnight he was knocked down by a motor-car.

The only injury he received was a grazed hand, which was treated at Westminster Hospital.

17.4

DAILY EXPRESS, Wednesday, November 20, 1929.

Daily Express

TO-DAY'S WEATHER: Stormy: warm.

NO. 9,222. WEDNESDAY, NOVEMBER 20, 1929. ONE PENNY.

HOUSE OF LORDS DEBATE ON EMPIRE FREE TRADE.

LORD BEAVERBROOK'S SPEECH LAST NIGHT.

VISION OF A UNITED EMPIRE.

"NOT ANOTHER CHANCE."

AN unusually large number of peers, and many members of the House of Commons, were present in the House of Lords last night, when Lord Beaverbrook opened a debate on Empire Free Trade. Mr. Churchill and Mr. Amery sat side by side on the steps of the throne.

Lord Beaverbrook's question was as follows:—

To ask his Majesty's Government if they will do anything to encourage the movement for Free Trade within the Empire.

Lord Beaverbrook elaborated the aims of the Empire Crusaders in a closely-reasoned speech, a verbatim report of which is given below. Every subsequent speaker paid a tribute, even in differing from him, to the great interest of his subject, and Lord Beaverbrook was warmly cheered from all sides of the House when he sat down.

Lord Arnold, the Paymaster-General, replied for the Government, and other speakers were Lord Cushendun, Lord Bledisloe, Lord Beauchamp, Lord Daryngton, Viscount Elibank, and Lord Parmoor.

LORD BEAVERBROOK.

DOMINION MARKETS WAITING.

"I RISE to put the question that is on the paper in my name," began Lord Beaverbrook. "In doing so I may be permitted, perhaps, to explain what we mean by Free Trade within the Empire. We mean

A movement which is to develop the resources, the industries and the commerce of all parts of the Empire to the fullest possible extent, and for that purpose, so far as may be possible, to make of the British Empire one economic unit, and to do everything in our power to break down all obstacles to Free Trade within the Empire, and to make the financial resources of the Empire more fully available for the benefit of all parts of the Empire.

"I suppose in these proposals we shall have general agreement, but when it comes to the method by which we hope to carry them out there may be considerable points of difference.

"We hope to carry them out by building up such a tariff against the foreigner as may be necessary to realise these ideals, and perhaps I may be permitted at once to say that our plan is not the plan put forward by Chamberlain in 1904. In saying that, I do not wish in the very least to say anything against the Chamberlain programme.

Chamberlain Programme.

"On the contrary, I was a supporter of that programme, and a humble follower of Joseph Chamberlain. Our plan does differ from the Chamberlain plan. We only wish to make out our case.

"It is said by the critics of the Chamberlain plan that it was four times rejected by the electorate. I do not agree with that statement at all, and I think most of those who think with me will disagree most profoundly with the suggestion.

"But at the same time, for the reason that the statement is made, we have the right to declare that our plan differs from the Chamberlain plan. It differs in this respect.

The Chamberlain plan proposed a tariff wall round Great Britain; it was insular Protection, and was subject to reciprocity in favour of the Dominions and Colonies.

Our plan is a tariff wall round the whole Empire, and our tariff wall will depend altogether upon, and is conditional upon, a reasonable response from the rest of the Empire.

Then, again, the Chamberlain plan proposed a duty on Empire foodstuffs. We do not propose any duty at all on Empire foodstuffs.

On the contrary, we declare that Empire foodstuffs shall be free of duty if our plan could be carried into effect.

"It is a fact that in 1906 a Chamberlain proposal was actually rejected, and the reason for rejecting it was that the burden that Great Britain would have to bear was so huge, and that because of her immense foreign trade Great Britain would be carrying a much heavier load than her foreign competitors.

"A manifesto recently published by Lord Melchett, to whom I am indebted for some figures which I will lay before the House, justifies our contention that the plan is worth while.

Imports and Exports.

"These figures are to the effect that

the total imports of the Empire amount to £2,200,000,000 yearly.

Of these total imports of £2,200,000,000 only £290,000,000 are moved from one part of the Empire to another, and £1,[illegible] are imported from foreign countries.

"We believe that that immense surplus ought to give us an opportunity which alone makes our plan worth while. We go further, and point out that

since the war the exports of Great Britain to the Dominions and Colonies and Dependencies have grown by 60 per cent., and exports to foreign countries have only gone up 16 per cent.

"These figures give us a further argument for our contention that the plan is worth while.

"Now I come to my next argument, the comparison with the United States of America. This competition has become a great menace to British manufacturing.

In fact, in 1913, the year before the war, the American exports of manufactured goods were only half those of Great Britain.

Now, in the year 1928, the American exports of manufactured goods are actually more than the exports of Great Britain.

America's Position.

"If ever there was a basic industry, it is the iron and steel industry. During these years the American position has changed to such an extraordinary extent that

the Americans now have three times the amount of iron and steel manufactures that we have in Great Britain, and under existing conditions America is actually fighting us in our own Dominions.

In the Dominion of Canada the imports from Great Britain have shown no development at all; in fact, if you take into account the different value of money between the period preceding the war and the present year the imports have declined by ten per cent., and all through these years the Canadian imports from the United States of America have grown constantly.

A similar comparison can be made of the position in Australia, and with very much the same results.

Australia in 1913 bought 52 per cent. of manufactured imports from Great Britain. In 1927, which was the last year which I have available, Australia only imported 41 per cent. of her imports of manufactured goods from Great Britain.

During the same period her imports from the United States of America were nearly doubled.

"What is the reason America's position has improved so rapidly as compared with Great Britain?

"It is due to the mass production in America, and this mass production is founded on the American domestic market.

We argue that the Empire, with a larger area, with a bigger population, has as good, if not a better, opportunity for the same development of mass production and for the same reliance upon a domestic market, but in order to obtain it economic fusion is completely essential.

"That brings me to a question that is very frequently directed to us: Can it be done? We think it can be done.

"We think so because it has been done. It has been done in Canada, for instance. In 1842 there were six different provinces in Canada, four separate tariffs.

"There were in the Dominion of Canada two races and two religions. The first effective step to union was made in 1867. Even so, the year before the union was founded, the province of which I am a native rejected it.

"When the union was brought about in 1867 two provinces refused to join it. The union was carried out, and one of the provinces joined.

"Not only that; when the federation took place the distances were great. It was a long journey from Eastern Canada to Upper and Lower Canada, and there were immense difficulties.

"In winter the eastern provinces had no access to the others at all. The waterways had to be relied upon in summer, and also great time was passed in reaching the various provinces. One province, British Columbia, was distant from Upper Canada by over 2,000 miles.

Tariff Walls.

"There was no communication between British Columbia and Eastern Canada at all; indeed, the area between Upper Canada and British Columbia was almost a desert.

"There was a great mountain range which made it inaccessible. There was no communication by telegraph or telephone, as there is now. There was no access except the waterways, and yet the union was carried out.

"We take great encouragement from the experiences of Canada and of Australia.

"Then there is the United States of America. After the War of Independence there were fifteen separate colonies in America, all setting up tariffs against one another. One State was actually charging heavy duties on the bottoms of ships of other States.

"Then, after the War of Independence, an effort was made to consolidate the various States. Great difficulties had to be overcome, but finally they all joined, and so we have the United States of America.

"These examples are, of course, familiar to you, but there is another which is perhaps more familiar to the people of this country than any other, and that is the German States. There there were separate tariffs, fiscal systems, and separate currencies, but now they have all been merged into what we now know as the German Empire.

Critics Answered.

"If I have made some headway in suggesting that union of the Empire can be secured because it has been reached by others in similar circumstances elsewhere, I would like to pass at once to the criticism directed against us most frequently.

That is: Will the Dominions consent to it? We believe they will.

"I will refer first of all to New Zealand. In the New Zealand House, on July 18, Mr. Cobb, Minister of Industries and Commerce, declared that he knew of no remedy for the state of affairs which had engrossed his attention during the debate except Free Trade within the Empire and a tariff against foreign nations. He went on:

The Empire of which we are a part should not be a mere counter for the display of the manufactures of other countries.

It may be said that we in New Zealand are actuated by selfishness. Are we to be blamed if in doing good for the Empire as a whole we also do good for ourselves?

"I think that represents the attitude of New Zealand. New Zealand not only looks on Empire Free Trade as something feasible, but as beneficial to New Zealand herself.

"Then I come to Canada. There a resolution has been put down by a member of the Progressive Party. This numbers about ten altogether, and has been an important factor in Canadian affairs for some years.

"That resolution proposes in the coming session considering the progressive increase of the British preferential tariff with the objective of free trade

PAGE TWO, COL. ONE.

THE Q-BOAT CAPTAIN TO A MOTHER.

WHY THE GERMAN OFFICER IS HIS FRIEND.

"GRATITUDE."

CAPTAIN HASHAGEN'S SYMPATHY.

COMMANDER NORMAN LEWIS, the English Q-boat captain whose ship was sunk during the war by a German submarine commanded by Captain Hashagen, yesterday sent a letter to the "Daily Express" in reply to the protest by A. L. F., the Liverpool mother, who lost two sons in submarine warfare and another in France.

The mother's protest was against making a hero of Captain Hashagen, who is now in England as the guest of his former enemy, Commander Lewis.

Commander Lewis' letter reads:—

Dear Madam,—

I have read with interest your letter in the "Daily Express," and can fully enter into your feelings as a mother who has lost three sons.

I myself have lost four brothers, and my sister lost her husband, all in the war, and I may tell you that she thoroughly endorses my attitude in the matter of Captain Hashagen.

I would like you to understand my motives in asking him here. The first is a personal one—gratitude for his treatment of me when I was his prisoner, and I cannot help feeling that you as a mother would have some such feelings if your son had been in the same position.

With regard to Captain Hashagen being fêted, the only fêting he has had has been at my hands. His only public appearance was at the Town Hall, Reading, where people could applaud or otherwise.

My other reason for asking him was that I considered it in the interests of peace, and that it was advisable that the British public should be told the true story of the behaviour of a U-boat captain. My experience is that they (U-boat captains) conducted a very distasteful duty in as humane a manner as possible.

I do not think this is a suitable moment to enter into the larger question of whether U-boats should be used for the torpedoing of merchant ships. Undoubtedly in doing so they broke the rules of war, but it seems to me open to question whether any country in a similar position would not have done the same thing.

With my greatest sympathy,

NORMAN LEWIS.

U-BOAT CAPTAIN'S QUERY?

Captain Hashagen, commenting on the letter, said to a "Daily Express" representative yesterday:—

"Why did you publish that letter? What good does it? Does it help towards the peace of nations, for which I came to England to speak at the request of my friend?

"Believe me, I can fully understand the feelings of that mother, and I am deeply sorry for her; but remember I only did my duty and carried out orders just as the officers and men of your ships.

"How do we know if it was I that sank the ships her poor boys sailed on? I can honestly say that I did not use unnecessary cruelty, and I always endeavoured to spare the lives of crews when I sent ships to the bottom. I do hope this English mother will believe me when I say in all sincerity that my only interest now is for everlasting peace, and that our German mothers suffered as did she."

READERS' VIEWS.

The "Daily Express" has received many letters on the subject, points from which are as follows:—

From Lieut.-Colonel Graham Deakin, D.S.O., of Birmingham:—

Captain Lewis seems to think that having had most of the brave men who were compelled to serve with him foully murdered, whilst he himself was saved, the offer to have a drink entitles their murderer to be considered a good fellow.

Personally, I should consider myself a traitor to the men with whom I was privileged to serve and who suffered and gave their lives while fighting with me if I adopted such an attitude. I am happy to think that this feeling is not typical of the majority of British officers, and that Captain Lewis is an unfortunate exception.

"Frightfulness."

It would be interesting to know how many hospital ships were included in Captain Hashagen's many successes.

Kew. A. B.

Names of His Victims.

I suggest that Captain Hashagen visits the memorial to seamen on Tower Hill. There he will see the names of every boat he torpedoed, together with the lists of crews whom he sent to their doom.

I also hope that some of his friends (British! save the mark) will go with him to cheer.

London, S.W.1. E. Carey.

"Past Cannot be Undone."

Will not that mother and all mothers try to understand that it was not the officers who were "cheered," but their earnest endeavour to make peace, in order that the sons of the present and future generations shall not be sacrificed? The past cannot be undone.

London, E.11. E. J. W.

"Treachery."

The fêting and feasting of Captain Hashagen is an act of treachery to the dead, who lie at the bottom of the sea and in the battlefields of Europe.

(Councillor) Henry Hinkley,
Trinity House Pilot and
ex-Mayor of Gravesend.

MADGE CLIFTON.

RICH FATHER KILLS HIS DAUGHTER.

"MERCY MURDER" OF DUMB CRIPPLE.

"Daily Express" Correspondent.

NEW YORK,
Tuesday, Nov. 19.

Mr. John A. Barton, fifty-four years of age, a millionaire resident of Two Harbors, Minnesota, and his daughter Beatrice, aged seventeen, who had been crippled and mute from birth, have been found dead with bullet wounds in a motor-car on a lonely road on the outskirts of Two Harbors.

The father's hand still clutched the revolver with which it is believed he killed his daughter as an act of "mercy murder," after repeated unsuccessful efforts to have her cured.

BANK FUNDS IN ORDER.

Mr. Barton was president of the First National Bank of Two Harbors. The funds of the bank were found in perfect order, and he had no known financial worries.

He took Beatrice and his two other daughters to the Presbyterian Church on Sunday, leaving Mrs. Barton at home. The two other daughters attended the church service, Mr. Barton saying that he wished to take Beatrice for a drive.

They did not reappear, and search was made for the motor-car, which was finally found several miles away with the two dead bodies on the front seat, Mr. Barton collapsed over the wheel, and Beatrice leaning against him.

COMMUNISTS IN S. AFRICA.

THIRD INTERNATIONAL ARRAIGNED.

"Daily Express" Correspondent.

PRETORIA, Tuesday, Nov. 19.

Mr. Pirow, Minister of Justice, speaking here to-night, justified the Durban police raids on native quarters, declaring that the Government possessed evidence that the native unrest had been fanned by organisations in touch with the Third International.

The influence of the unrest had spread to Rhodesia, and matters had reached such a stage that unless the unrest was checked it would lead to rioting by the natives so serious as to invite reprisals by Europeans.

Instructions had been given in writing by the Third International, Mr. Pirow added, that a fight against anti-native Bills should be waged in a revolutionary manner, that the mines should be penetrated by all possible means, and that a partial stoppage of work in all industrial concerns should take place on December 11, in addition to the demonstration to be held on December 16 ("Dingaan's Day").

In the light of these instructions the Government had decided to force the issue of the poll-tax.

"I am fully aware," Mr. Pirow declared, "that the present lull is only temporary. The root of the trouble is the agitator, and the Government are therefore proceeding at the earliest opportunity with an amendment to the Riotous Assemblies Bill."

NEW CANADIAN CABINET.

POSSIBLE RESHUFFLING OF POSTS.

"Daily Express" Correspondent.

OTTAWA, Tuesday, Nov. 19.

The return of the Prime Minister, Mr. Mackenzie King, from his western tour on November 24 will be followed by a reorganisation of the Cabinet in consequence of the recent death of Mr. James Alexander Robb, Minister of Finance.

Conflicting influences between Eastern Protectionists, who favour Mr. W. D. Euler, Minister of Customs, or Mr. James Malcolm, Minister of Trade and Commerce, for the post, and the Western low tariff interests, favouring Mr. C. A. Dunning, Minister of Railways, may result in a compromise by the selection of Colonel J. L. Ralston, the present Minister of National Defence, who comes from Nova Scotia.

MR. KELLOGG IN LONDON.

Mr. F. B. Kellogg, the former United States Secretary of State, accompanied by Mrs. Kellogg, arrived in London last night from America.

Mr. Kellogg, who is on a holiday visit, expects to remain in England about ten days.

SHIPYARD DISPUTE SETTLED.

A settlement of the shipyard joiners' dispute was reached at the Ministry of Labour last night, and the lockout notices were withdrawn.

DR. KNOWLES WINS HIS FIGHT FOR FREEDOM.

SISTERS' TEARS OF JOY ON HEARING APPEAL RESULT.

DR. Benjamin Knowles, formerly a soldier and a Government official, found guilty by a Colonial court of the wilful murder of his wife—once "Madge Clifton," popular music-hall comedienne—in a Gold Coast bungalow, will shortly walk out into the world again, through the iron-barred gates of Maidstone Prison, a free man.

His appeal against his conviction and sentence to imprisonment during the term of his natural life was yesterday allowed by the Judicial Committee of the Privy Council.

"We have decided," said the Lord Chancellor (Lord Sankey), president over a bench of four other judges, when he made known their decision in the Privy Council library above Downing-street—"we have decided that we will humbly advise his Majesty to allow the appeal and to quash the conviction. Our reasons will be given later."

ORDER IN COUNCIL.

Dr. Knowles, therefore, will be free when all the formalities have been completed—the advice to the King, the King's instructions by Order in Council to the Home Secretary, and the official order to the Governor of Maidstone Prison to "release forthwith one Benjamin Knowles, whom you have in safe custody."

He was told the news last night. A telephone message had been sent from the Home Office to the governor, who passed it on, with his congratulations.

Dr. Knowles was given privileges immediately. He was no longer regarded as a prisoner awaiting appeal. He had his own clothes handed to him, tobacco, cigarettes, newspapers—indeed, anything he wanted. He could do much as he liked until the signed parchment for his release came to the governor's hand.

The Privy Council Court, for once in its long course of important legal arguments and weighty judgments, gave a thrill of real human interest at the close of the appeal proceedings yesterday afternoon.

The five judges had listened the whole morning to the searching criticisms by Mr. D. N. Pritt, K.C., counsel for Dr. Knowles, on the long judgment of the judge of the divisional court at Kumasi, Ashanti, who, sitting without a jury, found the prisoner guilty of murder and sentenced him to be hanged.

Mr. Pritt played havoc with many points of that judgment, and it was obvious, from the interjected questions of the judges of the Privy Council, that they were in agreement with some of the submissions.

THE ATTORNEY-GENERAL.

Sir William Jowitt, the Attorney-General, was then called on for his reply for the Crown. Sir William spoke finely, as he always does, threw up the strong lines in the case for the prosecution, emphasised where, in his opinion, the judge of Ashanti was right, but plainly he had no heart in his advocacy.

He concluded with this sentence, in answer to a question from Lord Darling:—

I agree it would be wrong indeed that a man should spend all the remainder of his life in prison if there is any reasonable doubt at all about his guilt.

The court was cleared for a few

PAGE THREE, COL. ONE.

LATE NEWS.

Broadcasting Programmes on Page 13

17.5

SUNDAY SPECIAL

NEWS OF THE WORLD

No. 4,980 [Estab. 1843] Registered at the General Post Office as a Newspaper Telephones: Central 3030 SUNDAY, APRIL 9, 1939 Telegrams: Worldly, Fleet, London PRICE TWOPENCE

Certified Net Sale Exceeds 3,750,000 Copies Per Issue

MUSSOLINI PLANS "CONQUERING HERO" ENTRY INTO ZOG'S CAPITAL

King's Flight Through Greece With Queen And Baby Son

DAY OF TALKS IN DOWNING-ST.

(SPECIAL CABLEGRAMS TO THE "NEWS OF THE WORLD")

ITALY'S INVASION OF ALBANIA—THE STATE WITH TWO AEROPLANES AND TEN TANKS—CULMINATED YESTERDAY IN THE OCCUPATION OF TIRANA, THE CAPITAL, AND THE FLIGHT OF KING ZOG TO JOIN HIS YOUNG WIFE AND HER NEWLY-BORN BABY IN GREECE.

In London all available Ministers—nearly half the Cabinet—met at No. 10, Downing-street, to discuss the position.

After the meeting it was announced that the Premier had decided to cut short his holiday in Scotland and return to London by the night express.

Italy's attack on Albania was carried out by some 35,000 men, supported by scores of warships and hundreds of 'planes.

Messages from Albanian sources yesterday claimed that "ferocious resistance" was offered to the invaders, but there could be only one end to a struggle so pitifully one-sided.

In little more than 24 hours after their first landing the Italians were in occupation of Tirana, King Zog was in flight, and peaceful Adriatic towns had known the horror and devastation of modern war.

Piloting his own 'plane, Count Ciano, Italian Foreign Minister, arrived at Tirana later in the day, and is now supervising the formation of a new Government to replace that of King Zog.

Mussolini—"conquering hero"—will fly to Tirana either to-day or to-morrow.

Italy's action has the full diplomatic support of Germany, while Jugo-Slavia—the country most immediately affected by the invasion—has decided to do nothing, and was thanked by Mussolini yesterday for its attitude.

In America, last night, Mr. Cordell Hull, Secretary of State, denounced the invasion of Albania as "a threat to the peace of the world."

KING ZOG OF ALBANIA.

COUNT CIANO ORGANISING NEW GOVERNMENT

MAP OF SOUTH-EASTERN EUROPE, SHOWING THE POSITION OF ALBANIA.

MESSAGES from Jugo-Slavia last night reported that Albanian resistance, previously "very strong," seemed to have been broken.

It was stated that at Pogradesti, on the Albanian shore of Lake Okhrida, the road to Tirana was no longer passable owing to congestion caused by the motors and lorries of the Albanian troops and the flight of the population southwards.

Though resistance seems to have been smashed, occasional explosions and rifle-fire can still be heard from the mountains.

Lorries carrying exhausted soldiers and wounded have been passing through Pogradesti. Albanian refugees are already beginning to arrive on the Jugo-Slav bank of Lake Okhrida, which is reached by fishing-boats.

Mechanised troops under General Guzzoni had arrived at Tirana from the Adriatic seaport of Durazzo at 9.30 a.m.

A few minutes later relays of Italy's latest three-engined bombers began to land at the airport, watched by thousands of bewildered Albanians.

No sooner did the landing wheels come to a stop than tall, fully-equipped grenadiers stepped from the machines and lined up in parade formation on the ground.

REGIMENT ARRIVES BY AIR

By 4 p.m. an entire regiment of 3,000 grenadiers had been flown from the Grottaglio Airport, on the outskirts of Taranto, Italy.

Meanwhile Count Ciano, piloting his own 'plane, had arrived to supervise the formation of a new Government.

It was stated authoritatively that the Italians have decided to outlaw King Zog. If he is found in Albania he will be held for trial.

The new Government will depend entirely on Italy for foreign policy and national defence, but the new Albanian Cabinet will be constituted virtually on a "Home Rule" basis, which means that Albanians will be given a form of local autonomy.

It is even suggested in Italian quarters that King Victor Emmanuel will be given some sort of title in connection with Albania, which would be tantamount to making the country an integral part of the Italian Empire.

According to a dispatch from Tirana to the Italian news agency, the flight of the Albanian Government on Friday was followed by an outbreak of shooting and rioting in Tirana, which lasted nearly all night.

Order was restored, however, before the arrival of the Italian troops.

"For some hours," the communique stated, "the capital was at the mercy of convicts freed from prison and supplied with arms, who pillaged the royal palace and the residences of King Zog's sisters."—Reuter, Exchange, and British United Press.

YOUNG QUEEN'S ORDEAL

BEDSIDE APPEAL: "WORLD MUST HELP ALBANIA"

Athens, Saturday.—Fleeing from the overwhelming might of the Italian invaders, King Zog, his Queen, and their four-day-old son, left the town of Florina, on the Greek-Albanian border to-day.

Although some reports say they have arrived at Salonika, it is believed that they are on the way to the Hotel Theoxavia, in the small seaside village of Portavia, 90 miles south of Salonika.

Wearing civilian clothes, and looking weary and strained, King Zog had arrived at Florina just after noon to-day.

His 23-year-old Queen had preceded him last night, reaching Florina with her son after a nightmare journey from Tirana.

The King arrived with an escort travelling in 16 motor-cars and two motor-lorries. He immediately went to the bedside of his wife, and there was an emotional scene as he greeted her and his baby son.

Among King Zog's suite were 30 Army officers, dishevelled and unshaven, a number of high Civil Servants of Albania, and several women.

A crowd of several thousand Greeks silently watched the arrival, for which the police cleared the main square of Florina.

King Zog quietly greeted one of his sisters on the stairs of the hotel as he was on his way to the Queen's room.

APPEAL TO THE WORLD

Before her husband's arrival the Queen had sent a message to the world through her American-born grandmother, Mme. d'Estrale d'Ekna.

"The outside world," her message ran, "must do something for my Albania. Its brave people will resist to the end, but it is such a small country it cannot possibly hold out any length of time."

The story of King Zog's defiance of the Italians was told by Mme. d'Estrale d'Ekna to-day.

"Although the Queen was ill when King Zog decided that she must leave she pleaded with him to allow her to remain at his side," she related. "As we were preparing to leave, 57 Italian bombers were flying over Tirana dropping leaflets.

"The King had gone to the front. The Italians had already taken Durazzo, but the Albanian soldiers were resisting at several points outside that city.

"When the King reached the front an Italian 'plane landed near his headquarters, bringing negotiators from Mussolini. He received them. They told him that Mussolini wanted the Albanian Army to lay down its arms so that the Italians could move in quietly.

"King Zog refused to capitulate in any way, and said, 'I surrender to nobody.'

"So the negotiators departed, and the Italian attacks were renewed.

"Before we left Tirana we heard that one of the Italian ships had been sunk off Durazzo.

"Our party included all King Zog's sisters, and the wives and children of members of the Cabinet.

"We were accompanied by a detachment of Albanian cavalry, and had to move very slowly over the mountains because of the Queen's condition."—Reuter and British United Press.

MOTHER'S TERROR!

PREMIER'S ALL-NIGHT DASH TO LONDON

Mr. Attlee Asks for Recall of Parliament

(By Our Political Correspondent)

AFTER yesterday's meeting of Cabinet Ministers at No. 10, Downing-street, it was learned that the Albanian situation is regarded by the Government as a matter of the utmost gravity.

The principal reason for Mr. Chamberlain's decision to return to London is his desire to be in direct consultation with his colleagues. The Premier was due to arrive at Euston this morning after an all-night journey from Scotland.

It was only on Thursday that he left London to spend a few days fishing at the home of Lord Forbes in Aberdeenshire.

Another development yesterday was the announcement that Mr. Attlee, Leader of the Opposition, has decided to ask Mr. Chamberlain to recall Parliament immediately to consider the international situation, and particularly recent events in Albania.

The Liberals are urging a similar course, and their leaders sent a telegram to the Premier.

OFFICIAL STATEMENT

Yesterday's meeting of Ministers lasted an hour and a half, and at its conclusion the following official statement was issued:—

"The Ministers heard a report summarising the information at present in possession of the Government as to the position in Albania.

"The situation is still somewhat obscure in regard to a number of important factors, and it has therefore been arranged that the Ministers concerned should remain in or near London for the present.

"No further meeting has, however, been fixed."

In the absence of the Prime Minister, the chair was taken at the meeting of Ministers by Sir John Simon. Mr. Chamberlain was in constant telephonic communication with No. 10.

Lord Halifax spent a considerable time at the Foreign Office in the morning and called again in the afternoon, when he was visited by Mr. Attlee, M. Corbin, the French Ambassador, M. Kurti, the Albanian Minister, and Mr. Kennedy, the American Ambassador.

Sensational rumours were current in London last night regarding large concentrations of troops in certain parts of Germany.

The Dutch military authorities have taken all necessary steps for calling up reserves at a few hours' notice.

European States, large and small, are anxiously awaiting the reaction of Britain and France to the coup in Albania.

"Does this mean the end of the Mediterranean agreement between Britain and Italy?" was the question being asked in Embassies and Legations throughout the world yesterday.

No official pronouncement on this point was obtainable in the absence of the Premier from London.

Foreign diplomatic circles in London last night were gravely concerned with the future trend of events in the Balkans.

In particular, there was some apprehension in Greek quarters at the presence of Italian troops on the Greek frontier and the movements of Italian warships in the Aegean.

Considerable importance is attached in Paris and London to the hurried conversations in Istanbul between M. Gafencu, the Rumanian Foreign Minister, and M. Saradjoglu, the Turkish Foreign Secretary.

HITLER APPROVES

'PHONE TALKS WITH DUCE BEFORE INVASION

From all over the world yesterday came a spate of messages telling of warnings, threats, prophecies, diplomatic activity, and various reactions to the invasion of Albania.

Germany is backing up her partner in the Axis.

Italy's action has the full approval of Hitler. It is understood that Fuehrer and Duce had a long telephone conversation before the Italian troops moved.

Foreign political circles in Berlin connect the Italo-German staff conference at Innsbruck with the Italian move.

Berlin expects that it will prove an effective check to any possible Jugo-Slav move to join an anti-aggression front.

It is also pointed out that for the first time since the Dictators began their expansion policy Italy will on this occasion reap the sole benefit, while Germany threatens from the background.

Jugo-Slavia, which has a treaty of friendship with Italy, is taking no action.

The officially-inspired newspaper "Politika" stated yesterday: "In the spirit of her policy of friendship with all neighbours, Jugo-Slavia hopes that a rapid solution will be found which will give satisfaction to the two parties, without causing the least harm to Jugo-Slav interests.

"The latter are recognised by all, and are provided for by the agreements between Italy and Jugo-Slavia."

France is united in denouncing Italy, and the general opinion is that while the immediate repercussions of the new Axis move will be localised, its ultimate consequences may be very serious.

The moral is drawn that the British discussions for an anti-aggression pact must be pushed forward rapidly.

Anxiety is felt in the Paris Press as to whether the move in Albania is not the beginning of an Axis plan for a combined drive into the Eastern Mediterranean and beyond.

Russia read in the Government newspaper "Izvestia," that the invasion of Albania was designed to frighten the Jugo-Slavs and prevent them co-operating with Britain.—Reuter and British United Press.

TO-DAY'S WEATHER

FAIR (Official)

The weather forecast for to-day, issued from the Meteorological Office, is as follows:—

WIRELESS PROGRAMMES ON PAGE FOURTEEN.

QUEEN GERALDINE OF ALBANIA.

U.S. CONDEMNS INVASION

ACTION "IS THREAT TO WORLD PEACE"

NEW COUP BY HITLER EXPECTED SOON

WASHINGTON, Saturday.—President Roosevelt to-day denounced the invasion of Albania as a threat to the peace of the world.

The denunciation was contained in a formal statement issued by Mr. Cordell Hull, Secretary of State, after he had conferred by telephone with the President, who is at Warm Springs, Georgia.

"The forcible and violent invasion of Albania," the statement declared, "is unquestionably an additional threat to the peace of the world.

"It would be short-sighted not to take sight of this further development.

"Any threat to world peace seriously concerns all nations and violates the will of all peoples throughout the world that their Governments shall lead them not toward war, but along the paths of peace.

"It is scarcely necessary to add that the inevitable effect of this incident, taken with similar incidents, is further to destroy confidence and undermine the economic stability of every country in the world, thus affecting our own welfare."

QUESTION OF ARMS EMBARGO

Mr. Hull indicated that an arms embargo against Italy under the Neutrality Act was under discussion, but said that such action had not been considered officially at length thus far.

Diplomatic officials and experts of the United States Army and Navy regard the invasion of Albania as a prelude to larger military operations by the Totalitarian States.

Military officials here stated this morning that they were convinced that Germany would soon invade Danzig and the Polish Corridor, predictions being that this would occur *before April 15.*

It is also considered a strong possibility that Germany would simultaneously try to occupy all Silesia, since, with Poland resisting an invasion of the Corridor, there would be no extra risk to Germany in invading Silesia as well, and the spoils would be richer.—Reuter, Exchange and B.U.P.

THIS MAY BE A "TERROR" WEEK-END

Threats to Celebrate "The Rising"

("NEWS OF THE WORLD" SPECIAL)

IF opinions held in authoritative quarters are well-founded, then it may be that to-day and to-morrow Scotland Yard and the provincial police will find themselves confronted with an outbreak of organised sabotage on a scale far more serious than anything the I.R.A. terrorists have yet attempted.

It is to be an "anniversary celebration" of the disastrous Easter week rising in 1916.

"Squeakers," or informers, in various parts of the country have gone to the police with extraordinary stories of concentrations of men and explosives both in London and the Midlands.

Many of the reports are discredited, but from evidence in possession of the authorities, it is practically certain that outrages on a grand scale are contemplated.

A particularly disquieting rumour, which has reached the Special Branch, suggests that attempts will be made within the next 48 hours to emulate the exploit of George Gilmoure, an earlier member of the I.R.A., who in 1925 rescued 19 prisoners single-handed from Mountjoy Gaol, in Dublin.

Gilmoure, disguised in a policeman's uniform, walked alone into the prison, overpowered the gatekeeper, seized his keys and released every I.R.A. man under sentence.

As a final gesture Gilmoure relocked the prison gates as he left and threw the keys over the wall.

Dartmoor, Maidstone, Parkhurst, Pentonville, Wandsworth, Wormwood Scrubs, and Strangeways in Manchester have all been mentioned as prisons where demonstrations have been planned, and the authorities, naturally, are taking no chances.

EVERY MAN ON DUTY

Fully aware of the possibilities of "Easter Week" they have summoned every man to duty, and police reserves will stand by at the stations in the vicinity of the prisons.

Throughout the whole of this week every public building, every bridge, railway station, canal, power-station, pumping-station, gas works, and electricity concern will be guarded and patrolled night and day.

Leave has been stopped to uniform and plain-clothes police alike, and special constables will take over practically all the ordinary and routine duties.

As a matter of fact, the specials went on duty on Friday in order to give the regular police a "breather" before the week-end.

Windsor Castle, where the Royal Family is spending Easter, is to have a special guard, and similarly Scotland Yard itself, the Home Office, Downing-street, Chequers, and the residence of every Cabinet Minister and judge will be carefully protected.

Pedestrians and motorists will discover extra police on all the Thames bridges to-day, and every vehicle entering Blackwall and Rotherhithe Tunnels is to be scrutinised and possibly challenged.

Threats to bomb Woolwich Arsenal have been taken with some seriousness, and here again the normal guard has been strengthened.

In the meantime Flying Squad men are making a systematic search of the bed of the Grand Union Canal at Paddington, which has been drained for the purpose.

It is believed that a charge of gelignite has been deposited where it can be set off by a passing barge.

Yesterday the police of St. Heliers, Jersey, received a box, which was found to contain 56 detonators packed in sawdust. An accompanying note stated that it was "sent by an Irishman."

LATEST NEWS

17.6

of riots in the *Daily Chronicle* of 1930 (17.4) and the *Daily Express* of 1979 (16.2). You can extend your analysis of riots and demonstrations (for example) by taking published studies of the way they have been covered on different occasions, and comparing a current treatment with the findings of such studies. On demonstrations, see the discussion of 'News at Ten' in chapter 4 of this book; the analysis of the Grosvenor Square anti-Vietnam demonstration of 1968 in Halloran *et al.* (1970) or Murdock (1973); and the study of the May Day demonstrations of 1973 in Young and Brooke Crutchley (1977).

Time-based comparisons can also be used to set news-discourse into the context of historical developments. The *News of the World* of April 1939 (17.6) relates an event – the fascist invasion of Albania – which forms part of the build-up of international tension prior to the Second World War. Similarly, the *Daily Chronicle*'s report of May 1930 (17.4) on government proposals to deal with unemployment can be compared with those reported in the 1980s. In this context, the headline story in the *Daily Express* of November 1929 (17.5) is interesting – not for the story itself, nor for its presentation, neither of which are very remarkable – but for the prominence given to a speech by a peer in the House of Lords. Not only is it the lead story, but it is reported verbatim. This may be connected with the fact that the speech was made by Lord Beaverbrook, and that Lord Beaverbrook owned the *Daily Express*. But such overt accessing of the owner's voice is unusual nowadays. There has been a shift away from openly stated propaganda towards less easily contestable appeals to the ideology of common sense.

Comparisons across cultures don't always yield the differences you might expect. The *Daily Times* (18.1) looks more familiar (both visually and verbally) than does the *Morning Star* (18.2). But the *Daily Times* is Nigerian, whilst the *Morning Star*, though British, speaks from a position which is paradoxically more culturally remote from the mainstream of Fleet Street than the popular tabloid formula of the African paper. Similar to the 1929 *Daily Express* in both layout and in its overt championing of a political cause, the *Morning Star* is published by the Communist Party to provide a platform for the Labour movement.

4. *Compare media* Have a look at whether the treatment of a topic on television differs from the way it is treated in the news-

papers. To do this you can either take a particular topic (like youth, women, Northern Ireland, the economy, industrial relations); or you can take a complete sequence of TV news and see how the various stories are treated (if at all) in the papers. What do newspapers carry that TV news leaves out? Are the same stories regularly carried in both media? Do both media 'make sense' of events in similar ways?

5. *Compare experience* If a 'newsworthy' event like a march or a royal visit is scheduled for your area, go to it and take notes (several of you, if possible). Compare what you saw with the treatment given in the next day's papers. A good example of the use of observer notes is in Cohen (1980). Visit the nearest magistrates' or crown court, and compare the way you 'make sense' of the cases with the way they are told in the local evening paper.

Another accessible way of isolating material in the newspapers which you can then discuss is *content analysis*. This requires the collection of a reasonably large sample of stories (at least a week's output), which is then classified under various categories. You can find out how content analysis has been done by referring to Glasgow Media Group (1976 and 1980), to Fiske and Hartley (1978, chapter 2), to Fiske (1982) and to Williams (1966, chapter 3).

There is a further selection of projects on news in Cohen and Young (1973), where the final part of the book is devoted to 'Do-it-yourself Media Sociology' (pp. 369–83).

Television

Many of the questions and activities I've proposed for newspapers are of course relevant also to television news. But TV news is a special case – it is seen by more people than is news in newspapers, and it is often regarded as more impartial and trustworthy than they are.

The main problem in analysing it is of course its transience. If you are unable to record it any other way, it can still be useful to note down the main stories, 'key' words and images, and the weighting given to various segments of a story. Chapter 7 will provide you with a framework from which you can work. But it is obviously better to be able to analyse the real thing rather than a written record, because so much of TV news's meaning potential is generated by the relations between particular images and the commentary, and by the visual and verbal codes in operation. Monaco

Daily Times

THE INDEPENDENT NEWSPAPER

21,240 Monday May 17, 1976 10k

* THE seven wait as the members of the firing squad await the order to shoot.

7 EXECUTED

* GOMWALK at the stakes before the gun spoke.

COUP co-ordinator B. S. Dimka and ex-governor Joseph Gomwalk were among seven more people executed by a firing squad at the week-end for their part in the February 13 abortive coup.

The five others executed with them were Lt. S. Kwale, Warrant Officer, H.E. Bawa, Col. I. Buka, Major J. K. Afolabi and Mr. H. Shaiyen of the Nigeria Police Force.

Gomwalk, Dimka face the guns

The death sentences were confirmed by the Supreme Military Council last Friday along with other conclusions of the military tribunal set up to try those connected with the abortive coup.

On March 11, 32 persons, among them, Major-General I. D. Bisalla, who was the Commissioner for Defence, were executed by firing squads for their part in the attempted coup in which the former Head of State, General Murtala Muhammed, was killed.

Also killed in the abortive coup was the former Governor of Kwara State, Col. Ibrahim Taiwo.

The week-end execution which started at 4.20 p.m. lasted for 20 minutes. It was watched exclusively by soldiers, policemen and warders.

Eleven others tried along with the executed men got life sentences.

They include a former police commissioner for Kwara State, S. K. Dimka, brother of B. S. Dimka.

The rest are: D. Contulla, Gyang Pam, Captain C. Wuyep, Captain A. A. Maidobo, Warrant Officer II E. Izah, Sergeant I. Bupwada, second Lt. A. Walbe, Major A. K. Abang, S. Anyadofu and Mrs Helen Gomwalk, wife of the brother of executed J. D. Gomwalk.

Captain I. Gowon, younger brother of Yakubu Gowon, was jailed 15 years.

Also jailed was J. Tuwe who got 10 years while Lt. Col. J. S. Madugu was sentenced to two years' imprisonment.

Former Bendel State Governor, Mr Samuel Osaigbovo Ogbemudia and Squadron Leader Moses Bala Gowon were among those discharged.

Altogether, 56 persons were discharged out of a total of 219 military personnel and civilians recommended by the board of inquiry for trial.

Before the trial, 219 military personnel and civilians were arrested soon after the abortive coup.

So far, 39 have been executed while 15 got various terms of imprisonment.

Climax of Feb 13 coup bid

When does business die?

APPARENTLY, all businesses, big and small in this country, are struggling to exist, within this struggle many have already given up. Our own special correspondent and business analyst has, therefore, chosen this moment to ask: When does your business die? Find out his answers and hints from the BUSINESS TIMES tomorrow. In the same number, you'll know all about the deepening crisis in Federal Government's Warri-based Petroleum Institute.

18.1

★ **Morning Star**

Unite the left!

3865/14639 12p ★ INCORPORATING THE DAILY WORKER THURSDAY NOVEMBER 2 1978

DAILY Mirror THE Sun Another for 'tits' league DAILY STAR

THE STAR that will launch a thousand "tits and bums" appears on the news stands from today.

Its sale will be immense, enormous media excitement will be generated, and circulation black eyes will be given, for a day or two at least, to Sun and Mirror, the Daily Star's companions and rivals in the most miry end of the press stables.

Stars give light, energy, hope—that is their image. This new "Star" will give none of all that.

But the Star that is now in the middle of a tremendous effort to launch a thousand volunteers to help raise its circulation gives all three.

We should like to have been able to extend a special welcome to a new daily paper that spoke for the trade unions, for the women, for the young people, or for some other section of the millions unrepresented in the media.

The launching of the Express Newspapers' new paper merely rams home the need for all of us to win a new reader for the Morning Star.

Only "a moron in a hurry" would mix up the Daily Star with the Morning Star, Mr. Justice Foster said in the recent court case over the Star title.

Yet London's commercial LBC radio yesterday reported "growing excitement in Manchester where they are all ready to print their new paper, the Morning Star."

That court affair is over—though the possible confusion obviously remains—but the same David-and-Goliath contest goes on every day of the week.

Will you volunteer for it?

Who'll back the one ★ Morning Star that's different?

PREMIER STEPS UP WAR ON PAY

By MARTIN GOSTWICK

A FEROCIOUS declaration of war to the bitter end by the Prime Minister to force through phase four stunned Labour MPs yesterday.

Following his veiled hints of such an offensive during Labour's Blackpool conference, Mr. Callaghan yesterday spelled out in brutal detail how the government would use weapons in retaliation against those who breached the 5 per cent limit.

The Prime Minister started Labour's last year in office by leaving on the shelf his party conference's decisions for a reflationary strategy to revive Britain, and making clear that he would not budge an inch from his "three-legged stool" of economic policy—pay curbs, and monetary and fiscal policies.

TAX THREAT

Whatever is being offered to TUC leaders in the current secret talks on pay, Mr. Callaghan made it abundantly clear that the five per cent sticks, with fierce sanctions to back it.

"If the pay limit is breached, the government will be forced to strengthen restraints through the other two stools. This could include higher taxes. This is what the Chancellor might have to do."

It could also mean higher interest rates, and further cuts in public spending. Firms would find it harder to get credit.

"They would not be able to pay so much, or production might be slowed down."

Fords were first on the list for a clear hint of sanctions if the management settled above 5 per cent.

SCRUTINY

Mr. Callaghan challenged its management to "accept a public obligation and a public responsibility to account to the country" for any price increases attributable to a wage settlement of around 15 per cent.

Warning that any settlement's impact on Fords' prices would be scrutinised "very carefully," he asked: "If Fords get 15 per cent, who will get nought per cent? Will the consequences be that Leylands get nought per cent?"

PREMIER CALLAGHAN

He declared this would be a "make or break winter" for incomes policy, appealing to trade unionists not to make it "a winter of strikes."

The government would not evade its duty to warn or to take action if necessary to enforce its will. The country would support the government.

He hoped the public mood would not change when things got rough, with people then demanding "give them the money for the sake of a quiet life." No one had produced any evidence to persuade the government that a 5 per cent limit was not the best figure.

DEVOLUTION

Outraged by this blatant rejection and denial of all the government has been told by the labour movement this summer, left MP Eric Heffer (Walton) protested that 5 per cent was "ridiculous" for the low paid.

"They have a perfect right to very much higher wages than they are getting at the moment, and it is the government's duty to give them a square deal," Mr. Heffer declared.

Mr. Callaghan responded with yet more threats: "The faint hearts who say we should not be rigid, or that we are fighting the wrong battle, or that we cannot succeed, should make up their minds which side they are on."

The referenda on devolution for Scotland and Wales will be held in those two countries on St. David's Day, Thursday, March 1, 1979, after the completion of an updated register of electors in February, Mr. Callaghan announced.

Asked left MP Ron Thomas (Bristol NW) later: "What the hell does he mean, whose side are we on? We are on the side of the decisions of the Labour Party conference and the TUC."

Newly elected executive member Dennis Skinner condemned the missing of a "golden opportunity" in the Queen's speech to carry Labour into the next election with an alternative strategy of reflating the economy and redistributing wealth. But Labour MPs welcomed the positive commitment to more funds for the National Enterprise Board and marginally increased social provisions in the Queen's speech.

(Packed timetable: p.3)

Topless profit package

A BARE-BREASTED young woman gyrates before the camera as the photographer urges her to "look classy, very expensive . . . unattainable."

And so the preparation went ahead for today's new tabloid, the Daily Star, as seen on the BBC-1 television programme "Tonight" yesterday.

But newspaper tycoon Victor Matthews is not sure that he wants his new daily newspaper to be left lying around his home.

He admitted the paper would have "tits and bums" and didn't think he would want his "youngsters" to see a paper that his advertising executives have been telling all and sundry is specially designed for the "young readers."

The boss of Trafalgar House, the owners of the Express Newspapers group, told TV viewers last night: "My aim is to see a profit of something like £10 million a year from Express Newspapers."

But Express Newspapers which is producing the new paper in Manchester still has some stern problems to face.

Minutes before the television programme was on the air the company reached agreement with the National Graphical Association on a manning dispute which could have held up the new paper.

Lavish banquet

And these troubles may not be over since the situation must be reviewed in six weeks' time.

Mr. Derek Jameson, Daily Express editor who will oversee the production, was in chuckling mood, accusing one rival of "sanctimonious hypocrisy."

Crime correspondent Jimmy Nicholson was obligingly given dramatic beat background music and spoke of covering London assassinations.

Express Newspapers chief Victor Matthews was confident that the new daily would "find its place in the market." And preparations went ahead for a lavish launching banquet.

As for politics, "We will support any party that really believes in capitalist society," said Mr. Matthews. At the moment that meant "basically the Conservative Party."

The new tabloid was referred to as "The Star" throughout.

CANCEL VISIT TO IRAN —MPs TELL QUEEN

By Our Political Correspondent

MORE than 50 Labour MPs last night tabled a Commons motion calling on the government to cancel the Queen's proposed courtesy call on the Shah of Iran.

This was the immediate reaction to the announcement in the very first sentence of the Queen's speech that she is to visit Iran early next year.

At a meeting of the Parliamentary Labour Party on the speech, left MP Robin Cook (Edinburgh Cen) said this was, a piece of foreign policy completely out of tune with the government's support for democracy at home and abroad.

Ministers should consider that in supporting the Shah and supplying him with arms, they were not helping Iran to defend itself against external agression, but bolstering the Shah and his regime against their own people.

But Premier Callaghan cynically told the the PLP that if the Queen's foreign trips were limited to parliamentary democracies, "her tours would be fairly short."

Such tours by the Queen had an impact on Britain's standing in the world, and our our trade prospects beyond what many people appreciated.

As to Iran, there was no guarantee that the replacement of the present regime by the opposition to it "would be any more attractive to us."

(Shah: p.3)

Callaghan's brutality mutes cheers

By ANDREW MURRAY

SO BRUTAL and uncompromising was Premier Callaghan's onslaught on pay that the Labour faithful could only manage muted cheers at the end of it.

They had been hoping to give the Prime Minister and his colleagues a big send-off for the final lap up to the next election, but obviously found themselves disheartened and worried instead.

Left-winger Eric Heffer even went so far as to break the tradition of listening in loyal silence to the leader's speech by intervening on behalf of low paid workers.

The only consolation Labour MPs got from the opening of the debate on the Queen's Speech was the sight of Mrs. Thatcher tying herself in knots over her own attitude to pay policy in a desperate effort to paper over the cracks opened in the Tory ranks by Mr. Heath on the subject.

"A rigid percentage incomes policy at this stage cannot and will not hold but that does not mean you can abandon all restraint," she said to laughter from Labour MPs.

Control of the money supply was the main weapon for keeping down inflation, and on this there was a great deal of common ground between the Tories and the government, she added.

HEATH'S GLOOM

Praising Labour parliamentary chairman Cledwyn Hughes, who had moved the "loyal address" of thanks to the Queen, for his friendship with Tory MPs, she said: "It does not mean that those who have friends in the Opposition benches are any less loyal to their own party."

The House roared with laughter at this as the words seemed more appropriate to the mutinous Mr. Heath, who remained a picture of gloom below the gangway all through his leader's speech.

Ever Ready dismiss women strikers

The British-owned electrical goods firm, Every Ready, has dismissed 160 women strikers at its Port Elizabeth factory, it was announced there yesterday.

The women, all coloured (mixed race) workers, walked out on Monday over demands for better pay and conditions, and recognition of their union.

Their union, the National Union of Motor Assembly and Rubber Workers of South Africa, immediately called for a national and international boycott of Ever Ready products

Amin claims he holds a big slice of Tanzania

By Our FOREIGN STAFF

UGANDA claimed yesterday to have occupied 700 square miles of Tanzanian territory in a border war that seems to have been sparked off by a mutiny in the army of Ugandan President Amin.

More than 2,000 Ugandan troops, supported by some tanks and planes, have been engaged in the fighting, according to reports from Dar es Salaam, the Tanzanian capital.

Radio Uganda claimed that the Tanzanian territory — the bushland known as the Kagera Salient, west of Lake Victoria—had been occupied after invading Tanzanians had been driven out of Uganda.

The people of the area were told that they were now "under the direct rule of the conqueror of the British Empire" (Field Marshal Amin).

Diplomatic sources in Nairobi said that three weeks ago, when Field Marshal Amin first claimed Tanzania had invaded his country, a mutiny broke out in the Simba Lion battalion based at Mbarara, 30 miles from the Tanzanian border.

The rebels took to the bush and were pursued by loyal troops.

Eventually the rebels crossed into Tanzania and their pursuers followed them last Monday, taking the opportunity to hit transit camps for Ugandan exiles in the area, the sources said.

Two Ugandan aircraft and four Tanzanian planes were reported yesterday to have been shot down in the fighting. Both countries' air forces are equipped with Soviet-supplied Migs.

THANK YOU FOR £8,011

WELL, in spite of a really marvellous last-minute rally, we didn't make it. Such a pity! Not only for the paper but also for the many marvellous supporters who made such tremendous efforts.

We thank you all for your truly heart-warming support.

It seems difficult, doesn't it, to reach the target of £9,000 set in January this year? But you have come tantalisingly near to it.

So far this year the Fund total is 10 per cent greater than for the same period last year. But what is wanted is a 16 per cent increase. Clearly we need new supporters to help bridge that gap.

So how about it, all you who believe in the need for a paper like the Morning Star, but haven't yet sent? It's a good time to make a start.

Yesterday's grand post of £1,762.79 included £8 collected at the Hants and Dorset CP district congress, £16 collected at Yorkshire district's women's school, £40 from an Esher reader, £10 from Twickenham CP branch, £2 from a Manchester reader, £5 from a Carshalton supporter, saying: "our paper is the life's blood of progressive thought and reason, it must not be starved of cash."

Our warmest thanks to these and to all the others, too many to mention, who gave so generously this month.

MARY ROSSER

Try again, Jim

We say

THE Queen's Speech is most notable for what it does not say. But Mr. Callaghan did not leave us long in suspense on that.

The 5 per cent is to be driven through, come what may, he declared. Higher taxation and credit squeeze will be applied in an effort to force through the government's attacks on the working class.

Mr. Callaghan made it clear, in fact, that if necessary he was ready for open confrontation with the Ford workers.

To say the least, this is sheer madness. The Labour government depends on working-class votes to get re-elected in the next general election.

It was elected last time by the working people because Labour is expected to stand up for their interests.

It was not elected to beat its supporters into the ground with a massive great stick.

That can only lead to disillusionment. And it is certainly giving Mrs. Thatcher a card or two, which she tried to use yesterday by posing as the friend of free collective bargaining.

That, of course, is one huge tragic joke, in the worst possible taste. No Tory, least of all Mrs. Thatcher, is a champion of trade unionism.

Heathite or Thatcherite, they share one thing in common — hatred of the organised working class and its struggle for a better life.

That is not some peculiar perversion of theirs. It has a very real basis. This is the fact that the Tories are the servants of big business and always have been.

What is good for big business is certainly not good for the working class, who create all the nation's wealth by their labour, only to see it creamed off in private profit.

It is about time we stood up for our rights. Mr. Callaghan should be told to change course or make way for those who will.

'Bring the millions into action'

Morning Star Reporter

SPEAKING at a meeting in Slough last night, Mr. Gordon McLennan, general secretary of the Communist Party, condemned Mr. Callaghan's stubborn refusal to finish with the 5 per cent.

"Far from carrying out the TUC and Labour Party conference decisions, the Prime Minister is going in the opposite direction," he said.

"The only answer to this was to bring millions into action for and end to wage restraint and the other progressive measures which have been demanded by the TUC and Labour Party."

Mr. Callaghan was intervening directly against the Ford workers. This was the road to ruin for the government.

"The Ford workers were now in the front line of the struggle. They should receive maximum solidarity and support from all other sections of the movement.

"Unlike the government's policies, the demands of the Communist Party's campaign to cut the dole queues are fully in line with the TUC and Labour Party conference decisions.

"It is those decisions which should have been in the Queen's speech.

"The Communists' position is quite clear. Smash the 5 per cent. Win the 35-hour week. Expand the social and public services.

"This is what our campaign is arguing for. Remember that a £1,000 million increase in public spending on these services would create nearly 250,000 new jobs.

"And recall that the application of the 35-hour week throughout industry would lead to another 500,000 new jobs.

"Wage restraint makes such cuts in hours impossible. It holds down the purchasing power needed to expand the economy and create further new jobs and stimulate investment."

Oxygen union leaders prepare new challenge to 5% limit

By KEN FERGUSON

PRIME MINISTER Callaghan's pay policy looked to be facing another major challenge last night following the rejection by union negotiators at the British Oxygen Company of a "marginally improved" offer of 9 per cent.

Transport union national chemicals' officer John Miller said after talks in a Central London hotel that the situation "doesn't look too healthy."

The breakdown in talks followed a company refusal to consolidate supplements won last year worth £10.56, which would have taken the offer to 14 per cent.

Mr. Miller said that he had told the company that union research into the financial position showed that the 14 per cent claim "would not damage their viability."

The offer will now be put to branches tomorrow and Mr. Miller said that the union negotiating team were unanimously recommending rejection.

In the event of the majority branch vote for rejection, lay delegate conference comprised of senior shop stewards, would be reconvened to discuss the next moves.

If this happened and no improved offer came from the company, Mr. Miller said: "We are then facing trouble."

Last month lay delegates rejected unanimously an offer.

British industry gets something like 80 per cent of its industrial gases — used for jobs as diverse as welding, and food freezing from BOC.

Whatever the result of the dispute, it is clear that BOC workers are in no mood to settle for a pay offer within the government's 5 per cent guidelines.

18.2

(1977) gives a very full list of cinematic (visual) codes in *How to Read a Film* (pp. 147–80). Keir Elam (1980) isolates the codes operating in drama – many of which are exploited by TV; Fiske and Hartley (1978) analyse codes specific to TV (including those which originate in the culture at large, like gesture, certain conventional forms of behaviour, speech, etc.).

You can begin to decipher the codes operating in television news by putting them into classes as follows:

1. *Visual codes* These include (a) codes of composition, (b) codes of movement and (c) codes of sequence.

Codes of composition (in cinema these are called *mise en scène*). They include the codes which govern the way a picture is framed, coloured and lit. How many elements are on screen together, and what is their relationship? How does the way they are lit affect their signification or connotative qualities? How does the use of composition codes set news apart from other television genres?

Codes of movement govern movement within the frame of both camera and subject. One routine convention in newsfilm is the *pan* from an apparently insignificant object (like the flag on a ship's mast) to the 'real' subject of the report (like striking seamen gathered on the ship's deck). A similar device is the *zoom* from long-shot into big close-up on the newsworthy celebrity, or the hand-held camera doggedly following the star, the ball, the police, the petrol bomb into the thick of the action. In the 'News at Ten' analysed in chapter 4, one of the most striking effects (of nearly uncontrollable violence) is achieved by composing the picture in mid-close up/close-up frame and then following the police shove into the crowd as closely as possible. Had the camera operator stood where most of the crowd were, the scene would have looked a good deal calmer.

Codes of sequence are those associated with editing (compare with 'montage' in cinema). How quickly shots are changed, what images are juxtaposed, and how different aspects of a story are differentially edited into a sequence, can radically affect the 'meaning' of an event. For example, the 'News at Ten' story was edited in such a way that the two sides of the confrontation emerged as different in kind. The protesters were treated to a rapid sequence of very active shots, whilst the Prime Minister was only 'interrupted' once, by a shot of her audience applauding.

2. *Verbal codes* Many of these are not specific to television, being

derived from conventional speech, narrative and journalism. But of course that is one of the reasons why news can appear to be so 'natural'. However, the verbal element of TV news – especially the voice-over commentary – is unique in being closely associated with visual images. How do the verbal codes reinforce, undercut, or modify the visual elements? Find examples of places where the verbal discourse is 'anchored' by a particular visual image, and vice versa. How does this relationship help to produce ideological closure (p. 63), or a preferred reading for the event?

3. *Absent codes* Why are some familiar devices of television entirely absent from TV news? For example: music, dramatic reconstruction of events, studio debate. Compare a sequence from a TV drama series with a sequence of news film of similar length, and try to decide which codes operating in fiction are unlikely to appear in news. The list may be shorter than you think.

News photography

News photos play a crucial role in the construction of meanings for a story – partly because of their apparently 'unarguable' rendition of the world. They have long been used as part of the diet of news, as in the back page of the 1929 *Daily Express* (19.1). But today they are fully integrated into the main part of the newspaper and play a more dominant role. Certain stories, and even whole newspapers, are justified on the basis of their pictorial elements (19.2, the *Evening Standard*, May 1977; and 19.3, the *Daily News*, billed as 'New York's Picture Newspaper').

Here is a list of elements which help news photos to signify. All of them are derived from codes which govern both the selection of some photos rather than others for inclusion in the paper, and also our recognition of the 'meaning' of the chosen pictures. Look at the pictures in this chapter. See how the following elements contribute to the overall signification of the photographs, and thence of the stories themselves.

1. *Newsworthiness* Rarity, immediacy, topicality, conflict, personality, celebrity, human interest, glamour, familiarity, humour.
2. *Personal* Posture, attitude, pose, gesture, activity, expression, eye 'contact' with the reader, signs of social role or position.
3. *Situation* Background detail visible, props, secondary characters in the shot, the spatial relation between them, costume.

PETMECKY (24)

the World's most wonderful Gramophone Needle. 24 carat gold plated Chrome Alloy Steel—plays ten sides of a Record—multi-tone and modulating. Of all dealers and stores.

Sample direct from MURDOCH'S 59, Clerkenwell Rd. LONDON, E.C.1.

Daily Express

SATURDAY, NOVEMBER 30, 1929.

Buy your Children the "Daily Express" Prize Christmas Card Painting Book

Nine Greetings Cards to colour and send to friends. Christmas messages and stories, and free entry for a £250 Painting Competition—all for one shilling.

Obtainable at all Bookstalls, or 1s. 1d. post free from Books Dept., "Daily Express," 11, St. Bride-street, London, E.C.4.

GRIM END OF AFGHAN REBEL CHIEF AND HIS FOLLOWERS.

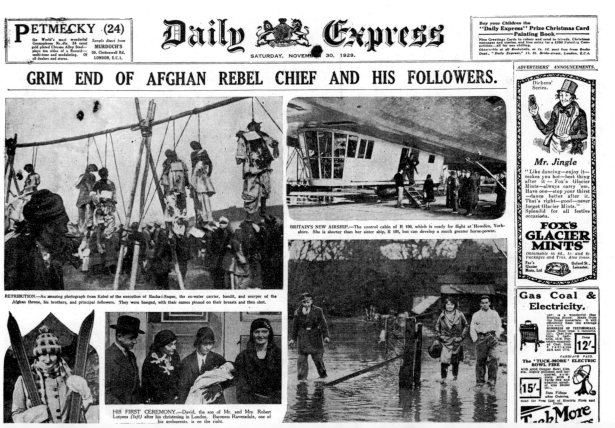

RETRIBUTION.—An amazing photograph from Kabul of the execution of Bacha-i-Saquo, the ex-water carrier, bandit, and usurper of the Afghan throne, his brothers, and principal followers. They were hanged, with their names pinned on their breasts and then shot.

BRITAIN'S NEW AIRSHIP.—The control cabin of R 100, which is ready for flight at Howden, Yorkshire. She is shorter than her sister ship, R 101, but can develop a much greater horse-power.

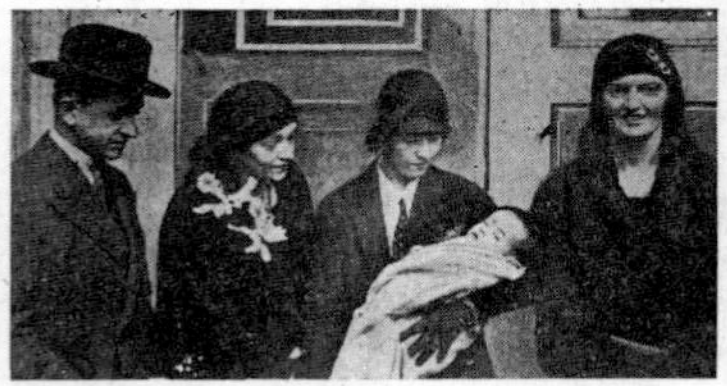

HIS FIRST CEREMONY.—David, the son of Mr. and Mrs. Robert Lutyens *(left)* after his christening in London. Baroness Ravensdale, one of his godparents, is on the right.

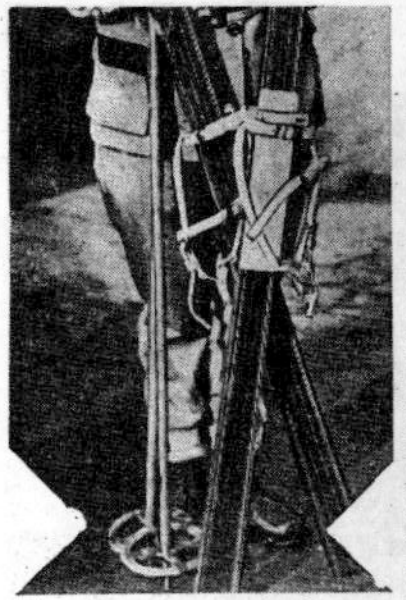

SHE OF THE SKIS.—A fascinating winter sports outfit shown at a London store.

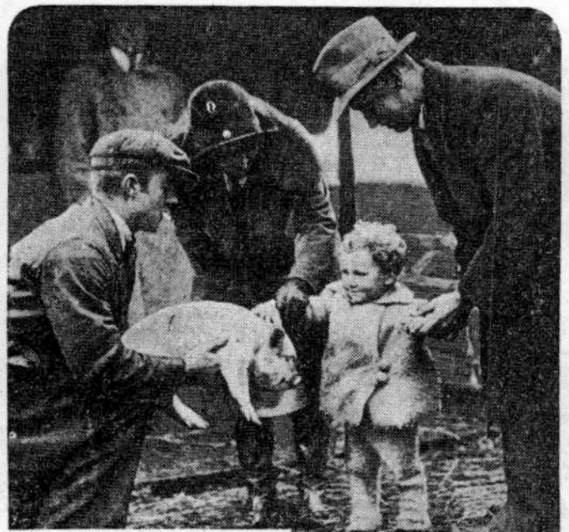

"THIS LITTLE PIG——"—The young visitor to Chelmsford market was delighted to find the nursery rhyme come true.

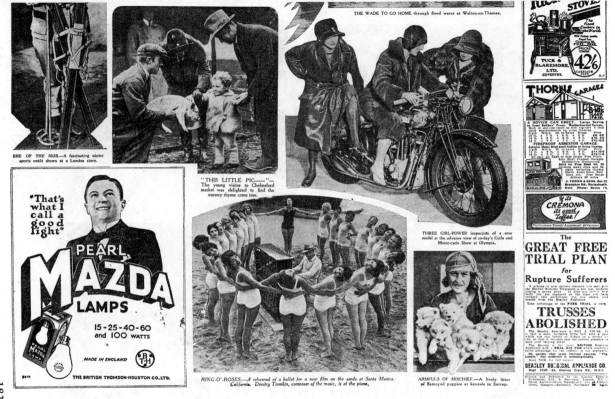

THE WADE TO GO HOME through flood water at Walton-on-Thames.

THREE GIRL-POWER inspection of a new model at the advance view of to-day's Cycle and Motor-cycle Show at Olympia.

RING-O'-ROSES.—A rehearsal of a ballet for a new film on the sands at Santa Monica. California. Dimitry Tiomkin, composer of the music, is at the piano.

ARMFULS OF MISCHIEF.—A lively litter of Samoyed puppies at kennels in Surrey.

Printed and Published by the London Express Newspaper, Ltd., 8, Shoe-lane, London, E.C.4; Great Ancoats-street, Manchester; and at Albion-street, Glasgow.—Saturday, November 30, 19[illegible].

I wanna riot! Fans smash 200 seats at punk show

RIP IT UP . . . Punk fans tear up seats and hurl them towards the stage.

NEWS ON CAMERA

REPORT:
James Johnson
PICTURES:
Chris Moorhouse

THE LATEST revolution in rock music exploded into disorder once again when the largest punk rock 'new wave' concert yet seen in London was staged at the Rainbow Theatre last night.

As top-of-the-bill group The Clash closed the four hour show, more than 200 seats were demolished by the audience in a bout of rowdy fanaticism.

The house lights were turned up but The Clash contined to play on regardless.

White Riot—I Wanna Riot thundered vocalist Joe Strummer, shuddering violently, as the broken seats tumbled up on to the stage beside him.

A search of the arriving audience had revealed a battery of items like knives. iron bars and assorted chains.

Release

The people who looked out of place were the gaggles of record company executives seated at the rear of the theatre, but their presence underlined the fact that punk rock has now become big business.

Despite the scorn and ridicule that accompanied the emergence of the new style, it has now become evident that punk, or new wave rock, has become the fastest growing commodity in the music business.

The Clash's first album entered the Top Twenty last month in its first week of release and was quickly followed into the charts by a record from another new wave group, The Stranglers.

"It's unprecedented for new albums by any group to get into the charts so quickly," said Maurice Oberstien, the British managing director of CBS Records.

"The record business has been looking around for a long time for something new, and this has to be it.

"I know people can be horrified by punk rock, but personally I am sanguine about the whole situation. For every person who says 'I hate it', you are going to find somebody who reacts the opposite way.

"I remember the days when the public was horrified by the Bill Haley-Elvis Presley era. Punk rock is just a new fashion and a new music. It is perfectly harmless."

To the ever-growing numbers of new wave fans, The Clash, from West London, have become known as the ultimate expression of an angry form of quasi-political nihilism.

The songs are blank negative diatribes against high-rise blocks, unemployment and general urban decay.

Guitarist Mick Jones once claimed that he had never lived below the 17th floor.

Their music has been dubbed the Sound of the Westway. A spluttering, high-speed, manic rush, it displays a release of energy normally stifled by living in Britain during an economic depression.

Groups like The Clash have suddenly emerged on the basis that there is probably more for young people to protest about in 1977 than in the 1960s.

None of the current new wave groups could claim to be great musicians or lyricists but last night's show and recent record sales suggest that they have become more relevant to a proportion of young rock audiences than superstar vocalists or virtuoso musicians.

● **Original 'New Wave' band moves quietly along — centre pages.**

PUNK protest . . . targets include unemployment and urban decay.

THE CLASH play on as broken seats land on the stage.

19.2

★

DAILY NEWS

15¢

NEW YORK'S PICTURE NEWSPAPER ®

Vol. 56. No. 165 Copr. 1975 New York News Inc. New York, N.Y. 10017, Friday, January 3, 1975★ Price 20c beyond 200 miles from N.Y.C.

PENN TRAIN RUNS SIGNAL; 187 HURT

Rear-End Collision in Bronx

News photo by Jack Smith

New Haven commuters leave train in Mount Vernon. It was stalled by derailment at Bronx Botanical Gardens.

Stories on page 3; other pictures in centerfold

CIA Snooped on Love Life of Agents

Story on Page 2

19.3

4. *Technical* Lighting, distance, definition, contrast, 'graininess'.
5. *Contextual* Composition into the page format; the page format itself (tabloid or broadsheet); relationship with headlines, story and graphics; the caption.
6. *Photogenic* Aesthetic code – realism, naturalism, fashion, 'art', etc. What echoes of conventional or artistic visual imagery contribute to the picture's aesthetic appeal – or, why don't your holiday snapshots look like news photos?

Take still photographs of TV news, and subject them to the same kind of close analysis. What differences are there between the two kinds of visual image? Then compare these results with those you obtain from analysing visual imagery in advertising (see Williamson, 1978 and Dyer, 1982): are the *same* codes operating?

Alternatives

In chapter 8 I discussed the alternative press. Compare the news values in these newspapers and magazines with those you find in the national/local established press. What differences are there between the topics covered, the modes of address, the codes of composition? Try to determine how many alternative sources of news there are available in your area, and where from. Use *Benn's Press Directory*, for instance, to find out who owns your local established press. Construct a 'map of information' for your locality, giving some indication of the ownership and control of the various concerns, and the differences in distribution between alternative and established papers.

Going beyond the press, there are a number of films available which offer alternative images to TV news. Hiring them is simple and cheap. Here is a brief selection.

News and Comment by Frank Abbott (1978); distributed by The Other Cinema.

Ireland: Behind the Wire by the Berwick Street Film Collective (1974), about Northern Ireland; distributed by The Other Cinema.

The Miners Film by Cinema Action (1974–5), about the 1972 and 1974 miners' strikes; distributed by Cinema Action.

Before Hindsight, by Jonathan Lewis and Elizabeth Taylor-Mead (1977), about the newsreels and documentaries of pre-war cinema, including much contemporary footage; distributed by the British Film Institute.

The War Game by Peter Watkins (1968), made for the BBC but still banned, about the effects of nuclear attack in Britain (and official secrecy about them); distributed by the British Film Institute.

It Aint Half Racist Mum by the Campaign Against Racism in the Media (CARM) and shown on BBC *Open Door* (1979), about racist 'codes' in television current affairs and entertainment; distributed on film or videotape by The Other Cinema.

Kino-Pravda (*Cinema Truth*) (Nos 21 and 22) by Dziga Vertov (1922–5), classic silent cinema newsreel from post-revolutionary Russia by one of the pioneers of cinema; distributed by Artificial Eye.

You can get the catalogues of these distributors from:

The Other Cinema, 79 Wardour Street, London W1.

Cinema Action, 27 Winchester Road, London NW3.

The British Film Institute Film and Video Library, 81 Dean Street, London W1.

The Artificial Eye Film Co., 211 Camden High Street, London NW1.

Making the News

Probably the best way, finally, to understand the news is to do it yourself. Producing a magazine, or a video (or super-8mm film) newsreel can be done on limited resources. Your local Adult Education service or Regional Arts Association will tell you what facilities are available in your area.

Advice on producing super-8mm films can be found in Huxley, D.R. (1978) *Making Films in Super-8: a Handbook for Primary and Secondary Teachers*, Oxford University Press. Advice on making television/video productions can be found in Burrow, Thomas D. and Wood, Donald N. (1978) *Television Production: Disciplines and Techniques*, Dubuque, Iowa, Wm C. Brown Co.

Further reading and study

News is not so much a cause as a symptom, and the same goes for this book. The approach I've used is not original, but it is not often applied to news. If you want to follow up the two related fields of semiotics and cultural studies, the following suggestions for reading should get you started. Most of the books listed are relatively cheap, accessible introductions to their particular concerns, and themselves provide useful reading lists to take you further.

Semiotics: language

Culler, Jonathan (1976) *Saussure*, London, Fontana. A good place to start, with an illustrated exposition of the European 'modern master' of semiotics.

Hawkes, Terence (1977) *Structuralism and Semiotics*, London, Methuen. Sets semiotics into its world-historical context, with lucid explanations of most of the influential writers in the field. Biased towards literature. Recommended as the best general introduction, with a full bibliography.

Barthes, Roland (1973) *Mythologies*, St. Albans, Paladin. One of the most influential and entertaining semiotic texts, comprising a series of short studies of contemporary myths (from Persil to wrestling), and concluding with the essay 'Myth today' which is the source of much subsequent work in the field.

Leach, Edmund (1976) *Culture and Communication*, Cambridge University Press. The structuralist approach to anthropology, with an enjoyable and helpful discussion of key terms, concepts and concerns central to semiotic theory.

Fiske, John (1982) *Introduction to Communication Studies*, London, Methuen. Many of the basic concepts of semiotics are defined and illustrated, along with other approaches to cultural 'texts' including content analysis. Introduces some of the issues raised by the contending perspectives, theories, etc. which are used in the study of communication.

Halliday, Michael (1978) *Language as Social Semiotic*, London, Arnold. More advanced reading, but a collection of papers in which the social determinants of language are explored by means of useful concepts; and the linguistic determinants of society are not forgotten. Good on Bernstein's codes, but less sure-footed on the class origin of linguistic/semiotic inequalities.

Semiotics: image

Barthes, Roland (1977) *Image-Music-Text*, essays selected and translated by Stephen Heath, London, Fontana. Included are 'The photographic message' and 'The rhetoric of the image', in which Barthes proposes methods for decoding photographs and advertisements. Recommended.

Hall, Stuart (1973) 'The determinations of news photographs', in Cohen, S. and Young, J. (eds) *The Manufacture of News*, London, Constable, pp. 176–91. An illustrated account of how news values and ideological values are 'cashed in' on the level of the photographic image. Recommended.

Fiske, John and Hartley, John (1978) *Reading Television*, London, Methuen. An attempt to use semiotic/cultural theories and concepts to understand the television image/message, with chapters on various popular programmes, from *Top of the Pops* and *Match of the Day* to *The Sweeney* and *News at Ten*.

Monaco, James (1977) *How to Read a Film*, Oxford University Press. A very wide-ranging study, readable and interesting, which applies semiotic concepts (among others) to a well-chosen variety of films. Recommended.

Eco, Umberto (1980) 'Towards a semiotic inquiry into the television message', reprinted in Corner, J. and Hawthorn, J. (eds) *Communication Studies: an introductory Reader*, London. Arnold, pp. 131–49. An early attempt (1965) to propose a system of codes and sub-codes at work in the television image, and still useful as a framework from which to begin analysis. First published in English in 1972.

Sontag, Susan (1979) *On Photography*, London, Penguin. An essay on the historical and aesthetic role of photography in the West. Excellent on the cultural codes and values associated with photography, and very stylishly written.

Camerawork, journal of the Half Moon Photography Workshop. Indispensable guide to current trends both in photography itself and in ideas about it.

Cultural studies

Hall, Stuart, Hobson, Dorothy, Lowe, Andrew, Willis, Paul (eds) (1980) *Culture, Media, Language*, London, Hutchinson. A collection of papers by members of the Centre for Contemporary Cultural Studies at the University of Birmingham. Includes Stuart Hall on Encoding/Decoding; Ian Connell on TV News; and Dorothy Hobson on housewives and the media. Highly recommended.

Hall, Stuart *et al.* (1978) *Policing the Crisis: Mugging, the State and Law and Order*, London, Macmillan. A large-scale study by members of CCCS (see previous study), which begins by tracing the media's construction of a 'moral panic' about mugging; it is a critical history of post-war British culture, in which the relations between the state, media and law enforcers are exposed in detail. Highly recommended.

Curran, James *et al.* (eds) (1977) *Mass Communication and Society*, London, Arnold. A 'reader' of numerous contributions, in which the cultural studies perspective is set against other approaches. Contains influential articles by Murdock and Golding, John Westergaard, Stuart Hall and others.

British Film Institute *Television Monographs*, amongst which are McArthur (1978), Brunsdon and Morley (1978) and Morley (1980) (see references section below), all of which are highly recommended. Other titles in the series are Pateman, Trevor (1974) *Television and the February General Election*; Collins, Richard (1976) *Television News.*

News

Cohen, Stanley and Young, Jock (eds) (1973) *The Manufacture of News: Deviance, Social Problems and the Mass Media*, London, Constable. Still among the most useful books on the news. A wide range of contributions from different perspectives and about different aspects of news. Entertaining, informative and highly recommended (entirely new edition 1982).

Boyce, G., Curran, J., Wingate P. (eds) (1978) *Newspaper History: from the Seventeenth Century to the Present Day*, London, Constable. A much-needed historical account of the British press, which includes a number of general overview articles as well as sections on specific periods.

Schlesinger, Philip (1978) *Putting 'Reality' Together: BBC News*, London, Constable. A sociological study of the production processes of television news, written from a complementary perspective to the one adopted here, and a valuable corrective to my semiotic 'bias'.

Glasgow Media Group (1976 and 1980) *Bad News* and *More Bad News*, London, Routledge & Kegan Paul. Not for the beginner, but influential in challenging broadcasters' own beliefs about the 'impartiality' of news on television. Uses the methods of large-scale content analysis.

Evans, Harold (1978) *Pictures on a Page*, London, Heinemann. A valuable source of news photos, compiled by the then editor of the *Sunday Times*. The commentary is an interesting insight into professional discourse, but often fails to do justice to the meaning potential of the pictures.

CONCLUSION

Everything is there – but *floating*
(Barthes)

Roland Barthes makes a distinction between two kinds of pleasure available from 'reading' texts: *plaisir* and *jouissance*. *Plaisir* is contentment, but *jouissance* describes a more explosive kind of joy – in French the word is synonymous with the joy of sexual pleasure. Texts which get near to producing *jouissance* are not usually associated with the news.

However, it is possible to move from mere *plaisir* towards a more active kind of intercourse with news if you take the initiative. This book is intended to provide you with some of the discursive concepts and strategies for approaching news texts which will help to get you started on a more productive role for yourself. Umberto Eco has provided a name for the game – it's called semiotic guerilla warfare. Critical resistance to the big battalions of the media is not necessarily simple or straightforward. But two possible outcomes of such action stand out. First, using the approach adopted in this book, a critical stance towards what the big battalions are up to can be developed and made more effective. Second, both critical activity and the production of news itself are closer to *jouissance* if you undertake them for yourself.

There is little point in bewailing the lack of a national, popular, commercially viable newspaper – like perhaps the *Daily Herald* – which will provide an alternative to the orthodox media. Times have changed since the *Herald* confidently announced in its first editorial (25 January 1911) that 'We have arrived. At last we have a daily paper of our own. If we differ at all from the orthodox daily press, it will be in the fact that we shall give the *correct* position of affairs day by day.'

One of the things that has changed is access to the technology of the media. It is getting easier to lay our hands on the means of film, video and litho-print production. And there is little room now for a single 'correct position' in any affair. Satisfaction is achieved by having your own say in what is said, preferably in like-minded company. The myriad voices of those localized, small-scale, ephemeral fanzines and music papers have shown what can be done outside the limits of 'correct positions'. Community video and film workshops are available in many cities, and are already used extensively to record alternative positions on the affairs of their areas.

It isn't necessary to be a professional to understand news. The apparent lack of national, 'professional' alternative media shouldn't blind us to the very real possibilities that are available. The politics and practice of alternative newsmaking and criticism includes a resistance to the ideology of professionalism with its associated news values and divisions of labour. In fact, such media – and criticism – should be distinctive and not just for disagreeing with the established view (the *Herald* position), but also for seeking to set up alternative discourses. And the *jouissance* of such struggles is that you won't simply have to watch the established media watchdogs. You can bite them back.

REFERENCES

Agee, Philip (1975) *Inside the Company: a CIA Diary*, Harmondsworth, Penguin.

Aldgate, Tony (1977) '1930s newsreels: censorship and controversy' *Sight and Sound*, Summer, pp. 154–8.

Althusser, Louis (1971) *Lenin and Philosophy and Other Essays* Harmondsworth, Penguin.

Annan (1977) *Report of the Committee on the Future of Broadcasting*, Cmnd 6753, London, HMSO.

Barthes, Roland (1968) *Elements of Semiology* London, Cape.

— (1973) *Mythologies*, St. Albans, Paladin.

— (1977) *Image-Music-Text*, London, Fontana.

Beharrell, Peter and Philo, Greg, eds (1977) *Trade Unions and the Media*, London, Macmillan.

Belsey, Catherine (1980) *Critical Practice*, London, Methuen.

Benn's Press Directory (1982) Tunbridge Wells, Benn Publications.

Bennett, Tony (1977) *The Mass Media as Definers of Social Reality*, Unit 13 of course DE 353: (Mass Communication and Society) Milton Keynes: Open University.

Berger, Peter and Luckmann, Thomas (1966) *The Social Construction of Reality*, Harmondsworth, Penguin.

Bernstein, Basil (1973) *Class, Codes and Control 1*, St. Albans, Paladin.

— (1975) *Class, Codes and Control 3*, London, Routledge & Kegan Paul.

Bodin, Jean (1576) *Six Books of the Commonwealth*, trans. Tooley, M.J., Oxford, Basil Blackwell, 1967.
Boyce, G., Curran, J., Wingate, P., eds (1978) *Newspaper History: from the Seventeenth Century to the Present Day,* London, Constable.
Brunsdon, Charlotte (1978) 'It is well known that by nature women are inclined to be rather personal', in Women's Studies Group, Centre for Contemporary Cultural Studies, eds, (1978) pp. 18-35.
Brunsdon, Charlotte and Morley, David (1978) *Everyday Television: Nationwide*, London, British Film Institute.
Burns, Tom (1977) 'The organization of public opinion', in Curran *et al*., eds (1977), pp. 44–70.
Cohen, Stanley (1980) *Folk Devils and Moral Panics*, London, Martin Robertson, (first published 1972).
Cohen, Stanley and Young, Jock, eds (1973) *The Manufacture of News: Deviance, Social Problems and the Mass Media*, London, Constable.
Connell, Ian (1978) 'Monopoly capitalism and the media', in Hibbin, ed. (1978), pp. 69-98.
— (1979) 'Television, news and the Social Contract', *Screen* 20, 1, Spring, pp. 87–107. Reprinted in Hall *et al*., eds (1980), pp. 139–56.
Corner, John and Hawthorn, Jeremy, eds (1980) *Communication Studies: an Introductory Reader*, London, Arnold.
Culler, Jonathan (1976) *Saussure*, London, Fontana.
Curran, James, Gurevitch, Michael and Woollacott, Janet, eds (1977) *Mass Communication and Society*, London, Arnold.
Curran, James (1978) 'The press as an agency of social control: an historical perspective', in Boyce *et al.*, eds (1978), pp. 57–75.
Drummond, Phillip (1976) 'Structural and narrative constraints in *The Sweeney*', *Screen Education* 20, autumn, pp. 15–36.
Dyer, Gillian (1982) *Advertising as Communication*, London, Methuen.
Eco, Umberto (1980) 'Towards a semiotic inquiry into the TV message', in Corner and Hawthorn, eds, (1980), pp. 131–149, Arnold (first published in English, 1972).
Elam, Keir (1980) *The Semiotics of Theatre and Drama*, London, Methuen.
Elyot, Sir Thomas (1531) *The Book Named the Governor*, ed. S.E. Lehmberg (1962) London and New York, Dent Dutton.

Fiske, John (1982) *Introduction to Communication Studies*, London, Methuen.
— and Hartley, John (1978) *Reading Television*, London, Methuen.
Galtung, Johan and Ruge, Mari (1973) 'Structuring and selecting news', in Cohen and Young, eds (1973), pp. 62–73.
Gilbert, W. Stephen (1980) 'The TV play: outside the consensus', *Screen Education* 35, pp. 35–45.
Glasgow Media Group (1976) *Bad News*, London, Routlege & Kegan Paul.
— (1980) *More Bad News*, London, Routledge & Kegan Paul.
Gramsci, Antonio (1971) *Prison Notebooks*, London, Lawrence & Wishart.
Hadwin, Arnold (1980) 'Objectivity is crucial – but is it possible to be objective?', *Journalism Studies Review* (University College Cardiff) 5, July, pp. 29–30.
Hall, Stuart (1973) 'The determination of news photographs', in Cohen and Young, eds (1973), pp. 176–91.
— (1973b) 'Encoding and decoding in the television discourse', *Stencilled Paper*, Centre for Contemporary Cultural Studies. Abridged in Hall *et al.*, eds (1980), pp. 128–38.
— (1977) 'Culture, the media, and the "ideological effect"', in Curran *et al.*, eds (1977), pp. 315–49.
Hall, Stuart, Connell, Ian, Curti, Lidia (1976) 'The "unity" of current affairs television', *Working Papers in Cultural Studies (WPCS)* 9, pp. 51–95.
Hall, Stuart, Critcher, Chas, Jefferson, Tony, Clarke, John, Roberts, Brian (1978) *Policing the Crisis: Mugging, the State and Law and Order*, London, Macmillan.
Hall, Stuart, Hobson, Dorothy, Lowe, Andrew, Willis, Paul, eds (1980) *Culture, Media, Language*, London, Hutchinson.
Halliday, M.A.K. (1978) *Language as Social Semiotic*, London, Arnold.
Halloran, James, Elliott, Philip, Murdock, Graham (1970) *Demonstrations and Communication: a case study*, Harmondsworth, Penguin.
Harrison, Stanley (1974) *Poor Men's Guardians*, London, Lawrence & Wishart.
Hartmann, Paul and Husband, Charles (1973) 'The mass media and racial conflict', in Cohen and Young, eds (1973), pp. 270–84.

Hawkes, Terence (1977) *Structuralism and Semiotics*, London, Methuen.
Hibbin, Sally (ed.) (1978) *Politics, Ideology and the State*, London, Lawrence & Wishart.
Hobbes, Thomas (1651) *Leviathan*, ed. C.B. Macpherson, Harmondsworth, Penguin, 1968.
Hobson, Dorothy (1980) 'Housewives and the mass media', in Hall *et al.*, eds (1980), pp. 105–14.
Hunt, Alan, ed. (1977) *Class and Class Structure*, London, Lawrence & Wishart.
Kennett, John (1973) 'The sociology of Pierre Bourdieu', *Educational Review* 25 June, pp. 237–49.
Kumar, Krishan (1977) 'Holding the middle ground: the BBC, the public and the professional broadcaster', in Curran *et al.*, eds (1977), pp. 231–49.
Lévi-Strauss, Claude (1968) *Structural Anthropology, I.* Harmondsworth, Penguin.
McArthur, Colin (1978) *Television and History*, London, British Film Institute.
McCann, Eamonn (1971) *The British Press and Northern Ireland*, Northern Ireland Socialist Research Centre, reprinted in Cohen and Young, eds (1973) pp. 242–61.
Minority Press Group (1980a) *The Other Secret Service: Press Distributors and Press Censorship*. London.
— (1980b) *Here is the Other News: Challenges to the Local Commercial Press.* London.
— (1980c) *Where is the Other News: The Newstrade and the Radical Press*. London.
Monaco, James (1977) *How to Read a Film*, Oxford, Oxford University Press.
Morley, David (1980) *The 'Nationwide' Audience*, London, British Film Institute.
Murdock, Graham (1973) 'Political deviance: the press presentation of a militant mass demonstration', in Cohen and Young, eds. (1973), pp. 156–76.
Murdock, Graham and Golding, Peter (1977) 'Capitalism, communication and class relations', in Curran *et al.*, eds, pp. 12–44.
— (1978) 'The structure, ownership and control of the press: 1914–1976', in Boyce *et al.*, eds (1978), pp. 130–48.

Parkin, Frank (1972) *Class Inequality and Political Order*, London, Paladin.

Saussure, Ferdinand de (1974) *Course in General Linguistics*, London, Fontana/Collins (first published 1916).

Spender, Dale (1980) *Man Made Language*, London, Routledge & Kegan Paul.

State Research (1978–9) 'The ABC Trial: a defeat for the state', *State Research Bulletin* 9, December–January.

Tunstall, Jeremy (1977) *The Media are American*, London, Constable.

Volosinov, Valentin (1973) *Marxism and the Philosophy of Language*, Seminar Press (first published in Russian, 1929–30).

Walton, Paul and Davis, Howard (1977) 'Bad news for trade unionists', in Beharrell and Philo, eds (1977), pp. 118–35.

Westergaard, John (1977) 'Power, class and the media', in Curran *et al.*, eds (1977), pp. 95–116.

— (1977b) 'Class inequality and "corporatism"', in Hunt, ed. (1977), pp. 165–187.

Westergaard, John and Resler, Henrietta (1975) *Class in a Capitalist Society*, Harmondsworth, Penguin.

Williams, Raymond (1966) *Communications*, Harmondsworth, Penguin.

— (1976) *Keywords*, London, Fontana.

— (1981) *Culture*, London, Fontana.

Williamson, Judith (1978) *Decoding Advertisements*, London, Marion Boyars.

Women's Studies Group, Centre for Contemporary Cultural Studies, eds (1978) *Women Take Issue: aspects of women's subordination*, London, Hutchinson.

Young, Jock and Brooke Crutchley, J. (1977) 'May the first, 1973 – a day of predictable madness', in Beharrell and Philo, eds (1977), pp. 23–31.

INDEX